A WOMAN OF COURAGE

The Journal of Rose de Freycinet on Her Voyage around the World 1817–1820

VENEZ...AMIS DES ARTS, QUE LE MARBRE FIDÈLE
SAGE DE NOS REGRETS DANS CES PAISIBLES LIEUX
RAPPELLE LA FÉNOUAL ET LE RENDE À NOS YEUX,
QUI, SOUS LES COUPS DU SORT, QUAND POUR NOUS
IL SUCCOMBA,
DE LARMES ET DE FLEURS JE COUVRIRAI SA TOMBE.

(Hymne De La Navigation)

A WOMAN OF COURAGE

The Journal of Rose de Freycinet on Her Voyage around the World 1817–1820

Translated and edited by
Marc Serge Rivière

National Library of Australia
Canberra 2003

Published by the National Library of Australia
Canberra ACT 2600
Australia

First Published 1996
Reprinted 2003

National Library of Australia Cataloguing-in-Publication data

Freycinet, Rose Marie de, d.1832.
  [Campagne de l' "Uranie" (1817–1820). English]
  A woman of courage: the journal of Rose de Freycinet on
  her voyage around the world 1817–1820.

  Includes index.
  ISBN 0 642 10767 X.

  Freycinet, Rose Marie de, d.1832—Diaries.
  2. Freycinet, Rose Marie de, d.1832—Journeys.
  3. Uranie (Ship). 4. Voyages around the world.
  5. Scientific expeditions.
  I. Rivière, Marc, 1947– .
  II. National Library of Australia. III. Title.

  910.41092
  910.41

Publisher's editor: Julie Stokes
Designer: Beverly Swifte
Cover designer (reprint): Cate Eggleton
Printed by Lamb Print, Perth

Cover: *'Île Timor: Réception à Diély [c.1818]',* colour collotype by Jacques Arago
Reproduced from *Journal de Madame Rose de Saulces de
Freycinet ...* (Paris: Société d'Editions Géographiques, Maritimes et
Coloniales, 1927), plate 1
Rex Nan Kivell Collection
National Library of Australia Pictures Collection

Frontispiece: Pierre Marie Nyon (fl.1859–1866)
Engraved title page of the official record of the *Uranie's* voyage,
featuring a vignette of a memorial to the French explorer La Pérouse
c.1825
engraving: plate mark 32 x 23.5 cm (S7221)
Louis-Claude de Freycinet, *Voyage autour du monde ... Exécuté sur les corvettes de
S.M. l'Uranie et la* Physicienne ... : *Atlas historique* (Paris: Chez Pillet Ainé, 1825)
Rex Nan Kivell Collection, National Library of Australia Pictures Collection

Contents

To Marc Paul

28.

Preface

The text published in this edition is a faithful translation of the journal of Rose de Freycinet, which was first edited and published in French in 1927 by Charles Duplomb (*Journal de Madame Rose de Saulces de Freycinet, d'après le manuscrit original accompagné de notes*. Paris: Société d'Éditions Géographiques, Maritimes et Coloniales, 1927).

The history of Rose de Freycinet's journal and how it came to be published in 1927 needs to be recalled briefly here. Rose's husband, Louis-Claude de Freycinet, submitted a proposal to the French Government in 1816 for a scientific expedition to circumnavigate the world, taking magnetic and meteorological observations and reporting on natural history. The Ministry of the Navy accepted the detailed proposal and Louis-Claude de Freycinet was appointed to command the voyage of the French corvette *Uranie*, which departed on its voyage of discovery the following year. Not wanting to be parted for a number of years, Rose and her husband conspired for her to stow away. Each day during the voyage of the *Uranie* around the world (1817–20), Rose wrote a series of intimate letters which took the form of a diary addressed to her friend Caroline, Baronne de Nanteuil, née Barillon. This diary was handed over to Caroline upon Rose's return to France in 1820 and was to remain in the archives of the Nanteuil family until 1910, when Caroline's grand-daughter, the Baronne de Rotours, passed it on to Henri de Freycinet (born 1857), the grandfather of the present Baron, and Rose de Freycinet's great-nephew.

On 5 April 1923 an erudite scholar, Charles Duplomb, wrote to the then Baron de Freycinet seeking permission to publish the journal 'in which, according to M. de la Roquette, Mme de Freycinet gave her impressions in a most piquant manner' (Archives de Laage—my translation). He added that the publication of the manuscript, which at the time was located in the Limousin region, would receive the blessing of the Société de Géographie de France and the Académie de la Marine. Henri de Freycinet replied on 6 April 1923:

I plan to go to the Limousin for a stay of a few weeks and shall be in a position to note everything that relates to the shipwreck of the *Uranie*. The journal in question concerns too many people to be published, and its extracts will have to be rigorously vetted, for its author had no thought of ever publishing it. It is written in the form of letters to an intimate friend, Caroline de Barillon, to whom, I think, she gave it on her return to France. I received it a few years ago from my cousin the Baronne de Rotours, née de Nanteuil, and a descendant of the Barillon family.

I had intended at some stage to publish a biographical sketch of my great-uncle, with extracts of the journal, but I have not yet found the time to execute this plan.

(Archives de Laage—my translation)

(opposite) Pinon dove, discovered at Rawak and named after Rose de Freycinet (née Pinon)

Jean-Louis Denis Coutant (b.1776) (engraver) and J.S. Prêtre (artist) *Colombe Pinon (Columba pinon N)* c.1822
hand-coloured engraving (S7352)
Louis-Claude de Freycinet, *Voyage autour du Monde ... Exécuté sur les Corvettes de S.M. l'Uranie et la Physicienne ... : Zoologie* (Paris: Chez Pillet Aîné, c.1830), plate no. 28
Rex Nan Kivell Collection; National Library of Australia Pictorial Collection

That the Baron relented soon after is clear; the manuscript, corrected and modified by the Baron de Freycinet and his uncle Charles de Freycinet (1828–1923), who had a distinguished career as a Minister in the French Government, was ready for publication in 1926. Only 500 copies costing 300 Francs each, and 15 luxury copies at 1000 Francs each, were printed; one of the former copies is in the collection of the National Library of Australia in Canberra. Moreover, the Duplomb edition contained a most informative introduction by the Baron de Freycinet, to which reference will be made in the pages that follow. It also presented original illustrations by the artists Jacques Arago and Alphonse Pellion, which until then had been in the safe-keeping of the Freycinet family; 13 of these were in colour and 12 in black and white.

However, there was a major lacuna in the manuscript of Rose, from 23 October 1818 when the *Uranie* left Timor until 18 November 1819 when she entered Port Jackson, that is, the period covering the *Uranie*'s visits to the Moluccas, the Caroline Islands, the Marianas and the Sandwich Islands—perhaps the section which contained the most colourful and interesting details of the journey, as far as the French-reading public of 1927 was concerned. In order to fill this lacuna, the editor of the journal, Charles Duplomb, relied on letters which Rose had written to her mother, Mme Pinon, each day during the voyage. These letters have not been found to date but constitute the essential source of Chapters 6–8 of this edition (Chapter 6 of the Duplomb edition). It will become clear to the reader of the text that the writing style changes and becomes slightly less intimate. On the other hand, details of an ethnographic and anthropologic nature are just as plentiful and are very much in keeping with Rose de Freycinet's vision and character. In order to fill a further lacuna in the Duplomb edition covering the

expedition's first few weeks in Port Jackson, I have added three letters by the artist Jacques Arago written to a boyhood friend in France—these appear at the beginning of Chapter 9.

This edition provides the first complete English translation of Rose de Freycinet's journal. Except for the three chapters containing Rose's correspondence with her mother, I have followed Rose's original in the division of chapters, the paragraphing and punctuation. Any modification or correction of factual errors made to Rose's original writing, for example in the spelling of proper names or of geographical locations, as well as any additions or explanations, which are not in the original but are vital to the understanding of the text, have been inserted within square brackets. As a rule, geographical locations are given in the English form, but in some cases the French version has been retained where there are no modern English equivalents.

The letters in the Epilogue following the main narrative have been included because they shed light on the life of Rose de Freycinet in Paris in the years after her momentous voyage. Through Rose's intimate and candid confessions to her sister-in-law Clémentine de Freycinet, Henri de Freycinet's wife, we witness her stoicism, already apparent in her journal, in the face of increasing solitude and intense pain from a stomach ailment. Her affection for the Freycinet family, in particular Henri and his wife, her maternal feelings for her nephews, and her deep regret and sadness at not being able to have children of her own complete the picture of a brave, kind-hearted and generous woman who was to bear the repercussions of an act of love for the rest of her life. She never recovered from the physical demands of the voyage upon which she embarked out of devotion for her husband, Louis-Claude de Freycinet, the captain of the *Uranie*.

These hitherto unpublished letters are to be found in manuscript form in the Laage Archives, now near Bordeaux at the home of the present Baron Henri de Freycinet. My translation would have been impossible without his kind hospitality and generosity during my stay at the family home. I cannot begin to express my gratitude to the Baron and his family for making me feel welcome and for his permission to use the family archives, in particular a large number of manuscript documents which provide the basis of the introduction.

I cannot end this preface without paying homage to the well-researched and exciting book by Lady Marnie Bassett, *Realms and Islands: The World Voyage of Rose de Freycinet in the Corvette Uranie 1817–1820* (London: Oxford University Press, 1962). Marnie Bassett retells the story of the voyage in the third-person narrative form in a most engaging manner, offering invaluable insights into the character and motives of the heroine through selected extracts of the diary. It occurred to me, however, that there was room for an English edition of the journal in which would be heard, without an intermediary, the unique voice of Rose de Freycinet—the ingenuous, slightly mocking, exuberant, almost wild and happy tone, as the curtain rises on a three-year journey, soon to be replaced by an increasingly grave, mature and philosophical tone, as the energy-sapping crossings took their toll and the vicissitudes of the voyage, and the shipwreck in particular, began to affect her emotionally.

It is thus my aim to allow Rose de Freycinet to hold the stage. Only by having direct access to her daily intimations is the reader able to grasp fully and ponder the unique life experiences, the resilience, the inexhaustible good humour and devotion to others, above all the bravery in adversity and the temerity of a 22-year-old woman who was prepared to flaunt conventions and challenge the French naval authorities by stowing away on an official maritime expedition. Such a woman so far ahead of her time deserves, in my opinion, to tell her own story.

Marc Serge Rivière
Townsville
August 1996

Acknowledgements

I would like to express my deepest gratitude to the following persons who have assisted me in the preparation of the book: Sandra Greville and the staff of the Pictorial Section of the National Library of Australia; Julie Stokes and the staff of the Publications Section of the National Library of Australia; Thuy Huynh Einam and Michelle Kuilboer for their help with proof-reading; Brian Pump of the Photographic Services of James Cook University. Above all, I owe an enormous debt of gratitude to M. le Baron and Mme la Baronne de Freycinet for giving me access to the family archives. Finally, I wish to acknowledge the unfailing support of my wife during the two-year project; like Rose de Freycinet, she showed a great deal of patience and steadfastness.

M.S. Rivière

Introduction

Unborn TO-MORROW, and dead YESTERDAY
Why fret about them if TO-DAY be sweet!

> Edward Fitzgerald,
> *Omar Khayyam*, I, xxxvii[1]

Rose de Freycinet, née Pinon (1794–1832)

Rose Marie Pinon was born on 29 September 1794 in the parish of St Julien-du-Sault, in the diocese of Yonne. She came from a modest middle-class background, her mother, Madame [Jeanne?] Pinon, being a teacher in charge of a boarding school for young ladies. Some information can be gleaned from a lengthy correspondence comprising 26 letters between Mme Pinon and Ruch Amboine Cucurron, Abbé Sicard (1742–1822), who in 1803 was inspector of schools for the deaf in the Paris district and became director of an institute for the deaf on 3 January 1807. In 1808 the Abbé was promoted to the post of Director of the Institut de Bienfaisance. This correspondence, which indicates a strong bond of friendship between Rose's mother and Abbé Sicard over many years, is to be found in the Archives de Laage (hereafter Laage), now in the care of the present Baron de Freycinet who resides near Bordeaux. In 1802 the Pinon family lived at 95 Rue d'Enfer near the Place St Michel, and it is clear, from a letter addressed by Abbé Sicard to Mme Pinon on 17 November 1802, that Rose's father was still alive at the time. However, in a subsequent letter

Rose Marie Pinon, later de Freycinet (1794–1832), Paris, 1812, aged 17
From an engraving of an original portrait in the possession of Baron Henri de Freycinet

dated 23 September 1803, Abbé Sicard thanked Mme Pinon for spectacles which he described as 'a relic of your dear husband'. This would tend to indicate that M. Pinon had by then passed away.

The same Abbé Sicard, writing on 23 November 1803 to Mme Pinon, who resided at the time at Rue de Sèves, praised her highly for the efficient manner in which she ran the institute for young demoiselles: 'How fortunate for those children to be entrusted to the best of mothers, to the most zealous of teachers, to one who possesses to an eminent degree, not only the most complete education, but also the rare talent of communicating this knowledge.' It was indeed the good Abbé who had encouraged Mme Pinon to open such an establishment and had lent her 500 Francs in August 1803 for that purpose, although he was quick to ask for a reimbursement one month later. The Abbé had met Mme Pinon at Versailles and had become her mentor and her financier in this bold undertaking for a lady of modest means.

Thus, young Rose Pinon would have grown up in a refined and fairly scholarly atmosphere, receiving the best possible education along with 40 other young Parisian girls. The numerous references in her journal to such French literary figures as Chateaubriand and Bernardin de Saint-Pierre are probably due to the classical training which was the order of the day in her mother's institution. Often she alludes to a thinker whose work she had studied with Mme Pinon, or she quotes a saying or axiom which she had learnt from the headmistress. We know that in 1808 the Pinon family lived 'opposite the Incurables, Rue de Sèves' in the Faubourg Saint-Germain district. Rose was the eldest child in the family and, after the death of her father, she must have shouldered a heavy burden of responsibility. Hence her constant preoccupation with the health and well-being of the mater familias throughout her journal. Her only brother was taken prisoner at Wilma in August 1814 and appears to have died shortly thereafter.[2] Her younger sister, Stéphanie, travelled to Mauritius in the vessel *La Caroline*, which left Le Havre on 4 April 1818, to be a governess with a French family. The ship docked in Port Louis on 17 July 1818, a day after the departure of the *Uranie*, which distressed Rose greatly. From Reunion Island, in a letter of 25 July 1818, she confessed to her brother-in-law Henri de Freycinet:

> For my part, I have just suffered a great hardship during which, I must admit, I have shown signs of weakness and acted in a feeble manner. Some financial setbacks deprived my mother of all she owned and forced her to urge my sister to accept an offer made to her by the nice Madame de Barillon, to travel to Ile de France and take up a position as private tutor to the children of a respectable and wealthy family. But it was even more terrible for me when the ship which transported her dropped anchor, without my knowledge, in Port Louis just 24 hours after our departure! What a painful and distressing circumstance! However, I am a little reassured as to the fate of my sister, since I have friends in Mauritius who will make her welcome and will ensure that the family with whom she is to stay, will treat her with all the consideration and respect which her position demands. (Laage)

Stéphanie Pinon returned to France in 1825, and three years later she married M. Maillard, a civil servant, who soon after repudiated her and returned to a life of debauchery.[3]

Mme Pinon, a lady of some standing in the Paris community and of strong principles, was clearly greatly admired by Abbé Sicard, who often addressed her as 'my dear kind friend'. In her own letters she showed herself to be a deeply religious and moral person who despised wealth and worldly glories. When she heard of the appointment of Henri de Freycinet as Governor of Reunion Island [Bourbon], she wrote to him at once on 10 August 1820: 'I send you my warmest congratulations, if the promotion pleases you; my way of viewing the honours of this world fills me with doubt as to their real value' (Laage 239–34). Moreover, her style reveals an excellent mastery of syntax and a great deal of fluency and polish. Brought up by such an upstanding and intelligent mother, Rose seems to have suffered from an interesting inferiority complex with regard to Mme Pinon and her sister, Stéphanie. In a letter dated 9 June 1828 to Clémentine, Henri's wife, Rose declared: 'It would not be fair, as I have frequently told you and as you will discover for yourself one day, to judge me by my mother and sister whom you have met, for the former has passed on to the latter her intellect and education, and poor Rose, devoid of the first of these assets, has acquired only the second with great difficulty, but Nature has largely compensated her by giving her a kind and loving heart' (Laage 240–29). She also describes herself as the 'most scatterbrained of all women; it is a defect that is innate in me' (Laage 240–34). And in her journal, she underlines the change which has come over her in the course of the perilous voyage, from a wild spirit to a more down-to-earth, serious and mature young woman: 'It is true that everything I have endured during the last two years has given me such a sombre outlook on life that I have become a philosopher and that the gay, wild and scatterbrained Rose has become serious' (Chapter 11).

Be that as it may, it was the lively, intelligent and somewhat 'wild' Rose who enchanted and married the aristocratic Louis-Claude de Saulces de Freycinet on 6 June 1814 in the parish of Montmartre. Rose was 19 and Louis de Freycinet 35 years old. The couple were to remain childless throughout their married life. For the bourgeoise Rose who married into an aristocratic family, it was a step up the social ladder. The Freycinets did not object to their son's choice in the slightest; instead, they grew to love their daughter-in-law. To her son Henri, Antoinette Elisabeth Catherine de Freycinet, née Armand (1756–1841), who had married Louis de Saulces de Freycinet senior (1751–1827) on 5 November 1776, declared:

> Thank you for your congratulations on the wedding of your brother Louis; this important event will determine their future happiness. We have been told many good things about our daughter-in-law; the letters which she has addressed to us confirm our opinion that your brother has made a very wise choice as regards the qualities of the heart and of the mind, but I might have wished that, in addition, there was more wealth. I know from my own experience that without material comfort, even in the most well-matched of marriages there can be no happiness. (Laage 239–15)

And when she eventually met her in-laws, Rose seems to have charmed them. On 3 July 1817, just before Rose embarked stealthily in the *Uranie*, Louis' mother wrote to Henri de Freycinet about the young woman: 'For the last five months we have entertained here our charming daughter-in-law who is very dear to me, for she displays qualities which make her both likeable and admirable. In addition to this, she has received the best possible education and has a charming face' (Laage 177C). Rose de Freycinet was to remain devoted to the Freycinet clan all her life, writing to them, from all corners of the globe,

more regularly during the voyage than did Louis himself. She also maintained a loving relationship with Henri and his wife until her death in 1832.

The de Freycinet family

Rose Marie Pinon never forgot that her husband came from an illustrious French family, which included both politicians and naval officers. The de Saulses [de Saulces] family can be traced back to the end of the thirteenth century, 1293, and came originally from Bordeaux. In 1623 Jacques de Saulses was 'Procureur' [Chief Justice] of the King at Valence and bought the domain of Freycinet in Mirmande in the Département of Drôme, hence the name de Saulses [Saulces] de Freycinet. His son René was Lord of Mirmande and died in 1699. Their direct descendant Louis de Saulces de Freycinet (1751–1827), Louis' father, held the post of Chief Administrator of Montélimar Hospital in 1788, was appointed Administrator of the Commune of Montélimar and was later elected President of the local administrative council on 18 November 1791.[4] In that capacity, he was sent on a diplomatic mission to Genoa and retired on his return to France. He received the Legion of Honour for his services to the state.

His eldest son, Louis-Henri de Saulces de Freycinet, born at Montélimar on 31 December 1777, had an illustrious career in the French Navy, from the moment he enlisted with his brother Louis-Claude in 1794. After serving on several ships in wartime from 1795 to 1800, he volunteered to sail in the *Géographe* under Baudin on her voyage around the world from 1800 to 1804. In the course of the circumnavigation, Henri de Freycinet was promoted to the rank of Lieutenant de vaisseau [Lieutenant] in 1803.[5] Put in command of his own ships upon his return to France, he took part on the *Voltigeur* in a sea-battle on 26 March 1806 off the coast of Santo Domingo and lost his right arm. A portrait, now at the home of the Baron de Freycinet, shows Henri looking very distinguished in his naval uniform without his right arm. Named Frigate Captain in 1808, he continued to command several ships, the *Elisa* (1808), the *Régulus* (1812), the *Patriote* (1813–14), until he gained promotion to the rank of Capitaine de vaisseau [Captain] in July 1818. Henri de Freycinet was destined to a brilliant career as an administrator, first as Governor of Bourbon Island from September 1820 onwards and then of French Guyana (January 1826). Made a Baron in October 1827 and an Admiral the following year, he took up the post of Governor of Martinique in December 1828 and was highly respected by the locals. He ended his career as Maritime Prefect of Rochefort from May 1834 until his death on 21 March 1840. He married Jeanne Clémentine Bézar (1795–1876), a native of Rochefort, and had three children, Henri (1816–19), Charles (1828–81) and Lodoix (1820–77), who was in Rose's care from 1828 to 1830 and is the subject of many letters to Clémentine.[6]

Louis-Claude de Freycinet's other brothers deserve but a brief mention. André Charles (1783–1823) is referred to by Rose in Chapter 3 on Mauritius. As indicated in the journal, he left the island shortly after the arrival of the *Uranie* and proceeded to Calcutta where he married a local, thereby causing a certain amount of distress to his parents. He appears to have been well liked by the Mauritians and by Rose herself. Little is known about Louis' younger brother, Frédéric-Casimir (1787–1862), except that he was a keen botanist and married Nancy Malet in 1816. From their union was born yet another outstanding administrator and politician, Charles de Saulces de Freycinet (1828–1923),

Louis-Claude's nephew, who was elected Senator from 1876 until 1920 and served as Minister for Public Works (1877–79), and as President of the National Council for several terms (1879, 1882, 1886, 1890–92). Moreover, he became Minister for War (1888–93, 1898–99) and Minister of State during World War I (1915–16).[7] He assisted in the preparation of Rose's manuscript for publication shortly before his death in 1923.

Of all the sons of Louis de Freycinet senior, Rose's husband, Louis-Claude de Freycinet (1779–1842), was arguably the finest navigator. Like his brother Henri, he was made Commander of the Legion of Honour in 1825 for his considerable achievements during the voyage of the *Uranie*. He too had volunteered to join Baudin; having embarked in the *Naturaliste*, commanded by Hamelin, Louis was put in charge of the *Casuarina* in September 1802 when it was purchased as a substitute for the former, which was sent back to France from New South Wales. In 1803 the *Casuarina* stayed in Mauritius and Louis de Freycinet returned to France in the *Géographe* commanded by Henri. Employed mainly in cartographic work between 1804 and 1807, Louis completed the official version of the voyage of Baudin following the death of Péron[8] and was promoted to the rank of Frigate Captain in July 1811. Then at his instigation came the expedition around the world in the *Uranie* (1817–20), described in detail by Rose in her journal. The publication of the official version of the voyage and the atlas preoccupied Louis de Freycinet from 1824 until 1839. That the Ministry of the Interior's attitude vexed and irked him is apparent from his correspondence, published by his friend Fr Grille; in a letter of 23 September 1823, he waxed indignant: 'However, to this day, I have not interrupted work on the composition of the narrative; I press on with a constancy which I believe deserves a better recompense, but I work with a heavy heart and with a feeling of disgust which you would deem quite justified if you considered the large number of obstacles which I have had to overcome.'[9] For his work in the field of cartography and his experiments on magnetism, Louis de Saulces de Freycinet was elected to the Académie des Sciences in January 1826. He later joined the Council of Works in 1830 and became one of the founders of the Geographical Society of Paris.

His career as a navigator is of direct relevance to Australia, not just because he had the temerity to remove from Shark Bay the Vlamingh plate, which he took back to Paris with him, but because his name was given by Baudin to a peninsula on the east coast of Tasmania, dominated by Mount Freycinet, 613 metres high. *The Australian Encyclopaedia* points out: 'Tasman named the peninsula Vanderlyn Island in 1642, but the present name honours de Freycinet, who explored this coast with Baudin in 1802.'[10] Louis' name is also linked with an island of the Tuamotu Archipelago (latitude 17° 43´ south; longitude 140°), which was discovered by Duperrey during the voyage of the *Coquille* in 1823.

In 1832 Louis de Freycinet fell seriously ill from an attack of cholera, which was rife in Paris; nursed by Rose and by his friend Dr Gaimard, who had sailed with him in the *Uranie*, he recovered. Not so Rose, who spent many days and nights at her husband's bedside despite a stomach ailment from which she had suffered for some time. She passed away within a few hours of falling ill on 7 May 1832 and was buried in Paris. Her body was later 'transferred to the cemetery of Saulces on 19 September 1849' and laid to rest beside Louis, according to a letter of the parish priest of Saulces to the Mayor of Mirmande (Laage).

As for Louis de Freycinet, after the death of his beloved Rose he is said to have pined away and to have become increasingly morose. His friend Grille remarked in 1853: 'Cholera deprived Freycinet of the wife whom he adored. Since that death, he only languished'.[11] In an anonymous obituary of Rose, which was clearly written after 1842, and possibly in 1849 when her body was transferred to the cemetery of Saulces, one reads:

> In 1832, Paris was in the grip of a cholera epidemic. M. de Freycinet was struck down but was fortunate enough to recover. Mme de Freycinet, who had been suffering from gastralgia for ten months and who had become exhausted from nursing her husband, herself fell victim to the dreaded disease and, in a few hours, was taken from her loving husband on 7 May 1832. M. de Freycinet never recovered from his loss; his health was subsequently always poor, and he died suddenly on 18 August 1842, struck down by a heart attack. (Laage 18–299)

Even as a young man, Louis had a fragile constitution; his parents continually expressed their concern about his health during the voyage. Indeed, the main reason alleged by Rose for secretly stowing away was that she wished to look after Louis. This she did in the Malouines during the weeks that followed the shipwreck.

Louis' death certificate lodged with the Commune of Mirmande, Département of Drôme, reads as follows:

> In the year 1842 and on 19 August at three in the afternoon ... M. de Lagarde, Charles-François-Maurice, aged 51, landowner, and M. Aubannel, Jean-Pierre, aged 50, geometrician, both residents of Mirmande, declared that M. Louis-Claude de Freycinet, aged 63, former Ship Captain, member of the Institute and Office of Longitudes, Commander of the Legion of Honour, living in Mirmande, the widower of Rose Pinon, died yesterday at 11 p.m. in the castle of M. de Lagarde, at Gazavel, also in this

Commune, and after the death certificate had been read to the witnesses, they signed before us. Mirmande, 6 August 1842

(Extract from the Register of the Commune of Mirmande, Drôme, no. 37 (Laage))

On his death, Louis left his whole estate to Blanche de Freycinet (1826–80), the daughter of his brother Frédéric-Casimir.

In the winter of his life, as he reflected on his achievements and on the way he had been treated since his return to France in 1820, especially with regard to the publication of the narrative of the voyage, Louis became more disenchanted and depressed. In an epilogue, or reflections, on the delay to the publication of the voyage, written in January 1839 and sent to his brother Henri, he mused:

> I have left behind in the Navy friends and comrades who are dear to me. I would like to convey to them here the fond memories I have of them and wish them far more happiness than I have experienced! Looking at my present existence and reflecting on a fast receding past, I can only quote the words of Tasso: 'Fame, which appears so attractive, whose seductive tones lure the proud mortals, is but a spectre, a dream, nay the very shadow of a dream which is so speedily dispelled!'
> (Laage 274C)

No wonder Henri wrote back to Louis on 3 April 1839 to urge him not to publish the epilogue in which the latter had attacked the Ministry of the Interior so openly!

The voyage of the Uranie

Louis de Freycinet's plan for the first scientific expedition around the world since Baudin's (1800–04) must be viewed in the context of France's attempt to restore her prestige following Napoleon's downfall in 1815. There was then a strong revival of interest in maritime exploration; between 1816 and 1830 France's expansionist policies were reflected in the fact that there were no less than seven maritime expeditions around the world. As John Dunmore has commented, 'national pride called for activities, now inevitably of a peaceful nature, that would help to retain France's position as a great European nation'.[12] Since geographical exploration was truly a thing of the past, after the great eighteenth-century voyages of discovery, the objectives of the proposed expeditions, from Freycinet's onwards, became essentially scientific, such as the verification of hydrographic data or the collection of botanical and zoological specimens. The initiative was taken by naval officers such as Freycinet, Duperrey, Dumont d'Urville, Hyacinthe de Bougainville, Laplace, Vaillant and Dupetit-Thouars, with a view to distinguishing themselves for the sake of advancement.[13] Moreover, a new spirit of adventure inspired those officers who sought to 'overcome the humdrum of office work and of anchorages and to draw attention to themselves by serving science'.[14]

A combination of all those motives probably led Louis de Freycinet to offer his services to the Ministry of the Interior. In August 1816 he submitted a detailed proposal to the then Minister, Lainé, for a circumnavigation of the world during which scientific observations would be his main goal: to measure the globe's southern hemisphere, to observe magnetic and meteorological phenomena, to carry out experiments relating to air pressure and to the temperature of the ocean at different depths. Freycinet also volunteered to report on natural history and on the culture and customs of diverse Pacific nations. His proposal was accepted without any major modifications by the Ministry of the Navy on 12 September 1816, although some aspects were developed further.[15] Since almost the whole of the Pacific had been successfully explored both before and during Baudin's expedition, Freycinet was instructed to verify and complete his former Commander's survey of the west coast of Australia, especially Arnhem Land. The plan of the voyage states: 'His Majesty recommends to M. Freycinet to explore that coastline, if as a result of favourable winds, his crossing were to be shorter than is usually the case ... He will reconnoitre in its entirety, or in part, the only coastline which is yet to be properly surveyed, in order that we may have detailed charts of the complete outline of Australia'.[16] The instructions of the Académie des Sciences largely reiterated Freycinet's proposed scientific goals and concluded that his was 'a vital voyage for the future of science and would add to the prestige of our nation and of the French Navy'.[17] There was no hidden political agenda in the instructions of the Ministry of the Interior, as there was to be later in the case of Louis-Isidore Duperrey, who was asked to find a suitable site for a French penitentiary settlement in the Antipodes,[18] or in the case of Hyacinthe de Bougainville, who was ordered to report on the military strengths of the British in New South Wales.

Louis de Freycinet chose to revert to Cook's and Louis-Antoine de Bougainville's practice of entrusting scientific duties to naval officers. He had not forgotten the unpleasant confrontations between civilian savants and officers during Baudin's expedition. Lamarche was his First Officer; Labiche, the Second Lieutenant, died at sea in the East Indies on 9 January 1819. Duperrey, an ensign, was to acquire a great deal of knowledge and experience which he put to good use during his own expedition of 1822–25. The other ensign, Laborde, died at sea on

23 February 1818. The surgeons, Quoy and Gaimard, were responsible for the natural history collection and Gaudichaud was an expert botanist. Requin, the purser, Gabert, the secretary, and Abbé Florentin-Louis de Quélen de la Villeglée, the chaplain, are referred to by Rose in her journal. Ten midshipmen helped out with the scientific work, making a total staff of 20. What is little known is that Dumont d'Urville, on hearing of Freycinet's expedition, wrote to the Commander on 21 January 1817 and volunteered for the voyage, but his request arrived too late, since the staff had already been chosen. Nevertheless, Dumont d'Urville insisted: 'I was sad to hear that you had selected all your officers and that there were no vacancies left. However, to explore all avenues so that I have nothing to reproach myself with, I have taken the liberty of writing to you directly to offer my services. I entreat you to include me, if at all possible, in your future undertakings' (Laage). The draughtsman Jacques Arago was the only civilian on board and was responsible for many of the 500 etchings brought back. Freycinet carefully picked his crew of 125, most of whom were southerners and were skilled tradesmen who proved very useful in the Malouines when it became necessary to repair the rescue ship *Mercury*. Freycinet had resolved to keep the costs of the expedition to a minimum, although Duperrey did even better in 1822 with the *Coquille* by restricting his crew to 12 officers and 58 sailors.[19]

In 1816 Louis de Freycinet was first offered the corvette which was later renamed the *Coquille* by Duperrey, but he chose instead the *Ciotat*, a corvette of 350 tons to which he gave the name *Uranie*. Gabarres and corvettes were considered at the time ideal for long circumnavigations because of their strong frames. The *Uranie* measured 112 feet long, 28 feet wide and 14 feet deep and carried two main cannons.[20] It is easy to imagine the cramped conditions in which Rose de Freycinet found herself in such a small vessel with 125 men, surrounded by a large amount of astronomic and other scientific equipment and more than 200 books, including *The Present State of New South Wales* by John Campbell, obtained through the French Consulate in London. Yet, Rose's husband had done his utmost to refurbish the ship for her sake; between 25 September and 31 December 1816, no less than 11 letters were exchanged by the Ministry of the Navy, the Ministry of the Interior and Louis de Freycinet concerning the urgent need to renovate the living quarters. Furthermore, a great deal of attention was paid by the Commander to hygiene, and he received detailed instructions from Dr Keraudren, the General Inspector of Health for the Navy. Food, the selection of adequate clothing, an emphasis on general cleanliness, the use of stills and iron containers, resistant to scurvy, for water and meat, and a large supply of Appert tins were all measures taken by the Captain to make the voyage as safe as possible for his crew. Many references to these items are to be found in Rose's journal. Little wonder that Freycinet lost only 11 crew members during the expedition, although 66 of the men deserted at various ports. Duperrey was to improve on this record; having learnt from the previous voyage, he took such stringent measures that not a single member of his crew perished during a three-year voyage.

Contrary to the original itinerary proposed by Freycinet himself and adopted by the Ministry of the Interior, the *Uranie* did not stop at King George Sound in Australia, nor at Dusky Bay in New Zealand, nor at Tahiti.[21] Nevertheless, the voyage was prolonged by a good six months, mainly because of the shipwreck at French Bay. What did the expedition achieve? There were no new geographical discoveries, but the crew

brought back an impressive collection of specimens in the fields of botany, zoology and geology: 25 mammals, 313 birds, 45 reptiles, 164 species of fish—many of which were unknown, countless shells, 30 skeletons including that of a Papuan, 1300 insects, 3000 plant specimens, a large number of which were new to the Muséum d'Histoire Naturelle in Paris, and 900 rock samples. Dunmore sums up Freycinet's and the crew's contributions thus: 'The scientific work, especially the study of terrestrial magnetism and weather observations, is far from negligible and deserves the praise which the Académie des Sciences bestowed on it in its report of 7 May 1821'.[22] This was all the more creditable since many crates had been lost during the tragedy that befell the *Uranie* in 1820. The French Government may well have been justifiably aggrieved on account of the large sums which it had spent on refurbishing the corvette—167 000 Francs, not counting the cost of replacing the *Uranie* with the *Physicienne* in the Malouines. Yet, the aims of the expedition had been more than adequately achieved. The total cost of the voyage has been put at 1 200 000 Francs, and it is not surprising that the Ministry of the Interior dragged its feet when it came to spending more money on the official publications, finally completed in 1839.

Such then was the significance of the voyage which, until the corvette ran aground in French Bay, had been crowned with success. Despite this catastrophe, far more benefits accrued to science during that voyage than as a result of Baudin's earlier expedition. Much of the credit must be given to Freycinet's professional approach, while other members of the staff, including Quoy, Duperrey, Gaudichaud and Gaimard, also played their part. Even Rose states in her journal that she caught the 'scientific bug' and started a collection of specimens, although she took no part in the scientific experiments which Louis carried out in the field of magnetism. The collection of books which belonged to Louis de Freycinet, and of which there is a catalogue in the Archives de Laage, indicates his strong preoccupation with magnetism and hydrography as well as astronomy. He was at heart a scientist, and although the recalcitrant Rose failed to comprehend, as she avows in her journal, the long detours decided upon by the captain of the *Uranie* in the name of science, it was predominantly the scientific observations and the natural history collections that won the approval of scientists and politicians alike on the return of the corvette to France in 1820. Perhaps they also helped to silence the once vociferous critics of Rose in official circles.

Reactions to Rose stowing away

All the evidence points to the fact that Rose's decision was not taken on the spur of the moment. In the anonymous obituary, the writer argues: 'Mme de Freycinet was gentle and shy, but she was always prepared to sacrifice herself for those she loved. Thus, it was she who first hit upon the idea of accompanying her husband; at first he objected to her plan, but then his affection for her swayed him' (Laage 18–299). Rose had probably decided on this course of action soon after October 1816, when her husband's proposal of a scientific expedition had been approved by the Ministry of the Interior. Grille, a friend of the family, stated that she had planned her campaign as early as 1815.[23]

On 17 September 1817, the day after she had gone on board, as the *Uranie* was making ready to sail, Rose wrote to Henri de Freycinet: 'There you are! Louis wanted to tell you of the plan which we had formed not to be separated during a long voyage and he is afraid that he might

have offended you by not confiding in you. Yet, his trust in you is complete and his love for you boundless.' As a postscript, Louis added the words: 'Adieu, Adieu, dear and kind friend! Forgive my silence; love me always as dearly as I love you. I am busy tacking between the channels in the harbour.' (Laage)

It was only when the *Uranie* was at sea that the actions of Rose de Freycinet became known to the general public. The conduct of the stowaway aroused indignation in official circles. Newspapers seized on a titillating front-page story and exaggerated the impudence of the 22-year-old who had flouted conventions and naval ordinances forbidding the presence of females on board state ships. The *Moniteur Officiel*, which on Friday, 26 September 1817, had proudly announced the launch of a new expedition, informed its readers on 4 October 1817:

> A few days after this departure, news broke in Toulon that Madame de Freycinet, who had accompanied her husband to the port of embarkation, had disappeared thereafter and, dressed as a man, had gone on board the ship that same night, despite the ordinances that prohibit the presence of women in state vessels, without official authorisation. This example of conjugal devotion deserves to be made public.[24]

Moreover, the Ministries of the Interior and of the Navy were at the time far less tolerant of such a flagrant breach of the rules and took some action, albeit too late, for Rose was already at sea. In an official letter to the Minister for the Navy, the Vice-Admiral, Commander of the port of Toulon, declared that he had been told of Rose's presence only after the ship had weighed anchor and that he had closely investigated the matter:

> I learnt that Madame de Freycinet had indeed embarked in the corvette *Uranie*. She left her

apartment during the night of the 15th and 16th around midnight, informing her hosts that she was leaving on the coach for Marseilles where she claimed she intended staying at the house of a merchant, M. Bonnet, to await the arrival of her father-in-law. The latter was supposed to come and take her to Freycinet in the Drôme. But M. Bonnet never saw her.

Her father-in-law never came to Marseilles. What is certain, however, is that upon leaving her lodgings in the Rue St Roch, she proceeded to others at 96 Rue Royale, where she remained until the night of the 16th to the 17th. Then she went in a boat disguised as a man and embarked in the *Uranie* at half-past midnight. The corvette set sail on the 17th at 10 a.m. The embarkation of Mme de Freycinet is thus confirmed.[25]

It would appear that a Lieutenant Leblanc [or Le Blanc] had disembarked at the last minute, allegedly to make room for Rose who was dressed as an officer. The Vice-Admiral reported to the Minister for the Navy that he had questioned Leblanc, who had admitted that he had suspected Louis de Freycinet's secret plan for some time. It may well be that the officer was saving his own skin by accusing the Commander after he had willingly been a party to the whole exercise. In the introduction to the Duplomb edition of Rose's journal, the Baron de Freycinet, writing in 1927, repudiated allegations that Louis had acted in an improper manner: 'There was a rumour circulating in Toulon that to accommodate his wife better, Commander de Freycinet had disembarked one of his officers (M. Leblanc) before his ship left port. The Maritime Prefect had no difficulty in refuting this slanderous report.'[26]

As to whether Louis knew of Rose's plan to stow away before he sailed, all the evidence points to the fact that the decision had been taken jointly by both spouses quite some time before 17 September 1817. The Vice-Admiral had

received several requests from Louis to have his private quarters extended. The Vice-Admiral wrote to the Minister for the Navy on 26 April 1817, without a hint of suspicion of the couple's plan:

> Monsieur de Freycinet, Frigate Captain in command of the *Uranie*, expressed to me the wish to have built on board a poop-deck which would be an extension both to his lodgings and to the quarters of other officers on the expedition. I pointed out to the officer in question that I was surprised that he had waited until the last minute to make his request, and that, in my view, such an extension ... by adding to the height of the deadwork, would have a detrimental effect on the manoeuvres and the stability of the ship. I did not, therefore, feel inclined to approve the construction, unless expressly ordered to do so by Your Excellency.[27]

Nevertheless, it would seem that in the end Louis obtained the Minister's permission to refurbish his lodgings, which indicates a calculated decision on his part to provide for the needs of his wife during the long journey that lay ahead.

Refuting newspaper reports that Rose had embarked without Louis' knowledge, the artist Jacques Arago declared in a personal tribute: 'Mme de Freycinet ... went on board with the consent of her husband; everyone knew this.'[28] The obvious irritation of the Ministry was exacerbated by the fact that it became aware of what it considered a serious breach of naval ordinances only after the departure of the *Uranie*. Rose wore her male apparel for several days and went thus dressed to visit the Governor of Gibraltar. The French Consul on the island, M. Joseph Viale, who is described by Rose as a braggard, reported much later on 11 February 1819 to the Minister for the Navy:

> M. and Mme de Freycinet and almost the whole crew came to pay homage to the Governor. His

Excellency received them in the most flattering manner. Mme de Freycinet did not wear a uniform but was dressed as a man in a blue frock-coat with trousers to match. If the Governor took offence at this, he did not communicate his feelings to me. Yet I feel that in view of his friendship for me, had he been upset, he would have confided in me ... I must point out to Your Excellency that, on the very day of the *Uranie*'s departure, Mme de Freycinet resumed her female clothes, and she would have come ashore thus dressed had the vessel not sailed on that day.[29]

The Ministry of the Navy was impotent to have Rose removed until the *Uranie* reached the first French port or territory, Reunion Island. In her journal Rose describes her trepidation about possible reprisals by French officials in Reunion (Chapter 4). By then, one year had elapsed and the Governor of the Island was conscious of the fact that he could not carry out the instructions of the French Government. He was, as Rose surmised, swayed both by the arguments put forward by Louis and by her own charms. Upon Louis de Freycinet's return to France, the matter of Rose's embarkation was not discussed at a special court martial convened on 16 December 1820 to examine the shipwreck of the *Uranie* in French Bay (the Malouines). The Commander was completely exonerated and Rose's presence never publicly called into question.

Yet, during the voyage itself, all crew members were extremely careful not to mention Rose de Freycinet's name, either in official dispatches or in their journals. Louis himself referred to the name Rose only once in his letters to the Ministry of the Navy; to the Minister he wrote on 17 December 1819: 'I have discovered to the east of the Navigators Archipelago a small island surrounded by strong reefs which I have named Rose Island'.[30] Moreover, he inserted a single reference in his official version of the voyage to the discovery of the island 'which

I named Rose Island, from the name of someone who is extremely dear to me'.[31] According to John Dunmore, this was not a new discovery, for the island had been sighted by Jacoob Roggeveen and named Vuyle Eyland, or Bird Island, in June 1722 on his way to the Samoas (latitude 14° 32′ 42″).[32] Much more tongue-in-cheek was Arago's comment on Rose Island in his highly readable version of the voyage, which was published in 1823, much earlier than the official version:

> Congratulate us, dear Batlle [sic]; it may be a short quarter of a league in circumference. Lengthened reefs surround it, and render its vicinity very dangerous. A few trees crown its summit, on which thousands of birds take refuge.
>
> Let us see, what shall we call it? Let it be a flowery name. Shall it be Green Island, Red Island, or ... No, I suppose it will be Rose Island.[33]

For all her courage and devotion during a dangerous circumnavigation, Rose is remembered for one islet to the east of the Navigators Archipelago and for one cape to the east of Peron Peninsula, near Shark Bay in Western Australia, which bore her name on French maps. In addition, during the voyage of the *Uranie*, the name Pinon was given to a dove in Rawak and to two ferns gathered by the botanist Gaudichaud and labelled by him: *Hibiscus pinoéanus* and *Fougère pinonia*. Two years after Rose's return to France, Duperrey, who had greatly admired his former captain's wife, named two parts of the New Guinean coast after her, Pointe Rose and Anse Rose. In his eulogy of Rose de Freycinet, Jacques Arago waxed lyrical: 'And in return for so much inconvenience, for facing so many dangers, for such deprivation, what recompense did she receive? What glory was hers? Alas! What did it matter to this brave lady, taken from her friends and from all her admirers at such an early age, that her name had been given to a small island a league in diameter at the most, to a sharp rock surrounded by reefs which we had discovered in the middle of the Pacific Ocean?'[34] In fact, it mattered a great deal to Rose, who could not hide her pride and joy in her journal: 'I am pleased to inform you, Madam, that the corvette *Uranie* has discovered, to the east of the Navigators Archipelago, a small island which does not appear on the most recent charts of these seas and which the Commander of the above-mentioned corvette has named Rose Island. It is done; my name has been linked with a small corner of the world' (Chapter 8).

The reactions of Louis' immediate family to Rose stowing away were more subdued, but betrayed a certain amount of apprehension about the likely repercussions of such a rash decision. Louis' parents had clearly been privy to their daughter-in-law's plan and had debated the point with their son. They were a little aghast at such a blatant infringement of the official rules, which had governed the life of Louis senior as an administrator. To Henri he wrote on 12 November 1817: 'Pray God that this voyage be a happy one! I was opposed to Louis' plan. The presence of his wife by his side on such a long voyage may have serious consequences, especially for the health of the young woman' (Laage). On 8 September 1817, Louis' mother confessed to Clémentine de Freycinet, Henri's wife, to being a little hurt and shocked: 'You are right to admire the courage of your sister-in-law. No doubt her presence will cause quite a number of problems for her husband. I hope that his health won't suffer as a result. May God protect them and grant them success on this long and perilous voyage' (Laage 177C). What seems to have rubbed salt into her wounds is the fact that Madame Pinon knew of the young couple's plans and had not attempted to dissuade them. To Clémentine, Mme de Freycinet declared:

I still believe that our dear daughter-in-law has presumed too much as regards her strength, by exposing herself to the fatigue of such a lengthy journey. We have nothing to reproach ourselves with; we tried hard to advise them against their proposed course of action; their minds were made up. Can you believe that they had the support of the Barillon family and of Madame Pinon? May God watch over these dear children and grant them complete success on this long and painful voyage! Like you, we took note of the malicious reports in the newspapers. (Laage)

It would appear that Caroline de Nanteuil was also in on the secret of the grand design and that Louis' family, with the exception of the one person in a delicate official position vis-à-vis the Ministry of the Navy, Henri de Freycinet, had all been informed of the intentions of the young couple before the *Uranie* set sail. Yet, all respected Louis' and Rose's wishes, some more disapprovingly than others. Caroline de Nanteuil had been told that she could expect a series of letters from all parts of the globe and Madame Pinon had obtained a number of maps on which to plot the ship's progress.

The hostile reactions of the press affected the Freycinet family far more than the Pinon family because the former were in the public eye. As for Rose, she was fortunate enough to be oblivious to the furore which her actions had caused in official circles, although she was perceptive enough to foresee the eventual condemnation by the Ministries. It was not until the stopover at Bourbon Island in 1818 that she had access to French newspapers. Soon after the *Uranie*'s departure, Frédéric-Casimir had written to his brother Henri on the subject: 'You must have read in the newspapers details of Rose's embarkation. I am quite sure that such notoriety will have distressed her greatly, for she was counting on the fact that her design would remain clouded in secrecy'.[35] Rose's actions were judged far more tolerantly by King Louis XVIII who, when told of the young woman's flighty action, was slightly amused and remarked that this act of conjugal devotion ought to be excused because Rose's example was unlikely to be followed by others.[36]

A courageous woman ahead of her time

In the main, both her contemporaries and subsequent generations have viewed Rose's momentous decision with a degree of sympathy and admiration. However, as had been predicted by Louis' parents, her presence on board did cause some problems. In *Realms and Islands*, Marnie Bassett has quoted Gabriel Lafond's report during his visit to the Marianas shortly after the stopover of the *Uranie*: 'she was also an apple of discord, thrown not just to three goddesses but to a crowd of young men whose jealousies and passions could not fail to be aroused'.[37] Today, Rose de Freycinet is likely to be remembered for being ahead of her time and for an unwillingness to conform to what she deemed to be irrational conventions. She also behaved with such a degree of decorum on board and with such fortitude that the crew came to hold her in the highest esteem. The *Dictionnaire de Biographie Française* sums up her conduct during the voyage thus: 'On board, she displayed admirable moral superiority over the crew'.[38] An anecdote about Rose's first few days at sea is recounted thus by Jacques Arago: 'She rarely walked on deck, but when she did, the crew, out of consideration for her, left the leeside of the ship to her alone, whilst beyond the main mast, unsavoury songs died in the throats of seasoned campaigners and long swear words of fifteen to eighteen syllables, which would have entertained the devils in hell, died on the lips of the most intrepid of men. Then Mme de Freycinet,

wearing her cool cornet, laughed at this strict discipline imposed on so many foul mouths, whilst sometimes her smile seemed to be saying "Thank you".'[39]

Fr Grille described her in 1853 as 'a remarkably intelligent, courageous and determined young woman'.[40] Dr Quoy, who sailed with her on the *Uranie*, said of Rose in one of his letters that she 'had a sharp mind' (Laage 259B), while her nephew Lodoix de Freycinet, who perhaps knew her better than anyone else, with the exception of her husband, praised her 'distinguished mind' and her 'charming personality' (Laage 12–259). The most moving tribute was paid by Jacques Arago in a passage quoted in the Duplomb edition of 1927. The artist stressed two aspects of Rose's character which will emerge clearly from the journal; first, her caring attitude and kindness towards others: 'When a poor sailor on deck fought against the torments of dysentery or scurvy, Mme de Freycinet never failed to enquire after the invalid's health, and pots of marmalade travelled to and fro with the permission of the doctor.'[41] Next, Arago highlighted Rose's bravery in adversity, especially during the shipwreck:

> Sad, unwell, but calm and resigned, she waited for death which threatened us from all quarters, without displaying any sign of fear ... And Mme Freycinet saw her apartment crowded with debris from the ocean and religiously guarded the biscuits which were half-soaked, having been removed from the hold under water, and she watched fearlessly as barrels of gunpowder floated by near her next to burning lanterns, and she forgot her own sad plight for the sake of the general misfortune. Mme de Freycinet is a truly courageous woman.[42]

Further proof of Rose's intrepid nature and steadfastness is provided in the anonymous obituary. Here the author describes the grave danger in which the *Uranie* found herself as she made for an anchorage point in the Bay of Bon Succès and recounts an anecdote which had come from Rose herself:

> Since then, she has told me that as the corvette was manoeuvring to avoid the reefs and passed perilously close to the reefs against which she might have smashed to pieces, Mme de Freycinet was fully conscious of the mortal danger. She had positioned herself to have a good view of what was happening. She propped her head against her hand, scarcely breathing, with one finger in her mouth so as not to betray her fear. The finger went between her teeth which bit into it so deeply that blood began to gush along her arm. This brought her out of the intense concentration which had prevented her from feeling any pain. (Laage 18–299)

As to whether Rose de Freycinet ever regretted exposing herself to such dangers and such discomfort and running the risk of public condemnation in the name of love, we have to turn to the testimony of Lodoix de Freycinet who quoted the following passage from a letter written by his aunt dated August 1828:

> I had to choose between my affection and general prejudices which could only be challenged with the certainty of being criticised by the majority ... I chose the solution which, in my view, would bring the greatest happiness to my friend [Louis] and to me. Life is too short! I wanted to brighten it up as much as possible, and I shall never regret the decision which I took, since on numerous occasions I was able to lighten the heavy burden of responsibility borne by my husband. This one thought now erases from my mind all the sacrifices which I had to make during those three long years. I now look back on my decision with a great deal of satisfaction, whereas had I acted differently, I would have nothing but regret. If only I were twenty today and if my health were as good as it was then, I would not be tormented by the prospect of another voyage.[43]

Those almost prophetic words were written just four years before Rose's life was cut short by the cholera epidemic of 1832. She was never to go on another voyage; neither was her husband, Louis de Freycinet, who passed away ten years after his wife. Both were to be reunited in the cemetery of Saulces in the Département of Drôme in 1849.

> Ah, my Beloved, fill that Cup that clears
> TO-DAY of past Regrets and Future Fears.
> > Edward Fitzgerald,
> > *Omar Khayyam*, I, xx[44]

Notes

Unless otherwise stated, all passages originally in French, especially those from documents found in the Archives de Laage and the Duplomb edition of Rose's journal, have been translated into English. Reference to a shelfmark has been provided for most of the letters and documents from the Archives de Laage where these have been catalogued. However, in some cases, where they do not bear a classification number, (Laage) has been inserted.

1   *The Oxford Dictionary of Quotations.* London: Oxford University Press, 1964, p.206.
2   'Notes of Admiral Lodoix de Freycinet on his aunt Rose de Freycinet' (Laage 12–259).
3   See Epilogue, Rose's letter to Clémentine, 29 May 1828 (Laage 240–28).
4   J. Villain, *La France Moderne: Dictionnaire Généalogique, Historique et Biographique.* Saint-Etienne: J. Thomas, 1908, Vol. 2, p.851.
5   Etienne Taillemite, *Dictionnaire des Marins Français.* Paris: Editions Maritimes et d'Outre-mer, c.1982, p.127.
6   See Epilogue.
7   Pierre Larousse, *Grand Dictionnaire Universel du XIXe Siècle.* Paris: Administration du Grand Dictionnaire Universel, 1872, Vol. 8, p.825.
8   Louis-Claude de Freycinet, *Voyage de Découverte aux Terres Australes exécuté ... sur les corvettes le Géographe, le Naturaliste et la goëlette la Casuarina ... 1800–1804.* 2 vols. Paris: L'Imprimerie Impériale, 1815.
9   Fr Grille, *Louis de Freycinet: Sa Vie de Savant et de Marin, ses Voyages, ses Ouvrages, ses Lettres, son Caractère et sa Mort.* Paris: Le Doyen, 1853, p.63.
10   5th ed. Sydney: Australian Geographic, 1988, Vol. 4, p.1351.
11   Grille, op. cit., p.15.
12   John Dunmore, *French Explorers in the Pacific.* Oxford: Clarendon Press, 1969, Vol. 2, p.50.
13   John Dunmore, 'Problems arising from social and political change in France' In J. Hardy and A. Frost (eds), *European Voyaging towards Australia.* Canberra: Australian Academy of the Humanities, 1990, p.65.
14   Jean-Paul Faivre, *L'Expansion Française dans le Pacifique: 1840–1842.* Paris: Nouvelles Editions Latines, 1953, p.259 (my translation).
15   Archives Nationales, Paris (hereafter AN), AN BB/4/998.

16   AN 5JJ 68.
17   AN BB/4/998.
18   See Marc Serge Rivière and Thuy Huynh Einam (eds), *Any Port in a Storm: From Provence to Australia.* Townsville: James Cook University, 1993, Introduction, p.18.
19   Dunmore, *French Explorers in the Pacific*, op. cit., Vol. 2, p.114.
20   AN BB/4/998.
21   Faivre, op. cit., p.265.
22   Dunmore, *French Explorers in the Pacific*, op. cit., Vol. 2, p.107.
23   Grille, op. cit., p.15.
24   Charles Duplomb (ed.), *Journal de Madame Rose de Saulces de Freycinet, d'après le manuscrit original accompagné de notes.* Paris: Société d'Editions Géographiques, Maritimes et Coloniales, 1927, Introduction, p.X.
25   AN BB/4/998.
26   Duplomb (ed.), loc. cit.
27   AN BB/4/998.
28   Duplomb (ed.), op. cit., pp.179–180.
29   Ibid., Introduction, p.XI.
30   AN BB/4/998.
31   Louis-Claude de Freycinet, *Voyage autour du Monde entrepris par ordre du Roi ... exécuté sur les corvettes de S.M. l'Uranie et la Physicienne 1817–1820.* Paris: Pillet Aîné, 1827–39.
32   Dunmore, *French Explorers in the Pacific*, ibid., Vol. 2, p.95.
33   Jacques Arago, *Narrative of a Voyage round the World in the Uranie and Physicienne Corvettes.* London: Treuttel and Wurtz, Treuttel Jun. and Richter, 1823, p.158.
34   Duplomb (ed.), op. cit., p.183.
35   Ibid., Introduction, p.X.
36   Ibid.
37   Marnie Bassett, *Realms and Islands: The World Voyage of Rose de Freycinet in the Corvette Uranie 1817–1820.* London: Oxford University Press, 1962, p.148.
38   Paris: Letouzey et Ane, 1969, Vol. 14, p.216 (my translation).
39   Duplomb (ed.), op. cit., p.180.
40   Grille, op. cit., p.15.
41   Duplomb (ed.), op. cit., p.182.
42   Ibid., p.183.
43   'Notes of Admiral Lodoix de Freycinet on his aunt Rose de Freycinet' (Laage 12–259).
44   *The Oxford Dictionary of Quotations*, op. cit., p.206.

Madame Rose de Freycinet stows away on the Uranie – Stopover at Gibraltar – Teneriffe – Santa Cruz harbour, Canary Islands – In quarantine – Crossing the equator

September 1817 – I shall begin my journal from the moment when, leaving my home in Toulon at midnight, I made my way alone to the house of one of my friends. There I spent a very restless night thinking of the somewhat daring adventure which I was to embark upon and the dear ones I was about to leave behind for so long and whom I might never see again.

Everyone in Toulon believed that I had left on the midnight coach, bound for Marseilles where I was to stay at the house of a relative of my husband.

I spent the whole of the following day writing my farewell letters and that night, around 11.30 p.m., I donned my male attire. Accompanied by Louis and one of his friends, I headed for the harbour to go aboard the ship. It seemed that the moon favoured my flight, for it disappeared behind the clouds, thereby preventing those present from recognising me. However, at the entrance to the dock, we had to stop and give the password; the sentinels brought a light and I did not know where to hide. At last, shaking all over, I reached the quay and climbed aboard as nimbly as I could. Forced to pass through a crowd of officers on deck, I was asked by some to identify myself: the friend who accompanied us declared that I was his son who, indeed, was about my height.

I tossed about in my sleep even more than usual that night. I imagined that I had been recognised and that the Admiral Commander, having been informed, would order my disembarkation. The slightest noise startled me and I continued to shake with fear until we were clear of the harbour.

17 September 1817 – At 7 a.m. we cast off to sail out of the main harbour, but as the wind was light, we were towed out by a harbour tug. A contrary wind forced us to tack as we rounded a promontory. In the evening, the wind freshened and we lost sight of our beloved homeland. Although it was almost night, I kept my eyes fixed on land as long as possible, and when

The port of Toulon, embarkation point for the *Uranie's* voyage in September 1817

Louis Philippe Alphonse Bichebois (1801–1850) *Vue du Port de Toulon* c.1836 lithograph; 20.3 x 30.5 cm Auguste Nicolas Vaillant, *Voyage autour du Monde ...* (Paris: A. Bertrand, c.1840), plate no. 1 National Library of Australia Pictorial Collection (S5178)

I could see only the sky and the ocean, it seemed to me that I was being parted from my friends a second time ...

I wept bitterly. I thought of my dear mother and of her misfortune at being cruelly separated from all her children, at a time in her life when their care would have been so important! For all that, I could not blame myself, as I was abiding by God's prescribed rule! Nevertheless, my heart was full of sorrow when I considered the sad state she would be in during the many painful years to come.

The weather changed for the worse in the evening and a rather violent storm arrived to disrupt our first night at sea. Besides being gripped by fear, I suffered difficulties which cannot be understood by someone who has never sailed. The rest of our personal effects had been brought to our quarters during the day; hence, they had not been arranged but dumped hurriedly in our small cabins. As a result, when the storm came and shook the vessel, the boxes and packages rolled onto the floor. Rising to try and safeguard some porcelain, I knocked a table covered with various articles. I myself would have fallen, had I not speedily reached my bed where I helplessly witnessed all the noise caused by broken crockery. Fortunately, at dawn, the weather improved and we were able to put everything away safely.

First page of Rose's journal, written in the form of letters to her dear friend Caroline, Baronne de Nanteuil (née Barillon)

Reproduced from the original held in the Laage Archives, near Bordeaux

SAULCE-SUR-RHÔNE. — Château de Freycinet

During the day, I became alarmed a second time. An Algerian corsair was espied at midday. It followed our ship for some time. We could not yet determine its strength and I feared that we might have to put up a fight, following which we would perhaps be enslaved. Although that prospect filled me with horror, the thought of a seraglio evoked even more unpleasant images in my mind, and I hoped to escape that fate thanks to my male disguise. I was still deep in thought when I was informed that the ship, which had sailed close enough for its inferiority to be ascertained, had veered off, not wanting to take on our guns.

As I had not yet met the officers since my arrival on board, and as I wished to attend mass the following Sunday, Louis invited them to take tea in his quarters. I received them with a great deal of pleasure and I had a good laugh listening to the various hypotheses which each one had formulated about my identity.

So long as we were close to the coast of Europe, Louis insisted that I keep on my male attire in the presence of the crew. Hence, I always attended mass dressed in that manner, until I thought of listening to it through the window of the sitting room which overlooked the deck, close to the spot where the altar stood. I much preferred this, as I felt uncomfortable in men's clothes.

On 21 September, the Spanish coast came into view, although it was too far away to be seen clearly. On 24 September, the island of Majorca was sighted. The same day, we were buffeted by a fierce storm, followed by a prolonged lull.

Tacking, we sailed past all the Balearic Islands. We drew nearest to Ivica Island; however, we did not catch sight of the capital, which was situated

Saulce-sur-Rhône,
the Freycinet family home
in the south of France

3

on the opposite side. That part of the island which we saw was woody and cultivated; it looked charming.

Contrary winds and calm weather impeded our progress to such an extent that it was not until 29 September that the Rock of Gibraltar came into view. But the strait was like the promised land to us; winds and currents denied us entry. After having battled for more than seven days, seeing his crew harassed and being himself exhausted, Louis resolved to drop anchor in Gibraltar harbour to await more favourable winds.

Almost at once, permission to enter was granted on Louis' word of honour that there was no illness on board. A Spaniard who acted as French Consul in that town came to enquire whether we were in need of fresh supplies. After taking orders for the crew, he offered his house to Louis and invited him to lunch the next day. I accompanied my husband and we were graciously received by his charming wife, who is French. He showed us all the unusual sites of the town, which is far more pleasant than is often thought. Seen from the sea, it has the appearance of an arid rock lacking any charm. Once ashore, one is pleasantly surprised to find charming houses, useful establishments and attractive walks.

The Governor, General Don, accorded a warm welcome to the officers of the *Uranie* and apologised for not being able to entertain them, because his kitchen staff and domestics were two leagues inland, but he offered these gentlemen everything he could to make their stay agreeable. As the fortifications, carved into the side of the rock and comprising several storeys, were one of the most extraordinary sights, he offered a guided tour by one of the engineers on his staff to those who were keen to visit them. Thus, we climbed to the summit of the rock, from where we had a magnificent view, and we were shown everything in minute detail.

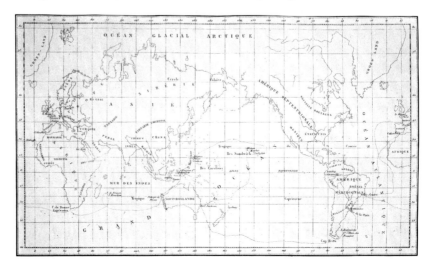

Route of the *Uranie* on its scientific expedition around the world (1817–1820)
From Jacques Arago, *Promenade autour du Monde pendant les Années 1817–1820* ... (Paris: Leblanc, 1822)

We also visited the officers' library, which was well stocked. The English officers showed us a number of works with colourful plates, among them *The French Victories under Napoleon*.

We enjoyed staying at the house of M. [Monsieur] Viale, our Consul, during our stopover. His family is charming, especially his 15-year-old daughter, who is extremely pleasant and well mannered. Several officers of the *Uranie* were smitten with her charms. We invited M. Viale to dine with us on board but were obliged the next day to cancel the engagement for him and our other guest, an English officer. The winds being most favourable for our departure from the strait, Louis thought it his duty to take full advantage of them. We set sail as soon as M. Viale had left and, in a few hours, we were out in the open.

During our voyage from Gibraltar to the Canary Islands, the weather was fine. On 22 October, we sighted land early in the morning. As Teneriffe was almost completely shrouded in mist, we were unable to have a clear view of the famous peak. Only the summit was visible above the clouds; on a clear day it can be seen at a distance of 20 leagues. That night, we dropped anchor in Santa Cruz harbour.

The *Uranie* was placed in quarantine due to an outbreak of the plague in the Mediterranean. Louis wanted to stop here for only six to eight days. He made his astronomical observations at the Lazaretto [quarantine station], while others were busy purchasing supplies and transporting them on board. In France, a Lazaretto is a pleasant spot where one finds houses supplied with all the necessities of life; several are furnished with gardens. It is where sailors and passengers spend the required time before the authorities determine whether they are carriers of contagious diseases. I therefore expected that in Santa Cruz, which is quite a pretty town, the Lazaretto would resemble these, but I was wrong. Its outskirts were dreadful; steep rocks were lashed by waves and visitors ran the risk of dying a thousand deaths upon disembarking, if the necessary precautions were not taken. Finally we climbed up those inhospitable beaches. We came upon a dilapidated cottage which looked like an old barn reduced to four walls, without even casements to protect us from the elements. The warden and two soldiers fled as we drew near and threw the keys at us from as far away as they could.

We could not possibly think of staying there. With observations completed before sunset, we returned on board by nightfall. Four times we had to stay in this pleasant cubbyhole. Beyond a yard full of rubble, the surrounding area was nothing but moors or rocks. One detail convinced us that the Spaniards paid little attention to military service. One of the officers on our staff noticed a pretty little bird and asked the sentinel to lend

Pinonia splendens, a fern named after Rose de Freycinet (née Pinon)

A. Poiret
Pinonia splendens c.1822
engraving
Louis-Claude de Freycinet, *Voyage autour du Monde ... Exécuté sur les Corvettes de S.M. l'Uranie et la Physicienne ... : Botanique* (Paris: Chez Pillet Aîné, c.1830), plate no. 21
Rex Nan Kivell Collection
National Library of Australia
Pictorial Collection

him his gun, with a little gunpowder and leadshot. Thinking that the sentinel was hesitating out of hope of gain, he showed him some silver coins, but in a rather pathetic manner, the poor man explained that he was unable to grant the French officer's request. He confessed that there were no cartridges in the guardroom, that neither his companions nor he had ever fired a shot nor seen any gunpowder; that all the military service in the colony was carried out by the island's militia consisting of local inhabitants, who were generally destitute and overburdened with taxes; that they cultivated the soil, but did not have enough to live on, except for some sort of taro paste and sometimes salted fish.

The guardroom contained two old rusty guns and old blue uniforms in rags with coloured flanges, worn by each of these wretches when he was on duty.

At the end of six days, on 28 October, having taken on board fresh supplies and all the necessary provisions to continue our voyage, we cast off with a fresh breeze and soon lost sight of the peak.

The weather was fine until 8 November when I began to feel some anxiety. The day had been stormy, and towards evening the heavy skies heralded bad weather for the night. Precautions were being taken on board and the wind was gusting when someone announced that the keel had been damaged. I must confess that at that moment I was shaking with fear. It seemed to me that the vessel was continually at the mercy of the wind and the sea. I could not think clearly and I did not know what to concentrate on ... I was even about to commend my soul to God when Louis came to reassure me and to inform me that all the necessary repairs had been carried out. The weather did not get worse and I slept peacefully, without thinking of the fear which had gripped me a few hours earlier.

As we neared the equator, the heat became most intense. Up to that point, I had felt quite well, but the high temperature gave me headaches and I was covered in small spots which made me continually itchy. Bathing and refreshing drinks rapidly eased my discomfort.

On 19 November, we crossed the equator. As a large number of men were doing so for the first time, the crew proceeded to organise the traditional ceremony.

To begin the ceremony, the previous evening, a postilion sent by the King of the Line climbed down from the top mast. The messenger's arrival was heralded by thunder, hail and heavy rain. The hail resembled the manna which met our forefathers in the desert; we could have eaten it, asit was nothing more than dried turkey corn. The thunder was in fact the sound of drums and the rain was seawater.

That envoy brought a letter from the King of the Line which stated that the *Uranie* would not be allowed to pursue its journey if all those not yet baptised did not undergo the ceremony. Louis replied gravely that he would give the necessary orders for His Majesty to be received the next day and that no-one would be opposed to his views.

In truth, the next morning, a throne was prepared for the King and his retinue, and next to it a seat was placed for those who were to be baptised. At 10 a.m., the King of the Line appeared, accompanied by his consort and his daughter. The two ugliest men among the crew had, on purpose I think, been chosen to play those parts; they were simply hideous. The King was preceded by six sappers and was followed by his chaplain, his attendant and a few other characters. Lucifer, surrounded by eight or ten small devils, brought up the rear; he was dressed in a dark skin with an iron hook on his shoulder. The small devils were completely naked, some wore red paint and others black, while others had rubbed a glue-like substance on their bodies and plastered themselves with chicken feathers.

As soon as the King had sat down, he sent his sappers to cut down the *Uranie*'s rigging, but Louis, crossing the palm of one of the attendants with a few silver coins, begged the King to spare his vessel. The sappers were then recalled and the congregation proceeded to the baptism of the infidels.

Thanks to the payment of a few Napoléons, I was let off during the ceremony. Almost all the crew had crossed the line already, and only a few officers had to pay their dues as I did. As for those who were unable to exempt themselves or who were less generous, the King of the Line ordered their faces to be daubed with paint; then the poor wretches were seated on a mobile seat and ducked into a tub of water, while at the same time a bucket of water was emptied on their heads. As for those who refused to undergo the ceremony, they were brought back forcibly and soaked according to the degree of resistance which they had offered.

This ceremony lasted all morning. The King and his retinue, having gone round the ship twice, went off to drink the double rations which Louis had granted them.

We dined that night in the officers' mess. They gave us a splendid meal and a very pleasant one, after which I watched the crew dance in masks and behave in an extravagant manner.

The weather, which had been rainy for a long time, was superb all day.

The following days were marked by violent winds and a sea far rougher than we had experienced since our departure from France. Although I do not usually suffer from any sort of seasickness, I grew weary as I had not yet become accustomed to it.

A Safe Haven Chapter 2

Stopover in Rio de Janeiro – Homage paid during the King's visit –
An outing to the outskirts of Rio – Portuguese women – A religious
ceremony – The Botanical Garden – A tea plantation – A visit
to the court

December 1817 – Upon leaving Teneriffe, Louis' intention was to proceed
to the Cape, but being dragged westward and having been delayed at
Toulon and in the Mediterranean, he resolved to change his strategy. This
change postponed our return to France by eight months. Hopefully God
will allow me to see the objects of my affection again ... He will not refuse
me, I hope, what I pray for each day ... to be reunited with you, to kiss
you, to hold you in my arms, and to be at my mother's side, to comfort her
and lend her support in her old age. For I can assure you that it is not for
the sake of pleasure and entertainment, which I shall be deprived of for a
long time, that I long so much to see my homeland again. Rather, I wish
to relieve my soul of the sadness that afflicts it and express my tenderness
for my mother and my friend.

We therefore made for Brazil and, on 4 December, we sighted the
coastline of America. I rejoiced at seeing this beautiful country, but at
that moment my thoughts were for France. I could imagine you about
to give birth and full of apprehension at this impending painful event.
How I regretted not being at your side; I would have been such a comfort
to you and would have lessened your suffering. Sometimes, morbid
thoughts came into my mind and I had to call upon all my reason not
to dwell on them. Besides, I pray so much to God for the health of my
Caroline and I have too much faith in His mercy to believe that He will
ignore my prayers.

On 5 December, we went round Cape Frio and, the next day, we entered
Rio de Janeiro's superb harbour. The weather was magnificent and we were
able to observe at our leisure the beautiful vegetation in this part of the
New World.

We had not yet dropped anchor when a boat came alongside. It was an
officer of the King's household, charged with the mission of verifying that
our ship was the *Uranie*, which had been expected in Brazil for some time.

Augustus Earle (1793–1838)
An ecclesiastic of Rio de Janeiro
c.1822
watercolour; 31.1 x 17.8 cm
Petherick Collection
National Library of Australia
Pictorial Collection (T140)

Part of the township
and a large aqueduct in
Rio de Janeiro

Jean Baptiste Réville
(1767–1825)
Vue d'une Partie de la Ville et du
Grand Aqueduc de Rio de Janeiro
c.1822
engraving; 23.8 x 32 cm
Louis-Claude de Freycinet, *Voyage*
autour du Monde ... Exécuté sur
les Corvettes de S.M. l'Uranie et la
Physicienne ... : Atlas Historique (Paris:
Chez Pillet Aîné, 1825), plate no. 6
Rex Nan Kivell Collection
National Library of Australia
Pictorial Collection (S7227)

He informed us that the King would receive the French to the best of his ability and would provide them with every necessity.

M. Lamarche, First Lieutenant of the *Uranie*, was entrusted with the task of paying a visit to the Admiral in charge of the harbour and to find out from the Governor's office if the salute would be answered. Having received an affirmative answer, he returned on board and, the next day at sunrise, the harbour and town each received a gun salute.

Louis went to see the Admiral in person and visited a few people for whom he had letters of recommendation. I remained on board alone, for the harbour was very safe and the weather was very fine. It was on that day that he met the Comtesse de Roquefeuille, a French émigré, who lived in Brazil where she received a royal pension. She is related to the Queen of Portugal. Her father, as well as her uncles and brothers, have all been in the service of the King of Portugal, and it was in those favourable circumstances that she was welcomed and granted a pension during the wave of migration to that country. As all her possessions had been put on sale, she lived off her royal pension. She longed to see her homeland but feared lest the King of Portugal might discontinue her pension without which she would have had no other means of subsistence.

She has with her a nephew whose father died in the King's service. Having been given a proper religious education, this young man has adopted a very pious attitude to religion and is willing to withstand ridicule in order to do his duty. Together with this quality, he has all the attributes which make him popular in society: a fine physique, a cultured and enlightened mind, and advanced knowledge of several sciences. He draws well and is an excellent musician; he plays several instruments, especially the piano.

When abroad, one derives a great deal of pleasure from meeting one's compatriots. Mme [Madame] de Roquefeuille has experienced this, having often found herself in such a situation. Consequently, she hastened to take us to the residence of the American Ambassador, M. Sumter, whose wife is French. On the same day that Louis was introduced to Mme de Roquefeuille, M. de Gestas, her nephew, took him to visit that amiable family.

I cannot refrain from writing to you at length about them and Mme de Roquefeuille, for in their company I felt happy for the first time since my departure. The latter treated me as a daughter, and the former became a very close friend within a few days. Our dispositions and conduct were so much in sympathy that one would have thought we had been childhood friends. Thus, the affection I feel for them will never change. It would be impossible for me to describe the attention and friendship lavished by those women on me.

Louis asked for their permission to introduce me, but Mme de Roquefeuille would not stand on any ceremony and invited us to dine with her the next day. Both women welcomed me most graciously and warmly. It seemed to me that I was among relatives once more.

Mme de Roquefeuille took us to the home of another French woman, who was extremely kind and whose husband served in the Portuguese army. But during my stay there this woman lost one of her children, so I scarcely saw her.

By 7 December, the French Consul had still to come on board. Louis was very annoyed about this, because it was important to find fresh supplies for the crew, as well as premises in which to carry out magnetic observations, which were the main object of our voyage. He sent a cadet to the home of the Consul, who had already been described to us as an eccentric.

The Consul came on 8 December and invited M. Lamarche, Louis and me to dinner the next day. We were not favoured by the weather, as it did not stop raining during our trip and we were soaked on arriving at his house. His first words to me proved that he deserved his reputation as a braggart: 'What! You came on foot! I thought you would have a carriage.

Rio de Janeiro harbour
E. Aubert
Baie de Rio de Janeiro: Vue de Praya Grande c.1822
engraving; 23.8 x 32 cm
Louis-Claude de Freycinet, *Voyage autour du Monde ... Exécuté sur les Corvettes de S.M. l'Uranie et la Physicienne ... : Atlas Historique* (Paris: Chez Pillet Aîné, 1825), plate no. 5
Rex Nan Kivell Collection
National Library of Australia
Pictorial Collection (S7226)

A Safe Haven

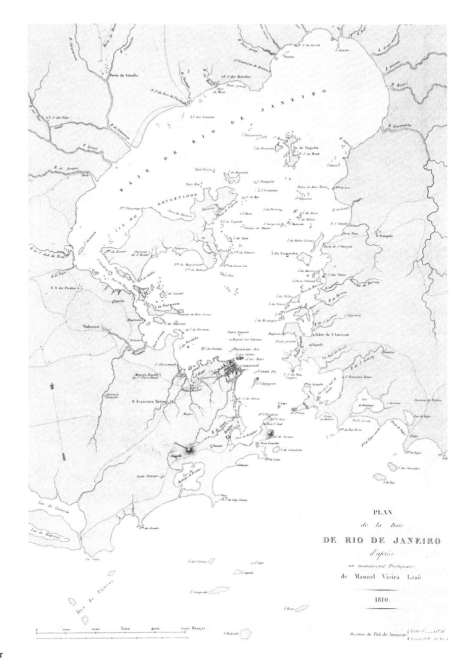

Map of Rio de Janeiro harbour

Manoel Vieira Leaó
Plan de la Baie de Rio de Janeiro
1810
Louis-Claude de Freycinet, *Voyage
autour du Monde ... Exécuté sur les
Corvettes de S.M. l'Uranie et la
Physicienne ... : Atlas Historique* (Paris:
Chez Pillet Aîné, 1825), plate no. 2
Rex Nan Kivell Collection
National Library of Australia
Pictorial Collection (S7223)

Had I known that, I would have dispatched mine to Madame, although it is true that I would have been in a quandary, not knowing where you were landing.' Yet, he knew full well the spot where we had come ashore, having chosen it for us himself. It appears that whenever someone asks him for a loan of his carriage, he pretends that his horses are confined to the stables or that his harness has been stolen. He has the reputation, on the whole, of being a rather unworthy fellow.

He emigrated in 1792, no-one knows why (for he was neither wealthy nor was he a nobleman); and he volunteered for the Portuguese army. He was accompanied by an aged mother who died, I think, during the voyage and by four sisters who were already grown up. The poor girls had not yet found husbands at the time, and although they must have given up all hope in this respect, they continued to spend money on heightening their faded charms at 40 or 50 years of age.

In 1814 he went to Paris to request the title of French Consul to Brazil and, thanks to M. Lainé, he was granted it. I ask you truly, is such a man capable of seeing to the interests of his country in negotiations with a monarch to whom he owes his fortune? One striking example will show that he is unworthy of that position.

It is customary in Portugal, as it is now in Brazil, for any person of whatever rank or age to kneel as the King goes by in public, even in mud; people on horseback and in carriages are not exempt from this humiliating ceremony. The present United States Ambassador, being of the opinion that it was too degrading for his country to lower itself thus in the presence of a sovereign to whom it had no obligations, refused to submit to that ceremony. This became the talk of the town. People wanted to force him to do so, but after he had explained his reasons to the King, he was given a dispensation. Other Consuls, being in a similar position, obtained the same dispensation. The French Consul thought that he too would follow in the footsteps of his colleagues. The Queen noticed it and in the presence of several people declared that, as French Consul, M. Maler [Maller?] was indeed under no obligation to pay her homage, but that he must not forget that he was in the pay of Portugal as a colonel and, as such, he was the King's subject and hence bound by the ceremony. However, if he did not wish to kneel, he would be considered a French citizen and would no longer receive his pay as a Portuguese colonel. Maler learnt this and for fear that it might be put into action, far from satisfied with kneeling on the first occasion the King passed by, he lay flat on the ground so as to be noticed by the whole court.

The dinner he offered us was very ordinary. He should have issued an invitation to the officers of the *Uranie*, but failed to do so. His actions ran counter to his duty.

Louis wished to be presented to the King and conveyed on several occasions to M. Maler his wish that he ask for an audience, as he could not be presented by anyone else, without infringing normal protocol. Maler asserted that, as the King's friend (it was yet another of his ridiculous claims that he was intimate with the King), he did not have to ask for permission and that he was received at any hour. Hence, on the day we had dinner with him, he suggested to Louis that he would take him to the court. As for us, we stayed behind the whole evening with the amiable sisters who bored us to tears. M. Lamarche was almost asleep and I yawned my head off, although from time to time I laughed at the antics of the youngest mademoiselle who was making eyes at the Lieutenant!

Louis came back indignant at Maler's bragging for, despite his intimate friendship with the King, they had not been given an audience. The lowly reputation of this man has unfortunate repercussions for his countrymen.

For a while my husband gave up the idea of visiting the King and decided instead to see to the setting up of his observatory. He urged Maler to find him a house; the Consul promised for eight days and did nothing about it.

Always eager to be of service to us, M. de Gestas found a charming house for us near the town and quite close to the residence of Mme Sumter. It belonged to the widow of a former Minister who had passed away in it and, for that reason, she was unwilling to live there. She was delighted to put it at the disposal of members of the French expedition.

The house suited us perfectly and the observatory was set up there. I was very comfortable in it; I had a superb apartment, a huge garden full of flowers and fruit. Situated on a small knoll, it enjoyed a magnificent view; the whole harbour was visible and the house overlooked most of the town. But the agent of the Comtesse, either out of spite because he had not been consulted or because he did not profit from it, succeeded in having us turned out.

We took up residence in a small house by the sea which M. de Gestas again found for us.

Mme de Roquefeuille, who some time beforehand had acquired a piece of land in the heart of the immense forests that surround the town of Rio de Janeiro, evoked such beautiful images of it that I could not resist visiting it.

Therefore, we gathered with the Sumter family and several of their friends and set out at 5 a.m. one morning. All the women were seated in a large barouche [carriage] drawn by eight mules, while the men travelled on horseback or in a cabriolet. The roads were full of potholes due to the heavy rain, and we were forced to leave the main road and take a path which led to the forest. We got out of the barouche so as not to tire the mules, which were to take us back to town that same night. Mules and saddled horses awaited us, but several of the women preferred to walk, as I did. On numerous occasions, we almost broke our backs; we sank into the mud up to our ankles. What amused us most in our predicament was a small person, the wife of the Dutch Ambassador, about whom I must say a few words.

Brought up in Paris, but in a rather liberal manner, her greatest pleasure was her clothes; she spent an inordinate amount of money on them. Nothing could stop her from being extravagant in her spending. Mme Sumter had urged her to dress very simply, assuring her that both she and we would be in linen or coloured silk. How surprised we were when we saw her arrive dressed in an Indian muslin dress, embroidered by hand, with a lilac spencer (in the style of Virginie), and a lot of trimmings and frills! Although she had been warned that we would be walking in the forest, which is always damp, she was wearing silk shoes.

It was comic to see her wade through the mud. Her shoes let in water and she had to be carried on horseback; her embroidered dress was black to the knees, as was her whole costume. When we told her how sad we were to see her in such a sorry state, she replied that she did not care, for she would receive other dresses from Paris. Fortunately for me, I was not dressed in a similar style; I would never have got over the loss of such a large sum for the sake of trinkets (she assured us that her dress had cost 600 Francs, not counting the rest of her outfit).

We were well rewarded for all those slight inconveniences by the beautiful view we enjoyed during the whole of our walk. The huge forests, in the middle of which the property of our countrywoman is located, are still virgin and one enters them by a path hardly wide enough for laden mules to pass through. They are identical to those described by our amiable M. de Chateaubriand in *Atala*. The foliage is of a thousand shades of green, enhanced by the bright flowers with which the trees are laden. Countless types of lianas, each one richer than the next in their elegance and the shape of their flowers, bind the trees together and make it difficult for visitors to penetrate into the interior where, however, one would be enchanted to venture in order to enjoy the charming music made by a thousand species of birds, all striking in their beautiful plumage.

I experienced such intense pleasure at finding myself in the midst of so many new and extraordinary things that I would willingly have remained there alone, if I had not noticed that all the others were hurriedly making their way towards the house, where lunch was ready.

I must not fail to mention a magnificent waterfall, located close to our friend's retreat. It hurtles down amidst lush vegetation on both sides; thousands of rocks lie in its path and add to its beauty. From time to time,

Augustus Earle (1793–1838)
View near Rio de Janeiro c.1822
watercolour; 16.1 x 24.2 cm
Petherick Collection
National Library of Australia
Pictorial Collection (R290)

it stops in superb pools where the water is crystal clear; it rushes down the small mountain on which the house of the Comtesse is located and ends up in a charming little valley. Before forming a waterfall, the stream skirts around the largest part of the property. Two or three other streams water the gardens around the outbuildings.

After a good lunch, we returned to the gardens which are most agreeably designed. Part of the forest has also been cleared to provide for a plantation of coffee and for other local crops. The temperature in these mountains is similar to that in Europe; hence, fruit trees native to our beloved France will soon bear fruit in this part of the new continent.

We would have spent a long time admiring those beautiful forests if we had not been obliged to take advantage of daylight to negotiate the bad roads. We reached the main road leading to the town before sunset.

We wished in turn to invite our French friends and the Sumter family to our humble abode. Our charming compatriots had shown us such kindness that we did not know how to repay it, and despite our rustic menage we wanted to enjoy ourselves a little. A slight indisposition prevented Mme Sumter from joining us and cast a shadow over our small party.

As the Consul had invited us to dinner once during our stay of two months, we felt obliged to invite him. It was a terrible chore which I was so glad to rid myself of that I could not help feeling the kind of relief described by dear Mme de Sévigné when she said farewell to her tedious visitors.

During our stay in Rio, we did not meet any Portuguese families. Louis was kept very busy by his work and the little time he had left was devoted to seeing our compatriots. However, on several occasions, we paid a visit to the Russian Consul, M. Landsdorf. His wife is a very good musician and I attended her soirées because she spoke French and had made several overtures to me. I was a little bored. I cannot personally comment on the customs of the Portuguese, as at no time did I visit a local Portuguese family. But I have heard enough to conclude that their manners would not appeal to me. These seem strange and even disagreeable. They are generally lacking in personal hygiene, a practice taken to extreme by the Hidalgos (the nobles). Scores of examples were mentioned to me, of which I shall cite only two.

A noble Portuguese woman, who had just employed a French maid, was on the point of dismissing her because the latter presented her with a bowl to wash her hands in. She replied very angrily that a lady of her rank did not need to wash her hands because she did not touch anything dirty, and that it was only the populace and servants who needed to wash themselves.

One of the most powerful people in the kingdom suffered from a rather serious ailment affecting his leg. Several Portuguese doctors, after using their knowledge to no avail, were replaced by a French ecclesiastic who dabbled a little in medicine, especially in curing sores. He convinced the illustrious personage to wash his leg. He took a lot of persuading, as that remedy appeared extraordinary to many. It succeeded and, as a result of a few trivial recipes to close up the wound, the ailment disappeared in a few days. But, once cured, the person stopped washing his leg and had a relapse. The monk was then recalled and prescribed the same cure, which appeared so disagreeable that the doctor was sent packing with his weird remedies. And while we were in Rio, this illustrious personage was still unable to go out, housebound because of the same sore leg.

In the households which I visited regularly in Rio, I did not have an opportunity to meet any Portuguese women. They are allowed to leave their homes only to go to church; hence, they do so often. Moreover, it would appear that the Church provides them with many such opportunities, for there are festivals almost every day, especially at night. The women put on their finery as befits the occasion.

I attended one such brilliant assembly, which I cannot call a religious festival as it resembled more an operatic performance. The church was

decked with silk material embroidered in gold and was lit up superbly.
At the appointed hour, the priests made their entry next to the main altar where, before starting the *oremus*, they turned towards the congregation which they ought to have shunned rather than looked at, and searched for faces known to them. Then, they bowed or smiled or made other gestures of acknowledgement.

Women, who are deprived of spectacles, usually look upon these festivals as substitutes; they turn up in all their finery and in low-cut dresses as though they were at a ball. Their main concern is to be attractive rather than to pray to God. I saw many beauties there; they are quite provocative brunettes.

After two or three prayers had been recited, I thought that the ceremony was over. I was about to leave that place where I had witnessed such extraordinary scenes, when voices which appeared to come down from heaven reached my ears. They seemed so pure, one might even say celestial, and I could not understand why. Those voices, though far too sweet and melodious to belong to men, had a virile force and a vigour which were not characteristic of women's voices. I was overwhelmed. I thought that I had been transported to Heaven among angels singing of the glory of the Supreme Being. And I would have remained in such a state of ecstasy if the chants had not made way once more to prayers. Thus, I considered asking someone where those voices emanated from. The answer conjured up a cruelty I could never have imagined before that day.

At the end of our stay, the weather was a little less humid and we seized the opportunity to make some interesting trips. I visited the Botanical Garden two leagues from Rio. For the first time, I saw growing, planted in the ground out in the open, cinnamon trees, nutmeg trees, pepper trees, and so on ... and breadfruit trees. I also saw a large field of tea which the government had just planted. It is an experiment which cannot fail, as the mild nights are most propitious to it. Chinese labour has been imported to cultivate and harvest those new crops. Our visit coincided with the harvest. The supervisor of the garden, thinking rightly that we would be interested in the various stages through which tea goes before it is ready for sale, ordered the Chinese to give us a demonstration. The ovens were lit and it was with great pleasure that we witnessed the details of this process.

January 1818 – On 24 January we made our farewell visits, while our baggage was carried on board. Louis planned to set off the next day, but calm weather and a visit by the King delayed us a few days.

On the day of the King's visit I intended bidding farewell to the Comtesse de Roquefeuille. But upon going ashore, we were buffeted by a dreadful storm. The rain came down in torrents and, as there was no way of finding a carriage, we had to proceed on foot. The drainage in the streets is so well managed in the town of Rio that, when it rains a little heavily, the streets are under two feet of water!

For half an hour, we paddled through water which came up to our knees. The Abbé [chaplain] accompanied us, and although I did not wish to conform to the local custom of allowing myself to be carried by blacks, I urged the Abbé to put himself in the hands of these people. But they almost let him fall, so that we had no choice but to travel on foot.

We reached Mme de Roquefeuille's residence in a piteous state. She hastened to make us change into dry clothes, served us supper and refused to let us return on board. We spent the night at her house and Louis went to pay his respects the next day. He was well received by the King, but it would appear that he was a man of humble means and would have been readily taken for a fool, if he had not been the King.

At last, on 30 January, we sailed out of this beautiful harbour, with ample supplies and in a good frame of mind.

The death at sea of one of the officers – Cape Town – Dinner at the Governor's residence – Ile de France, Mauritius – A visit by palanquin to the Chief Judge's home – Creole society – The Oval Table literary society – Dinner on board an English frigate – Horse racing in Mauritius

February 1818 – On leaving Rio, we had rather favourable winds. M. Laborde, one of our midshipmen and the third-ranked officer of the *Uranie*, a very interesting and charming young man who was well loved by Louis, was slightly ill during the voyage. He had a weak chest and he met with an accident which proved fatal. While giving orders for working the ship, he broke a blood vessel in his chest and, unable to cough up the blood, he choked to death after ten days.

Being a good friend and a distinguished officer, his death saddened all the officers and the whole crew. What touched me most was the courage, the steadfastness and the resignation he showed in his last moments. Endowed with such qualities and having high hopes for the future, he must have loved life. He left it as a Christian philosopher would; he himself asked for the last sacraments and died as a saint.

On 5 March, we sighted the summit of the mountains of Africa and, on 7 March, we dropped anchor in Table Bay harbour, opposite Cape Town.

M. Delêtre, a French merchant, sent his son on board to invite us to stay at his house. As there is no furnished hotel at the Cape, foreigners usually take lodgings in the homes of local residents and he offered his home to us in his capacity as a French national. Several former visitors to the Cape had assured us that it was a very pleasant house.

We left the ship around 2 o'clock and went ashore to the home of M. Delêtre. His wife and daughters did not come to greet me, because we were told that they were unwell (the truth is that they were not yet dressed). After a while, I saw a young lady enter with four women as stiff and straight as rods. I thought that it was an official visit, until M. Delêtre introduced them as his wife and daughters. I was shocked by their singular air, but I hoped that once they realised that I hated formality, they would abandon theirs. Nothing of the kind. Mme Delêtre did not budge an inch. She was a Dutch

Natives conveying a passenger in a palanquin, Mauritius

T. Choubard (fl.1807–1830)
Ile de France: Palanquin c.1824
hand-coloured engraving; 23.7 x 32 cm
Louis-Claude de Freycinet, *Voyage autour du Monde … Exécuté sur les Corvettes de S.M. l'Uranie et la Physicienne … : Atlas Historique* (Paris: Chez Pillet Aîné, 1825), plate no. 10
Rex Nan Kivell Collection
National Library of Australia
Pictorial Collection (S7231)

Creole, born at the Cape. Her daughters, the youngest of whom was at least 24 years old, were less formal, especially in their mother's absence.

I felt no warmth in this family; their hearts were as dry as old parchment. I, therefore, remained in my quarters almost permanently. At an hour when I knew the sitting room to be vacant, I would sit at the piano and spend many enjoyable moments playing.

I must, however, give them their due, in so far as they were kind towards me; but this cost me dearly. The father, on the pretext that purchasing supplies would tire me, asked me for my lists and took charge of everything. I was embarrassed by his kindness and told him so on many occasions. He received my apologies in a rather self-effacing manner and assured me that he was only too glad to assist me. He was well repaid for his labours, for instead of us spending 700 to 800 Francs, as we had done at Rio de Janeiro, the dear man presented me with a bill for 2000 Francs, which we had to pay. I have since found out, by comparing my purchases to those of the officers of the *Uranie*, that this honest fellow made me pay for everything at twice the normal value.

In Rio, we had bought almost as many supplies and we stayed more than two months, catering for four to six people and sometimes more, and yet it had cost me only 800 Francs, while at the Cape we spent only 22 days ashore. If ever we have the good fortune to return to the Cape, I will not lodge at the house of such self-interested people!

On 3 March in the morning, after taking me to the Delêtres' home, Louis went to visit the Governor, who made him welcome; when my husband asked him for permission to present me, he invited me to dine at his country residence, two leagues from the Cape. We went there, but I was not impressed by the outskirts of the town, which were very sandy. Yet, one league from the town, the countryside was green and charming.

The Governor's residence is a magnificent house in a delightful location. It is sheltered by a high mountain from those horrid winds which are so distressing for the locals. He is treated as a viceroy in this country, has considerable wealth and lives like a prince.

On arriving, we were received by the Colonel-in-Chief. His Excellency and his daughters were returning from a hunt and were getting dressed. But very little time elapsed before Lord Somerset and his daughters came into the sitting room. They seemed a little shy and unaccustomed to visitors. I discovered that night that their mother had died very recently. Besides, they were only 17 or 18 years old. I found them a little cool; since then, I have had a chance to learn that it was their shyness of speaking French which caused them embarrassment. As for me, I did not dare address them in English for fear of hurting their feelings. Hence, our conversation was limited to a few words of French which I had to guess, so poor was their pronunciation. They are quite attractive, especially the second sister who bears a striking resemblance to Blanche Day, in both her looks and character. The eldest sister is a little too dark, and bushy eyebrows make her face look hard. I believe them both to be well brought up, as are generally all young English girls from good families.

Milord seemed to me a little stiff and cool, but this trait is common to almost all his countrymen. They do not have the affable manner which they condemn as frivolity in the French. Lord Somerset's manner is a poor indication of his real character, for he is most kind and very gallant. He spoke to me all evening with such kindness and such consideration as can only emanate from his adoration of women. He is even taken to task for loving them a little too much.

I was also very impressed by a colonel named Ware, who at once formed a friendship with Louis. Subsequently, he saw a lot of us during our stopover at the Cape. His wife, a charming woman, was ill and, as a result, I saw little of her. She was staying in the country.

We were feted by the Governor in a most lavish manner. The meal was magnificent. It was the first time I had witnessed such a ceremonious dinner. We spent the night in the country, as the Governor was afraid that a journey by night would be too tiring for me. We set out on the return trip the following morning, after having been overwhelmed with kindness.

Cape Town would be most pleasant if the wind from inland did not make a stay there tiresome. When it blows, one does not walk in the streets, nor along the promenades, without running the risk of being blinded by fine sand. One may even be injured by small stones scattered by the wind. The streets are straight, clean and lined with charming houses which are well built and extremely clean. The Company's Garden provides an exquisite walk for the locals and, on the parade ground, a large square surrounded by two rows of trees, one can take a breath of fresh air on hot still nights.

The theatre was being refurbished; it reopened only two days before our departure, and we did not think of getting tickets until the last minute. We were shown to empty seats which, in fact, had already been reserved and we were forced to move elsewhere. I chose to retire early and consequently I can comment only on the theatre, which is small but quite attractive. However, I did not miss much, for the officers of the *Uranie* assured me that the plays performed were in bad taste. One of them was *John Bull*, a burlesque comedy of the kind performed at the Variety Hall.

On 2 April, we returned on board. Louis intended leaving the next day but contrary winds were so strong that our departure was delayed until 7 April.

One must blame our host's family for the depression which I experienced at the Cape. The darkest thoughts came into my mind; all my letters bore the mark of that melancholy. Fortunately, none of my fears eventuated during our voyage. The sea was very rough but, without mishap, we rounded the Cape of Storms, which was so dreaded in bygone days, but which is frequented by so many ships nowadays. We hoped to arrive at the next anchorage to make the acquaintance of a brother of Louis, whom he had not seen since the age of 12.

On 5 May, we anchored in the harbour of Ile de France.

It was almost night, so we could not make contact with the town. As soon as day dawned, the health inspector came on board with my brother-in-law Charles, who had obtained permission to accompany him.

We went first to visit the Governor and, the next day, we accepted an invitation to lunch with the Chief Judge and President of the Court of Mauritius, Judge George Smith, to whom my brother-in-law was private secretary. That kind stranger sent his palanquin to the landing spot to convey me to his house, for in the Ile de France one uses carriages only to travel to the country, and women cross town either in palanquins or in sedan chairs. I had never seen a palanquin before and did not know how to sit in it. To give you an idea of this type of vehicle, imagine a box 5 feet long by 3 feet high, with blinds all round, painted green and well padded inside with silk or leather of the same colour. At both ends of that box there are two long sticks which blacks carry on their shoulders. One is seated as one would be on the ground, and the box, lifted by the blacks, is three feet off the ground.

It is quite a pleasant way to travel, especially if one does not remain inside too long, for keeping one's legs level with the seat is tiring and causes numbness. I also found that frills on dresses get crushed. Sedan chairs are preferable in this respect. Nevertheless, I preferred the palanquin because Judge Smith's men, being very strong, moved well in unison, while the motion of sedan chairs was less agreeable and rougher. There are more sedans than palanquins in Mauritius. The former require two men, while four carry the latter. Moreover, the palanquin is a luxury and owners compete with each other as to the manner of dress of their blacks. M. Smith's were always dressed with great taste; all four wore a small white skirt gathered up and tightened around the waist with yellow belts. Their chests and legs were naked. Such was the fashion then.

We were received by M. Smith as by a loving father. He told us that his whole house was at our disposal. He gave us a superb apartment, as well as lodgings for our chaplain, for Louis' secretary and for the officers on duty at the observatory, which was set up in a corner of his house. 'I shall be your butler,' he declared to Louis, 'and all you will do is rest.'

After refusing several times, my husband was forced to accept our friend's kind offer. He supplied me with a black woman as a servant, provided a domestic for Louis who refused, having an attendant already to whom he had grown accustomed. The palanquin was at my beck and call, at any hour of the day, with four blacks to carry me and a servant to follow me and open the door. Our dearest friend offered us all this with a kind heart, assuring us that he would treat us like his children and that he loved us a great deal on account of Charles, whom he called his son. I may add that he was unfailing in his feelings of affection and that he never wavered in his kindness despite the fact that our stay, which was supposed to last only 20 days, was extended to two months.

As soon as we arrived, the kind M. Smith invited the wife of the Public Prosecutor to make my acquaintance. I was delighted to meet this very amiable woman and, above all, such a good mother.

During the days that followed, M. Smith also wanted to invite other female acquaintances, but his invitations were refused for the following reason. Someone drew his attention to the fact that in Mauritius it was customary for foreign women to pay a visit, on their arrival, to all the people they wanted to see and that this was the reason for the refusals. Hence, I went on a general round of visits, even though these were an inconvenience to me. I must say that I received a warm welcome wherever I went. Creole women are very kind-hearted; some are educated, but they are in the minority. In general, they are rather superficial. On the whole, they become excellent mothers.

I saw most of the young people of Mauritius at a ball given in our honour by M. Smith, which was quite splendid but a little crowded. I cannot refrain from mentioning that, considering the dreadful calamities which had devastated the island and had hit all pockets, it was hard to believe the luxury that was displayed in Mauritian society. I believe that Creole women are very misguided, for they would look much better in simple dresses than in the finest silks. There are many pretty women among them, but few who are truly beautiful. Well shaped, they have nice figures, but they have lost that charming simplicity which has set them apart until now; they are pretentious and very calculating in their deportment. At a ball given by M. Smith, I saw one of these beauties, well known for having superb hands and arms, make a show of not only removing her gloves each time she waltzed, but also placing her hand in the most advantageous pose possible. Having returned to her seat, she would enquire of her mother if her hand and arm had been in the most favourable position. Even in our most debauched towns, one does not witness such behaviour! Yet, these are simple Creole women, who are said to be devoid of all artifice and adorned only with natural graces.

I must add that one of them seemed to me to be endowed with all the charms likely to draw attention to a young woman. Naturally quick-witted, she has been well brought up. She is very devout, a rare quality among Creole women, who receive very little religious education. I formed a friendship with that nice woman because I liked her a lot, and I must confess that she owed it all to her resemblance to you. It was Caroline as a brunette, the same mind, the same sensitivity, the same thoughtfulness. I spoke to her so often about that resemblance that she wanted at all costs to see your portrait. She was so thoughtful that, in our quite lengthy conversations, she always asked about you and my dear mother, knowing that it was my main concern. I think that I have won her friendship; our temperaments were well suited to each other. She is about my age and has been married for 14 years to a colonel on the Mauritian staff. She has no children as yet and regrets it, as I do.

I would have liked to have shared my time in Mauritius between that nice woman and another young lady, a cousin of Mme Barillon, who is very kind, although she does not have one hundredth of the merit of Mme Lindsay. But I had to cultivate M. Smith's acquaintances, several of whom I liked.

I greatly enjoyed being in the company of our host. He is a first-rate fellow and, in spite of his age, his cheerfulness is engaging. He speaks French perfectly well. Moreover, he presides in French over a tribunal and makes impromptu speeches with the greatest of ease. Louis was able to witness this at a meeting of freemasons called in his honour, which was chaired by M. Smith as deputy to the Grand Master, who was absent. Our friend made a speech in perfect French, worthy of a Frenchman.

At the time of our arrival in Mauritius, the country was in dire straits. Scarcely had the inhabitants recovered from the horrors of a fire, which had destroyed half of the capital, and of a cyclone which had devastated the countryside, than they had to endure the severity and injustice of a General who was Acting Governor during M. Farquhar's absence. Having perpetrated some injustices, the General wanted the Chief Judge, M. Smith, to give his approval, but that honest man refused. He was divested of his powers and was thus impotent to protect the local inhabitants against the Governor's harassment.

I must add that the Interim Governor, M. Hall, hates the French, having been taken prisoner by them and having spent seven years in France. I was rather vexed by those problems, for M. Hall's wife is a very agreeable woman who speaks French fluently, and I wanted to get to know her better. As we were not involved in those disputes, we accepted the General's invitation and were received by him as well as his unsociable nature would

allow. I found his wife charming, from both a physical and moral point of view; she had acquired French habits during her stay in France with her husband. Each time I met her, I found her to be the same, but I could not help thinking that she must have been unhappy with such a husband. She is said to be as wicked as he is, but I cannot share that view. She is far too intelligent to be impolite towards the local people, and I believe her to be incapable of inflicting suffering.

On our third day, we were invited by a lawyer friend of Charles to a large dinner party given in honour of Louis' arrival and of his brother's departure. It was offered by a man who had recently made his fortune and who did not come from a very good family. He was silly enough to want to invite a large number of people to his very small house. Moreover, he deemed it polite to serve an excessive number of dishes; he offered us a dinner with three sittings, each of which would have fed 20 guests. The table was so overloaded with dishes that none of the guests knew where to put their glasses. The smell of the dishes, the heat caused by the smallness of the venue and by the lights, and his insistence on serving us almost made me leave a number of times.

Natives carrying a palanquin, Ile de France, Mauritius

Nicolas Eustache Maurin (1799–1850)
Un Palanquin de l'Ile de France c.1822
hand-coloured lithograph; 14.5 x 23 cm
Jacques Arago, *Souvenirs d'un Aveugle: Voyage autour du Monde* (Paris: Hortet et Ozanne, 1839), vol. 1, plate facing p. 264
Rex Nan Kivell Collection
National Library of Australia
Pictorial Collection (U5509)

M. Smith and several friends gave parties to mark Charles' departure, which occurred on 12 May. One of M. Baudin's botanists had stayed behind in Mauritius because of his poor state of health. Being a very able chemist, he opened a pharmacy, which is the only one in Mauritius, and made a fortune; despite having lost 300 000 to 400 000 Francs in the great fire, he still has 600 000 left, which he is busy transferring to France where he wants to settle. He has married a rich Creole woman. I socialised with the family because the husband had been friendly with Louis aboard the *Naturaliste*.

I shall not bore you with details of all the different homes where I was received and which were nothing out of the ordinary. I wish, instead, to tell you about a fine expedition which I made inland.

We left on a splendid day at 5 a.m. in a barouche drawn by four horses; we were accompanied by several friends on horseback. We headed for one of the most pleasant districts of the island two leagues from where M. Smith had his country residence. It is located in a picturesque spot on a knoll and it overlooks enchanting little valleys graced with charming dwellings. From there one catches a glimpse of the sea and a number of the islets which are close to Mauritius. A magnificent waterfall borders the largest part of the property and provides water over its entire length.

We had lunch there and left our carriage, the horses being exhausted by the arduous climbs. After lunch, having toured the whole estate, some of us left in a palanquin and others on horseback, and we went together to the Réduit ['The Retreat'], the Governor's country residence, where my husband and I were to pay a visit to the General. The latter, being most gallant, had my palanquin bedecked with flowers, knowing that I would be travelling in it for a while.

Having then rejoined our friends, we set off together towards Plaines Wilhems where we were to spend two days at the home of acquaintances. We reached our destination around 4 p.m. and were warmly welcomed by the parents of a young Creole woman, named Saulnier, whom I had often seen in Paris, where she was educated. They were extremely wealthy and received us sumptuously. Having been warned, I had brought some dresses and linen clothes.

The next day, we attended a very fine ball at which I danced with far more pleasure than at M. Smith's residence, because it was not as hot, because there was less of a crowd and because the dances were similar to the ones we danced in Paris, while generally in Mauritius they have such odd styles of dances that I was confused on the first few occasions I attempted them.

The following morning, we left to pay a visit to a charming family who were friends of M. Smith. They are very respectable people who reside in the country. We were generously entertained, albeit modestly; an air of ease and freedom pervaded their house. I was charmed by the two women and a young person whom I met there. They were musicians and were kind enough to play the guitar and sing for us. The mother is said to have a talent for the harp, but I could not vouch for it, as several strings were missing from her instrument and it is difficult to obtain them here.

To my deep regret, we spent only one day at their home; the simplicity of the women appealed to me greatly. As the road was difficult and very hilly, we had to take our leave early.

We also visited a family whose eldest son has a collection, which would be deemed most precious in France, of Indian fruit in coloured wax. The imitation is so perfect that one would take them for the real things.

While in the country, I also went to the home of a highly respected merchant. He offered us a very fine dinner in a greenhouse. Unfortunately, the occasion was marred by the presence of his wife who, as a former comedienne, had caught the eye of this gentleman. The dear man had a daughter by her and, under the pretext of caring for her daughter, the woman agreed to give up her career in the theatre on condition that he marry her. Being a good father and having only his daughter's interests at heart, he agreed, but this woman is so lacking in manners that hardly anyone visits him.

Her husband suffered from a liver disorder; he had just undergone surgery between two ribs and was close to death. I had a conversation with her about his illness and asked her if the wound had healed. She answered almost jokingly: 'Madame, is he cured? No, not really; his wound is still wide open. The poor man almost died and I had already got my mourning dresses ready. Fortunately, at the time I came across a piece of good quality taffeta.'

I also went to Pamplemousses, a district which I knew so well even before reaching Mauritius. M. Bernardin had aroused my interest so much that I longed to visit it. But I will not highlight here the inaccuracies of which this charming author was guilty. For all that, his work is enchanting and those minor blemishes do not diminish its value.

A few days later, we visited the Botanical Garden where are gathered a host of tropical plants.

There is also a very fine sugar mill where I observed all the stages of sugar production, from the time when the cane is harvested to the delivery of that foodstuff for retail.

Of all the parties and meetings organised in our honour, I must mention one which will amuse you. As you know, in the colonies less attention is paid to the origins of families than to their present wealth.

One of the men, who had arrived in Mauritius with nothing but a saucepan to make his fortune (which often eludes such men), was lucky enough to amass so much wealth over such a long period of time that he became a multi-millionaire. He was, accordingly, highly thought of by everyone, and his riches made people forget that, only 26 years before, he had been a boilermaker who had roamed the streets.

We received an invitation from this very wealthy man, who owned a magnificent house and did not know what to do with his money. He dreamt of having two dining rooms, a rare luxury indeed; the object was to be able to eat dessert in the cool and avoid not only the sight of the meats being cleared, but also their unpleasant smell. But the fellow overlooked the fact that he was completely ignorant of such things.

The dinner was sumptuous, although there were far too many guests present. There was a terrible crush, and no-one did the honours nor showed us around. As soon as the second course was over, everyone rose and the master of the house took me by the arm and invited me to move into the dessert room. The orders had been given and executed so well that, as we were about to enter, nothing was ready and the room was still in darkness. The dessert was charming and served with extraordinary luxury; the gold, the silver, the pieces of crystal and the chandeliers made a splendid effect. But the hosts were so unequal to the service that cheerfulness did not reign in the midst of all this luxury and everyone appeared relieved when it was time to leave.

Several Creoles, lovers of poetry and wits for the most part, had founded a society which met under the name of the Oval Table. People had spoken highly to me of their witticisms and especially of their talent for composing pretty ditties. At one of M. Smith's dinners, attended by some of the members, new songs were discussed at the end of the dinner, and my brother-in-law, who has a good singing voice, was asked to perform some of his new compositions for us. He could not remember anything good in Creole but sang a rondo with taste and wit. Despite my repeated pleas to the members of the Oval Table, no-one could find anything worthy of a Parisian woman. However, a Creole vowed to present to me in a few days some verses composed by him. He did indeed send me the following piece:

Couplets addressed to Mme Rose de Freycinet during her stopover in Mauritius in June 1818 to the tune of 'Lover's Charm etc ...'

First Verse

Of all wives the charming model,
Forsaking games and laughter

Because of too faithful a love.
What! You desert Paris.
Helen, Phaedra and other beauties
Have defied the oceans like you,
But history never said of them
That it was to follow a husband.
...

I won't tell you what I think of those verses. Here they are, you can
judge for yourself. But you must not judge all members of the society by
this one example. Some are better than others. The day I made M. Pitot's
acquaintance, I had seated beside me at the table an officer of genius, who
informed me, in a most grandiloquent tone, that he had the great honour
of being an overseas associate member of the Oval Table, and without
waiting for me to ask him for some productions inspired by his grey-haired
Muse, he declared that the night before he had offered to his colleagues a
short piece most remarkable for its witty and original quality. At once, he
recited that masterpiece, and he prefaced it by stating that its subject was
Thought. He mumbled a few words which completely baffled me. He hit
himself on the forehead with his hand, raised his eyes to the sky as if to
read there the masterpiece which had escaped his mind and which had

A grinding wheel for making
coconut oil, Mauritius

Victor-Jean Adam (1801–1866)
*Ile de France: Moulin à Faire
l'Huile de Coco* c.1822
engraving; 32 x 23.5 cm
Louis-Claude de Freycinet, *Voyage
autour du Monde ... Exécuté sur les
Corvettes de S.M. l'Uranie et la
Physicienne ... : Atlas Historique* (Paris:
Chez Pillet Aîné, 1825), plate no. 9
Rex Nan Kivell Collection
National Library of Australia
Pictorial Collection (S7230)

perhaps taken refuge in Heaven, but all his efforts were in vain. He began the same verse several times, without once being able to complete it. At last, cursing his treacherous memory, he assured me again that it was most charming and that he was mortified to be unable to treat me to it.

Louis became friendly with a judge who belonged to the same society. The gracious manner in which he offered me a sample of his poetry was too refined for me not to mention it here.

He is the head of a family and is highly respected for the way in which he raises his children. Religion, so universally ignored in Mauritius, is both revered and practised by M. Mallac. Unfortunately for him, the fire has almost completely ruined him and deprived him of the money he needs to provide a proper education for his children. Undaunted, though reduced to borrowing money in order to furnish his house, and having no other resources but his limited stipend as a judge, he asked for his friends' help to set up a printery intended for his children. His eldest son, quite advanced in his education, is now the printery's manager. This child, in truth, displays intelligence and reasoning powers far in advance of his age. As you may well imagine, the father oversees everything. In brief, the business is doing so well that I have no doubt that the young Mallacs will restore the family fortune through it.

I wanted to view these printing presses, made in England, and I expressed that wish to M. Mallac, who gave me a guided tour of the workshop. It was proposed that something be composed and printed in front of my very eyes. The intelligent manager personally manned the press, explaining each procedure in the minutest detail. As soon as his work was finished, he presented the paper to me and invited me to admire the fine characters. To my great surprise, I read the heading, 'To Madame Rose de Freycinet', and the following lines:

> Of Orion, brilliant stars,
> You children of the Peda dear to voyagers,
> Stars which pierce the dark veil of Night,
> Do not hide your light from those observers,
> Who travel, guided by the *Uranie*,
> To take to distant shores,
> Both bravery and genius.
> Zephyr and you, Venus, do watch over their destiny.

I was very touched by his gesture and judged the good intentions rather than the end product. I have read other verses by M. Mallac, which I have deemed better than the above; he enjoys the reputation of being witty. I do not have much to say about his wife, whom I did not get to know very well, but she seemed to me to be of the stuff of which good mothers and good educators of children are made, as all Creole women generally are.

Our visit to Mauritius coincided with that of an English frigate whose captain is a fine man. His very young wife travels with him, but how different is his mission compared to Louis'. He sails the Indian Ocean to protect merchant ships against pirates; he puts into port whenever and wherever he wants. In all settlements, he is provided with a fully furnished house and servants ashore. Sometimes, he leaves on short cruises and entrusts his wife to friends, so as not to tire her by too long a voyage. She had just given birth on her arrival in Mauritius, where the frigate was undergoing repairs. She was a charming and well-mannered young woman. We felt drawn to each other by our similar situations.

Some time before our departure, the captain returned from a cruise near Madagascar. He wanted to give a party for us aboard his frigate the day before we planned to leave Mauritius, and I was pleased that we were unable to postpone our departure in order to return their invitation on board the *Uranie*. We would not have been able to entertain as lavishly and in as distinguished a manner. Our ship was far too small to hold all the people we would have had to invite and our finances were somewhat depleted as a result of our considerable expenses in Mauritius.

To facilitate the crew's comings and goings, the ship was moored near the coast. It was a 'mystery' lunch which was supposed to start at 2 p.m., but we only sat down after it had struck 3 o'clock. The table was set up in the battery and was surrounded by flags, which formed a pretty lounge. All the officers of the *Uranie* had been invited, as well as a large number of English families in Mauritius. I was the only French woman. But many of the women I had met during my stay were present; they spoke French to me and I ventured to speak English to them. There were about 80 of us at dinner and the 'mystery' meal was very well served and was very pleasant, although the length of the table only allowed for private conversations.

I was seated between two of M. Smith's friends who were well known to me. After we had drunk toasts to the Kings of France and England, to princes and princesses, to the English and French navies, etc ... and shouted hurrahs which are endless at this type of dinner, we withdrew to the lounge, leaving behind all those who wanted to drink each other under the table.

Soon after, we went to take a breath of fresh air on the deck, where the band was playing very pretty quadrilles. The deck was lit with lanterns and each man chose his partner. Until midnight, they went on hopping about in English reels. I did not feel like dancing and retired early on the pretext that we had to leave at dawn the following morning, but in fact it was because I was a little bored.

Ten days before, a race meeting had taken place, which was a very festive occasion for the English. Large bets were laid. The Champ de Mars, a bare and treeless area, which is called a promenade, was chosen as the venue. Barriers were erected to mark the course and the finish. Stands were built for the women, so that they might overlook the whole scene. Our good friend M. Smith had a superb stand erected. The spectacle lasted three whole days.

This form of entertainment is greatly appreciated by Creole women who seize the opportunity to wear their finery and to spend money. Protocol requires that one wears a different dress on each of the three days. The mulattos themselves display a luxury of which it would be difficult to estimate the cost. All those pretty and well-shaped girls are kept by the rich men, young and old, of Mauritius. I shall add that, to the great shame of men, even fathers lavish on those wretches luxuries which their own children often go without. Can you believe, dear friend, that one would not find two men here who do not keep one of those girls in fine quarters, fine clothes and served by five or six black servants? As all this costs the women nothing, they flaunt an excessive luxury. When they have caused one man's ruin, they find another who is better off. The day of the race meeting, I saw a number of those women dressed in white or pink satin, with tops made of embroidered tulle, covered in diamonds, and wearing cashmere scarves which cost 1000 to 1200 piastres. Others were dressed in beautiful silk clothes or in magnificently embroidered muslin.

Some men even set up home with these women, have a dozen children by them and have no other house but theirs; these men are not married. By their actions, they are forced to withdraw from society, for these women are never received publicly. They provide a good education for their children, who are almost white; several even send them to England and France. Many of these young people, who have been well brought up, are charming. They have a talent for learning all manner of things, especially music.

What is to become of this population? Will they always be completely segregated from the whites? Creole women generally abhor those women who cause the ruin of their families and the breakdown of so many marriages. Several wealthy men, wishing to ensure their children's or their mistresses' future in the event of their own deaths, buy land in their names. A few women already own substantial properties in their own right.

Until now, the government has not favoured that class, for although these women and children are born free, and therefore have the same rights as the whites, they share a special register with slaves and have no association with the whites. Not one of them is welcomed into society and their places are clearly marked in churches. At the races, they also have their seats reserved and the gallery of so-called brown half-castes was more dazzling than that of the white Creole women.

On the occasion of the races, there was a ball which I was obliged to attend. As I had no intention of rivalling the Creole women in luxury, I dressed simply, wishing to put in an appearance and retire early without dancing. I wore a gauze dress with blue satin panels and trimmed with ruches of tulle. I always wore a scarf, which strangely enough offended all the Creole women, as all the ones I met, laughingly or mockingly, urged me to remove it.

Mme Lindsay alone not only found it most becoming but would have liked to imitate me; however, she was afraid that her husband might not allow it, for, as you know, English women wear low-cut dresses even for dinner. I cannot begin to tell you all the gossip that my scarf gave rise to; there were some who claimed that undoubtedly I must have had some blemish on my breasts, or some scar that was hidden by the gauze. Others had learnt from one woman that I had nothing to hide, as she had seen me one day wearing a low-cut dress and had noticed nothing untoward, and so on ... But all joined forces to make fun of my reserved nature, giving me the nickname of 'Mrs Virtue' or other similar names, to which I can assure you I paid no attention whatsoever.

Having been starved of dances for some time, the Creoles were most eager to attend this ball. It was a huge crush. The stewards had no idea how to do the honours; accordingly, nothing at all made sense. Seeing that I was not enjoying myself, our friend asked at midnight if I wanted to retire, which I did most gladly. I have been told that the supper room was so small that there was a great crush and that chairs were flying here and there in a most undignified manner.

To mark the King's birthday, there was another ball at Government House, to which M. and Mme Hall invited us. On that occasion I was forced to wear a brand new dress which was in keeping with my position, a finery which would certainly have cost me 400 Francs (clothes are four times more expensive here than they are in France). As I could not have cared less about going, I pretended to be indisposed and excused myself.

Louis did his best to apologise on my behalf to Mme Hall, who was already in a bad mood because of the small number of people attending her ball. The Creole women, whose husbands had been badly treated by M. Hall, were indeed not present at this gathering. Mme Hall ascribed my refusal to the advice of M. Smith, who was at the time in open conflict with the General. I deplored this, for the only motive for my absence was economy. I had all the more reason to believe that she had been upset as, on several occasions prior to that ball, she had asked me to spend a few days at her house, while subsequently she did not ask me once. Louis did not mind at all, as he did not like M. Hall's personality, and he would only have gone to his house reluctantly.

When we bade them farewell, she received me cordially, but the General, who a few days before had fallen out with Louis over a quarrel that occurred between several of our sailors and some English soldiers, was very cool towards my husband.

You must be surprised to see that I have made no mention of music after spending two months amidst Creoles, who are almost all musicians. However, I found that, on the whole, they are not very talented. They are better at the harp and the piano than at singing. There are no good master singers here, nor do Mauritians go to the theatre to develop their taste. I heard several ballads sung, such as 'Coming Back from Pontoise', without any kind of expression or the correct pronunciation. It would indeed be strange if things were different in Mauritius, for several Creoles who were discussing a young Parisian woman with me, declared that she sang well but rather as an actress playing a part. Mme Lindsay, who had heard her, assured me that she had sung with the correct expression.

If, however, Creole women generally fail to achieve a high degree of accomplishment in music, I must cite as an exception M. Pitot's sister-in-law, who has succeeded in overcoming the greatest difficulties on the harp. She would even surprise our artists in Paris. Her nimbleness and lightness of touch on her instrument are amazing, though not completely enchanting because she lacks expression.

One of her relatives was renowned for her superb voice, which she demonstrated exceptionally by singing great operatic arias. Alas, for my poor ears, she demonstrated a sample of her talent! Good God! Such screams! My ears are still ringing from them!

I too was asked to perform, but I must confess that I did not care to do so. Besides, because I had not sung since my departure from Paris, my voice was a little rusty and my pride would have been hurt if I had not done myself justice. Accordingly, I declined.

The repairs to the corvette had now been completed; the difficulty of unloading and reloading everything on board had been overcome. The ship was rigged and ready to set sail on 15 July. I paid my farewell visits, some of which, I must admit, caused me sorrow. I was sad at the thought of leaving that fine gentleman for whom I felt a daughter's affection. His kindness, his obliging and generous behaviour towards us could be explained only by his great affection for my brother-in-law, which was transferred to us. I was all the sadder because I did not think I would see our friend the kind judge again. He assured us, however, that having always wished to live in France, he was now more determined than ever to realise his dream, and that he would be drawn there by his dear children.

The next day, 16 July, M. Smith accompanied us on board and refused to leave until the ship was under sail. At 4 o'clock, favoured by a light breeze, we sailed out of the harbour, and I must confess to you that it was with deep sorrow that we bade farewell to our friends for the last time.

In Saint-Denis harbour, Bourbon Island — Receptions at the residences
of the Administrator and the Governor — Description of Saint-Denis —
The Botanical Garden — Bourbon Island's female society — Saint-Paul
and surrounding districts — An accident at departure time

July 1818 – We made for Bourbon Island [later named Reunion Island]
where we intended taking on board fresh supplies from the King's stores.
The wind was quite fresh but contrary, and we had a long and unpleasant
voyage. We had on board several passengers, two of whom had been
warmly recommended to us. One was a colonel in command of the
artillery on Bourbon Island; the other a civil servant in some government
department unknown to me. Both were seasick and our apartment
resembled a hospital. My servants themselves were not in the best of
health. I did nothing during the whole voyage but send broth, cups of
coffee, and so on ...

As we had to tack and as the sea currents were very strong, we made little
headway. At last, after a voyage of three days, which could have been
completed in a few hours with a favourable wind, we dropped anchor on
19 July at 5 p.m. in the harbour of Saint-Denis, the capital of Bourbon Island.

That night, I received a letter from Mme la Baronne de Richemont, the
wife of M. Desbassayns de Richemont, Intendant [administrator] of Bourbon
Island.

M. Desbassayns is a Creole, the son of a wealthy Bourbon Island
planter. Early in his life he embarked on a career in commerce and became
a merchant in India with considerable success. He came to Paris, while
still a young man, to continue in large-scale business. There, he married
a charming French woman.

In 1814, thanks to some influential friends in the Ministry of the Navy,
he was appointed to the post of Administrator in Pondicherry. In addition,
he was responsible for taking to England the treaty of trade with the Indies.
As a result, M. Desbassayns received the title of Baron de Richemont from
the King.

Mme de Richemont has an 18-year-old son; she cannot therefore be in
early youth. I estimate her age to be 36, but she is truly so pretty and well

Bourbon Island [later named
Reunion Island]

Jacques Arago (1790–1855)
Ile Bourbon: Vue de la Batterie
de la Possession c.1818
colour collotype; 14.5 x 21.4 cm
Journal de Madame Rose de Saulces de
Freycinet ... (Paris: Société d'Editions
Géographiques, Maritimes et
Coloniales, 1927), plate no. 5
Rex Nan Kivell Collection
National Library of Australia Pictorial
Collection (U8139e)

preserved that she could easily be taken for a younger woman. She is quick-witted, is most pleasant and has all the attributes that would make her stand out among members of her own sex.

The events of 1815 happened before M. de Richemont had been able to leave France. Then everything changed, I cannot say why. But he was stripped of his administrative position before taking it up and subsequently was named Intendant of Bourbon Island, sharing the administrative duties of the colony with General Lafitte, the island's Governor.

Her letter offered us an apartment in her home and invited us to occupy it, although she herself was unable to meet us at the harbour. She was staying in the country and was only due to return in the course of the next day.

It was far too late to think of going ashore. Besides, I found the sea to be too rough to risk getting off at that spot, where landing was extraordinarily awkward. As the harbour is very open and there is no port, the sea lashes the coast. One is forced to use small canoes, that is, small boats of medium length, pointed at both ends and only two feet wide. When one reaches the shore, one waits for the arrival of a big wave. Soon after, without raising the oars, one is almost carried ashore, where blacks grab the canoe and drag it onto the beach.

When the sea is rough, landing is impossible, for even if the weather is passable, canoes can be seen overturning, and people can drown or be dragged out to sea.

The wind abated during the night and, on 20 July, the sea was quite calm. The pilot who was to guide us had informed Louis that the sea was at its best early in the morning, and I had to leave the *Uranie* and try my luck. I would have preferred to await the return of Mme de Richemont, but there was no time to waste. I was terrified and the trip from the ship to land was most unpleasant for me. However, nothing untoward happened to us and we landed safely.

The harbour master came to greet us as we landed and offered me his arm to lead me to the administrator's residence. He showed us into a sitting room and, a short while later, a maid came and offered to take me to my apartment. I hastened away, as I wanted to dress before Mme de Richemont's arrival.

I had scarcely finished dressing when a young woman was introduced to me as her envoy; it was her daughter's governess. She seemed witty and stayed with me until 10 a.m. She made me promise to come to lunch, assuring me that Mme de Richemont had urged her to invite me, if she herself was late. I went reluctantly, fearing that the Baroness might arrive during lunch, which would have embarrassed me greatly. We had been seated for barely 15 minutes when she entered. Her welcome was gracious and friendly; she apologised profusely for having delayed my lunch.

I found the Baron a little cool; he appeared gloomy and absent-minded, which surprised me. But I have since observed that he purposely put on an air of being overwhelmed by the numerous problems of his administration. His affectation is so pronounced that everyone is aware of it. He goes as far as to sign letters at the table in order to show that he cannot spare the time to have his meals in peace.

After lunch, I retired with the Baroness into a small drawing room where we spent several hours chatting. She told me, among other things, that the Governor, M. Lafitte, intended to detain me and prevent me from going back on board because the orders he had received demanded it. She led me to believe that he was a wretch and that once he had set his mind on this, it would take all my rhetorical skills to convince him to do otherwise. She declared to me that he had warned her of his impending visit in the morning to meet me.

I was determined to avoid meeting him, not wanting to put up with such an unpleasant assault, and I was about to leave the room, asking Mme Desbassayns to excuse me, when he was suddenly ushered into the drawing room where we were, thus making my retreat impossible. I had to put a brave face on things. I bowed to him as graciously as I could and received his compliments with gratitude. I prepared the way by trying to arouse his interest in my fate, in order to make him less ruthless and to deceive him just this one time. I was shaking with fear; what would become of me far from my family, my friends, in a colony that was so alien to me? But, instead of finding a critic of my conduct intent on rehabilitating me, all I had to do was to ward off the compliments of someone who was full of admiration for my courage, and so on ..., who resorted to all those clichés which my poor ears have been subjected to so often. He invited us to dine at Government House the next day and left declaring he was happy to be able to receive a heroine such as me in his home!

Mme de Richemont was dumbfounded. She asserted that my pretty eyes had been my advocates. Yet, the real reason for his change of heart was that my dear Louis had reasoned with him a few moments before he entered the drawing room. The Governor understood full well that if he did not allow me to leave of my own free will, I would still do so in spite of him.

The invitation to dinner also surprised her; since his arrival on the island, the Governor had never had a female guest at his table. Until dinner, we spent the time visiting some of Mme Desbassayns' female relatives.

Cape Bernard and the
township of Saint-Denis,
Bourbon Island

Jacques Arago (1790–1855)
*Bourbon 1818: Vue du Cap
Bernard et d'une Partie de la Ville
de Saint-Denis* 1818
collotype; 15.2 x 20.8 cm
*Journal de Madame Rose de Saulces de
Freycinet ...* (Paris: Société d'Editions
Géographiques, Maritimes et
Coloniales, 1927), plate no. 4
Rex Nan Kivell Collection
National Library of Australia
Pictorial Collection (U8139d)

The streets of Bourbon Island are badly paved, crooked and as a rule too
narrow for carriages. Nevertheless, the Baroness' barouche, which is so light
and small, copes quite well.

The town of Saint-Denis is ugly. All the houses are built of wood and are
unsightly. Only government buildings are made of stone and, as they are
usually badly located, they do not add to the appearance of the town.

Port Louis in Mauritius, prior to the fire that consumed the most
attractive district, must have been much more pleasant; there are large
numbers of stone houses, a few of which are very well built. But there is
not a single promenade, while in Saint-Denis they have had the foresight
to plan a charming one, which I went to see that night after dinner. It is in
a Botanical Garden, remarkable not only for its rare plants, but also for its
sheltered paths, which the sun never reaches. Those avenues are formed
by mango trees whose stature and shape recall those of our horse chestnut
trees. We walked in moonlight; the rays, scarcely penetrating the foliage,
left some areas in profound darkness. I felt inclined to dream, and it seemed
to me that I would have been happy to have been left in the small nook
where I had withdrawn, not alone but with you, my dear, for whenever
I experience some sweet pleasure, you always share every moment of joy.
I imagined how ecstatic I would have been if I could have had but
two hours of conversation with you in this charming solitude. Mme
Desbassayns jolted me out of these thoughts by making fun of the sad and
melancholic mood which had come over me in those Creole avenues.

The next day, a grand dinner was organised at the administrator's residence, to which all the town's public servants and the officers of the *Uranie* were invited. But the latter were so soaked during landing that almost all had to excuse themselves.

I spent part of the next day, 22 July, in my apartment finishing my letters for France. At 3 o'clock, I was told that I was expected in the drawing room prior to going to Government House. I went down and found Mme de Richemont there, who joked with me about my scarf and assured me that my dress, quite pretty otherwise, was marred by those pieces of gauze which covered my bosom. I had taken care, indeed, to neglect nothing which might embarrass the Baroness. I wore a white satin petticoat which highlighted a beautiful dress of embroidered gauze, very light and trimmed on the hem with rolls of red satin.

The Governor was waiting impatiently for us. He came to help me out of the carriage and led me into the drawing room. He showed me in detail the whole of Government House, which is more spacious than elegant. However, I was in raptures over the two drawing rooms, which would provide a splendid venue for balls. I believe that he would have been swayed, had he not also thought that he would have had to spend a lot of money on such functions. At such a thought, our good General's face took on such a sombre look that the Baroness and I dropped the subject.

His dinner was sumptuous. The table was big and well served, but there were not enough guests. He would have done himself more credit by inviting 25 guests rather than 15, for the table seemed empty. One thing shocked me, about which I had not been forewarned, namely that he had in his service a woman who seemed to belong to the pantry and yet held the position of housekeeper. We were seated at the table when she entered with her daughter through the door of the pantry and came to take her place beside us. That the General in private should eat his meals with his housekeeper, as do parish priests, I can't see anything wrong in that. But that, at an official dinner, she should be seated at the table is completely ridiculous. The Baroness whispered a few words to me on the subject after dinner and I noticed that her viewpoint concurred with mine.

We returned to the drawing room after a few minutes. Mme Desbassayns invited the General to come and spend the evening at the administrator's residence. He accepted, all the more willingly because he did not have any means of entertaining his guests and was delighted to be spared the task of doing so.

Several invitations were sent out and that night a large company gathered at the residence. To give me a sample of Creole music in Saint-Denis, Mme Desbassayns asked them to play and sing. I shall make the same observation about it as I did about Mauritius; Creole women don't know anything about singing. Mme Desbassayns wanted to plead in their defence, but I must admit that I did not show the same leniency, and I found it to be in very bad taste.

The Creole women of Bourbon are far less agreeable than those of Mauritius; they are not as pretty and are brought up more simply. I would compare the Creole women of Mauritius to Parisian women and those of Bourbon to our provincial women. One can make the same distinction between them. I could only judge them by their appearance, as I saw them for only a few days, while I spent two and a half months in the company of Mauritian Creoles.

I paid several visits to Mme Desbassayns-Montbrun, sister-in-law of the Intendant. She is a very pretty Parisian woman, and a very interesting one at that, who is languishing here until her husband's business is completed and she can go back to live in Paris.

In Bourbon Louis found one of his friends who had been a botanist during the expedition of M. Baudin. He had remained in this colony and had married a sister of Mme Desbassayns. They invited us to dinner on 23 July and received us like real friends. In the evening, we went to the administrator's residence where there was another large gathering of Creoles. We played games and spent a very pleasant evening.

The following morning, I received a visit from the captain of the *Rosalie* [the *Caroline*], the ship in which my sister had made the voyage. He is a sailor without pretensions, whose manners are as down to earth as his profession. I asked him countless details about my sister and, in spite of myself, a few tears ran down my cheeks. Would you believe that the man stood up angrily, declared his intention of leaving and stated most brusquely that he did not like to see women cry? He sat down in the hope that I would be more sensible. After an interesting conversation which lasted about an hour, I begged him, as he was leaving, to come back and see me again before setting sail, but he replied rather harshly: 'Yes, I shall do so, but only on condition that you do not cry, for otherwise, if I see your eyes all red, I shall leave at once.'

As all the supplies had been taken on board on 25 July, Louis planned to cast off the next morning. We were ready to leave when the harbour master informed us at 10 a.m. that the sea was so rough that any communication with the ship was impossible. Louis went to the beach to judge for himself and, seeing indeed that it would be difficult to board, he sent the agreed signal to M. Lamarche, the First Lieutenant, that he was to sail without us. He then returned to the administrator's residence to arrange horses so that we might proceed by land to Saint-Paul, another town on

Bourbon Island, where the *Uranie* was to take on vegetables, poultry and refreshments for the sick and the officers. Several hours elapsed before we were able to get both the horses and the blacks who were to carry our baggage. I rejoiced at the prospect of this small expedition, though it was more tiring than by sea, for I would be able to see the interior of the island which, I have been told, is superb. But as the wind and sea died down a little towards 2 p.m. and no decision had yet been taken concerning our journey by land, Louis convinced me to be brave enough to go on board, as this was the simplest and shortest route and as he could not wait to leave the colony and continue his voyage. Moreover, if we did not take advantage of this fine weather, we would probably lose several days. With terror in my heart, I resigned myself, wanting to be faithful to the resolution I made on the very first day I set foot aboard, never out of fear or a whim to prevent Louis from doing his duty.

I therefore had to board in that wretched canoe, in which I was told we had the best pilot and the bravest blacks ... there was nevertheless some danger! I did not try to conceal the truth from myself and it took all my courage to endure that painful moment. I shall never forget the sinister thoughts that came into my mind when, almost lying down in that boat with my head on Louis' knees, I could hear nothing around me but the

Burning off on Bourbon Island

Jacques Arago (1790–1855)
Ile Bourbon: Vue du Grand-Brûlé
c.1818
collotype; 14.4 x 21.5 cm
Journal de Madame Rose de Saulces de Freycinet ... (Paris: Société d'Editions Géographiques, Maritimes et Coloniales, 1927), plate no. 6
Rex Nan Kivell Collection
National Library of Australia
Pictorial Collection (U8139f)

45

frightening noise of the raging sea lashing the shore and the shouts of the pilot who urged that the blacks work in unison and properly in order to propel this frail piece of wood into the first wave which reached us. I was terrified but arrived on board safely!

We set sail at once and the following morning dropped anchor in the bay of Saint-Paul, which is on the opposite side of the island. There, a lieutenant who was the harbour master came on board. After taking lunch with us, he encouraged us to go ashore where we met M. de Villèle, the brother-in-law of M. Desbassayns de Richemont. Once again, it was necessary to slip into a small canoe, but the weather was fine. The sea did not break as violently in this harbour as in that of Saint-Denis.

We found M. de Villèle waiting for us on the shore. He was kind enough to bring a palanquin for me. Louis and he rode on horseback as we headed for his mother-in-law's home, located at the far end of the town of Saint-Paul, half a league from the spot where we landed. I was received simply but most warmly by his wife, as his mother-in-law had not yet arrived.

Louis and M. de Villèle returned to town to pay a visit to the fortress' commander, who came in person to greet me a few hours later. He is the father or the cousin of a man well known in Paris for his poetry, M. de Parny. He too is reputed for his wit and kindness. He is a lieutenant-colonel and the Army Commander of the town of Saint-Paul. After squandering part of his fortune in Paris and losing his wife, the beautiful Contat, he obtained this position as a Creole from Bourbon, as much to restore his fortune as to recover a few properties left here. He married a very wealthy young Creole woman, with whom he has had two children.

That evening, I made the acquaintance of Mme Desbassayns, about whom I had heard so much. She is the mother of the Intendant and of Mme de Villèle. She displayed a blend of common sense, natural wit and Creole simplicity which would surprise most French women. At first, I found her manner of dress strange; a red Madras scarf, tied simply, was all she wore around her hair, and a black silk dress, in as unsophisticated a style as one could imagine, completed her costume. When she goes out, the contrast is striking, for she wears a magnificent veil of black lace worth 50 to 60 Louis and a cashmere which would turn our elegant Parisian women green with envy.

Mme Desbassayns lives almost permanently inland, where she has large properties. Her magnificent town house is occupied by her daughter. Everything in the family exudes affluence and their simple habits are in sharp contrast to the silver service on the table. I spent three very pleasant days in their family home and I have nothing but praise for the manner in which I was received.

Mme de Villèle is very sweet and kind by nature. She has three lovely children whom she brings up extraordinarily well. She asked me for permission during our stay to continue supervising her children's homework, and I can assure you that nothing pleased me more than to see her small 7-year-old daughter, after finishing her homework, come with her spindle and cotton and sit beside her mother and work with the poise of a 20-year-old.

The surrounding districts of Saint-Paul are very picturesque, and M. de Villèle wanted us to go on a trip each morning to judge for ourselves. As the roads were not pleasant for walking, we went on quite long treks on horseback. On those occasions, I realised how much can be lost through lack of practice, for I did not feel very confident on an old mare which perhaps had never galloped in her life.

We also visited the church which is quite attractive, as well as the presbytery which is striking in its beauty and the size of its gardens.

The government has set up a number of very interesting schools in Saint-Paul. The girls' school is run by the Sisters of Mercy; the inborn talent of young mulattos for learning is amazing. I have seen some at the age of 8 who could read and write quite well after only three months of schooling. The boys' school is managed by ignorant brothers who have not yet adopted the Lancaster method practised at the girls' school. Their institution does not seem to be as successful.

M. de Villèle personally took charge of our supplies, which were collected and taken aboard on the second day of our stay in Saint-Paul, but the next day, 27 July, the weather was so inclement that we could not dream of casting off. The corvette dragged its anchor and had to drop a second one. In the evening, the weather seemed calm and we returned to the *Uranie* to board her once more. The wind, though light, favoured our departure from the bay and we planned to get underway soon after we boarded. As we reached the ship, the *Cybèle*, a French frigate arriving from China, anchored in the harbour a few cables length away from us. She manoeuvred so badly that she broke one of our side anchors and caused other damage, which forced us to stay an extra day to carry out the repairs.

On 28 July, with repairs completed and a favourable wind, we left behind our compatriots, our hearts wrung by emotion at the thought that a considerable amount of time would elapse before we saw French people again.

Shark Bay, New Holland – Anchored in Dampier Bay – The Uranie aground on a sandbank; refloated, she heads for Timor – Arrival in Kupang Bay, Timor – Setting up an observatory – The houses and the heat – Chinese festival for the full moon

September 1818 – We had to contend with adverse winds for several days and were able to make good headway towards New Holland only six days after leaving Saint-Paul. We sailed south where we experienced a little cold weather.

As we were not expecting to find fresh water at Shark Bay, Louis set up a still, which would be ready for action when we caught sight of the low and arid lands of New Holland. The furnace was lit and all seemed to be going well. The water was plentiful and its taste confirmed to us that it was drinkable, when an unexpected accident caused general consternation and struck fear into some of us: a fire started in the pipe of the still's chimney and the deck in turn became heated and caught fire. Prompt emergency action allayed our fears, but my poor Louis, in his eagerness to extinguish the fire, seized a red hot iron bar and scalded his whole hand.

I spent many anxious moments in a quandary, not being able to go to Louis' aid. He did not want to leave the battery before everything was secure and it was impossible for me to enter that melee. Fortunately, the vigilant and skilled care of the doctors provided immediate relief and the burn did not have any serious after-effects.

Although it was not much longer than others we had experienced so far, this crossing was one of the saddest. Until now, as I went from A to B, I spent half my time recollecting the place I had just left and the other half looking forward to the pleasures of the next port of call. But the charm of our destination could not distract me, and I resolved to busy myself with endless tasks which left me no time to think about the huge distance I had to cover, deprived of news from home for 17 to 18 months, as I would not be able to receive any further news until we reached Port Jackson.

I had come on board in Toulon with a guitar which I had made little use of until now. Having taken only a few lessons in Paris with regard to the position of the hands, I had a lot to do before I could be satisfied with

Anarana, a young Malay woman, carrying water, Timor

Nicolas Eustache Maurin (1799–1850)
Anarana, Jeune Malaise Portant de l'Eau, Timor c.1825
hand-coloured lithograph; 14.5 x 23 cm
Jacques Arago, *Souvenirs d'un Aveugle: Voyage autour du Monde* (Paris: Hortet et Ozanne, 1839), vol. 2, plate facing p. 74
Rex Nan Kivell Collection
National Library of Australia Pictorial Collection (U5519)

Inside a Timorese home, Kupang

The game being played is tchonka, one much enjoyed by Louis de Freycinet

Jean Nicolas Lerouge (b.1776)
Coupang, Ile Timor: Intérieur d'une Maison Timorienne c.1822
hand-coloured stipple engraving; 23.2 x 31 cm
Louis-Claude de Freycinet, *Voyage autour du Monde ... Exécuté sur les Corvettes de S.M. l'Uranie et la Physicienne ... : Atlas Historique* (Paris: Chez Pillet Aîné, 1825), plate no. 18
Rex Nan Kivell Collection
National Library of Australia Pictorial Collection (S7239)

my progress. I spent one hour each day learning to play, one hour on my journal, one hour studying English, one hour on my sewing. Thus, the end of the day was upon me without my having been bored.

I had yet another distraction. A friend of Louis, who had been forced to leave Mauritius, had entrusted to foster parents a young child whom he had had by a mulatto. Louis, who is very fond of that friend, thought that the child would benefit greatly from joining us on board and being educated by me. As a rule, these children have innate intelligence, as if Nature wished to offer them such compensation by endowing them with special skills. But that particular child was unfortunately quite an ordinary student. He was 7 years old when we sailed from Mauritius, and could neither read nor write. Although he caused me a lot of trouble, as he was a slow learner and especially because he had never been taught to obey, he nevertheless provided me with a little diversion, and when Louis was forced to leave me by myself, his presence prevented me from feeling completely alone.

On 12 September at 5 o'clock, we anchored at the entrance of Shark Bay, near Dirck Hartog's Island. That same night, the still was lit and produced a continuous flow of water. But my fears that a fire might start persisted, all the more because the deck where the furnace stood became alarmingly hot. We had to wet it continuously. It appears that the furnace was a little too big for the size of the ship. Louis has kept all the data and observations on the subject. For all that, the experiment was highly successful, and there was an abundance of fresh water.

On 13 September, Louis sent a boat to Dirck Hartog's Island to remove an inscription left behind by the Dutch to mark their landing around 1600 [the Vlamingh plate]. It is a precious object which we plan to take back to Paris.

Soon after the departure of the boat, we made way under sail to move further into the bay. At 6 p.m., we dropped anchor in Dampier Bay in five fathoms of water. The next day, a rowing boat was sent ashore to set up our observatory.

Louis was a little astonished that the boat sent to the island had not returned, for the party had just enough supplies to last until the evening of the 14th and could not expect to find any food or even a drop of water on that wretched land.

On 15 September, M. Duperrey set out in a boat to do a geographical survey of the coast. The observatory was set up in another place. Louis and I went ashore the next day.

That trip was not entirely enjoyable, for the sea was so low that half a league from the shore, the dinghies did not have enough water to float.

I had to be carried by two sailors to the beach and the gentlemen were forced to trail through the water. At last, we set foot on land in a spot which my husband deemed the most suitable to pitch camp.

As soon as we arrived, we noticed at the top of the sandhills which lined the coast several figures whom at first we took to be members of the crew on a hunting expedition. But drawing near, we realised that it was a band of natives, all naked, armed with assegais and spears. They threatened us, signalling that we were to return to the ship. Louis had with him only one officer and the two sailors who had carried me ashore; the others were on board ship. He wanted to go and meet them, but not knowing how many there might be, he decided to send for the sailors from the other camp, which was about one league away, before proceeding in numbers towards them to offer them greetings. He had resolved to resort to force only if they were hostile towards us. It was then that I recalled what you once said in a letter in Toulon 'that I would hide behind Louis' shirt-tail at the first sight of natives'. In truth, I must confess that I was afraid and would willingly have hidden myself.

Back at the spot where we had landed, we found that our lunch had arrived, and after putting up a canvas to provide us with some shade, we ate a healthy meal, not just on what had been brought from the ship, but also on excellent oysters which we found on the rocks, oysters far tastier than all those I had eaten, sitting at a table in comfort, in Paris.

We returned to the ship in the evening, fully expecting to find the boat back from its expedition. But those on board, by now very anxious, informed us that they had had no news of it. Louis was determined to

First meeting with natives at Shark Bay, New Holland (Jacques Arago is shown playing his castanets)

Jacques Arago (1790–1855) *Première Entrevue avec les Sauvages* c.1818 collotype; 15 x 21 cm *Journal de Madame Rose de Saulces de Freycinet* ... (Paris: Société d'Editions Géographiques, Maritimes et Coloniales, 1927), plate no. 8 Rex Nan Kivell Collection National Library of Australia Pictorial Collection (U8139h)

Observatory and camp set up
by the *Uranie's* crew, Shark Bay,
New Holland

Rose and the Mauritian boy
are at the door to the tent on
the right; Louis de Freycinet
is at work at a table close by.
In the same scene featured in
the official record, Rose and
the boy do not appear.

Alphonse Pellion
*Baie des Chiens-Marins:
Observatoire de l'Uranie* c.1822
colour collotype; 29.5 x 34.8 cm
*Journal de Madame Rose de Saulces de
Freycinet ...* (Paris: Société d'Editions
Géographiques, Maritimes et Coloniales,
1927), plate no. 7
Rex Nan Kivell Collection
National Library of Australia Pictorial
Collection (U8139g)

dispatch a boat to look for them the next day, when at about 2 o'clock they
were seen on the horizon.

On 18 September, I went ashore with Louis and we spent several days
sleeping under a tent. That stay on land was not a pleasant one for me, the
country being entirely devoid of trees and vegetation. One could only go for
a walk on burning sand. When the heat died down a little, I would collect
shells, of which I have an impressive collection. I spent the rest of the day
in the tent reading or working.

On 21 September, M. Duperrey brought us enormous turtles which
greatly pleased us, for one can make excellent broth from them and their
flesh was rather delicious in a stew.

The natives, no doubt frightened off by the number of people coming
ashore, had retreated on the day we first saw them. The previous day,
after much hesitation, they had come up to men in the first camp and
had exchanged their weapons for tin, glass necklaces and so on.

Several crewmen, anxious to see the natives, resolved to go on an
expedition inland and, most imprudently, without any supplies. The party
split up; two of the wisest, realising the distance which had been covered
and thinking of the return journey, made their way back to the camp. But
as the country was uniform and covered with sand dunes which all looked
alike, they found their way only after a long trek made more difficult by the

heat and lack of water. All the others returned the following evening after spending two days without food and drink, except for the blood of a bird.

When all the observations had been made and enough water had been stocked up, we weighed anchor at 11 a.m. on 26 September with a fresh breeze, and headed for Timor. Around 6 p.m., as we were continually taking soundings, the water became shallow all of a sudden and, a few minutes later, although quite far from the shore, we struck a sandbank. You can imagine the state I was in at that moment, shipwrecked on such a horrible coastline without any resources. All my courage deserted me and I envisaged nothing but calamity. I thought that if the wind freshened up, our poor *Uranie* would shatter into a thousand pieces on the rocks ...

My husband came running to reassure me and convinced me that there was no real danger and that we would soon be on our way. Since his presence was required on deck, I was left alone, preoccupied by my fears. Our chief surgeon, realising that I would be all by myself, was kind enough to come and reassure me and keep me company. I must admit I was most touched by his thoughtfulness. He allayed my fears a little by pointing out that there was no real danger. Indeed, we immediately dropped several anchors and with the rising tide the ship, which had been made lighter, was afloat. All night, the corvette lay in one or two inches of water.

The next day, at dawn, Louis sent out a party to take soundings. Having found a channel, we made way under sail after hitting the bottom gently on two or three occasions. At midday, we were in 12 to 15 fathoms of water, free from any danger. We then steered a course into the open sea and headed for Timor, where we were to stay for some time.

It was as if God wished to compensate us in this crossing for all the afflictions we had endured in New Holland. We could not have hoped for finer weather and more favourable conditions: no rough seas, a fair wind all the time and not a single day of foul weather.

On 7 October, the island of Roti came into sight and, the next day, we were close to Semau near Timor. How happy we were to see the lush vegetation of these islands! We feasted our eyes on all the greenery after the sand dunes and the dry and scraggy shrubs of New Holland.

On 9 October, Louis dropped anchor in Kupang Bay, a Dutch settlement on the island of Timor. At last we would find fresh water without running the risk of setting fire to the ship to obtain it. I must say that the most anxious moments I experienced on board the *Uranie* were when the still was lit. Twenty times a day, it was reported that the deck was becoming heated under the furnace and, on several occasions, we were ready to hack the surrounding wood to make certain that it did not catch fire. Hence, I was overjoyed to find fresh water in Kupang.

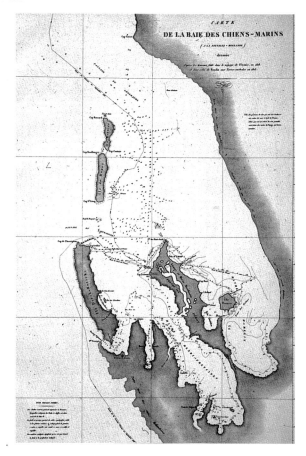

Map of Shark Bay,
New Holland

Louis-Claude de Freycinet
(1779–1842)
*Carte de la Baie des
Chiens-Marins* 1818
Louis-Claude de Freycinet, *Voyage
autour du Monde ... Exécuté sur les
Corvettes de S.M. l'Uranie et la
Physicienne ... : Atlas* (Paris: Chez
Pillet Aîné, 1825), plate no. 1
Rex Nan Kivell Collection
National Library of Australia Map
Collection (RA 260)

We realised afterwards that the water contained many unhealthy properties, because of the climate, which was itself very insalubrious due to the humidity that prevailed; many of the crewmen on board contracted dysentery. Louis kept a few barrels of distilled water for our table; he deemed it to be healthier, and it was thanks to that precaution and to other measures made necessary by this unhealthy climate that we were not affected by that dreadful disease.

Upon our arrival in Timor, Louis made me promise not to eat any manner of fruit. In spite of the temptation, I kept my promise. I was only allowed to eat mangoes, a fruit which I cannot compare to any other which we have in France, because they are not as refreshing.

On the day of our arrival, the Governor was in the interior, in command of his troops, trying to repulse a King who, not satisfied with gaining independence from Dutch rule, wanted to encroach on the territory of Kupang. It was the Governor's secretary who showed us two houses, one for the observatory and the other for the officers. We occupied them, taking our personal effects and equipment with us.

I paid a visit to Mme Tielman, the secretary's wife. She is a half-caste from Java, whose father was French. She was brought up in Samarang. She knows Dutch, understands English a little and is something of a musician. I found her manner of dress a little strange. She wore a large black petticoat, pleated to the feet in the manner of priests' robes; over this she wore a type of black camisole which reached her knees. Her long straight hair hung down over her shoulders.

The day she came to see me, she was in European clothes. She is not pretty but has beautiful black eyes and a sweet and kind demeanour. She spoke a few words of Malay to me, but as my knowledge of that language is very limited, our conversation was brief. In the course of her other visits, to entertain me or so she claimed, she played the piano, but this fell short of her goal since she knew only as much as a 9-year-old schoolgirl after six months of private lessons.

On other occasions, slaves trained in music gave concerts for us. She had in her service, among others, a charming, young Timorese girl who was 12 years old and who played a small harp quite well, holding it quite differently from the way we do in France. She sat holding her harp at such a low angle that the strings were horizontal rather than vertical. Other musicians played the violin and the flute; occasionally someone sang. Every evening we took our coffee, tea or other refreshments there.

Our house had wooden shutters with openings at the top to let in some light when the heat of the sun required them to be shut. There are a lot

Visiting the Tilleman [Tielman] home in Kupang, Timor

Alphonse Pellion
Ile Timor: Visite chez M. M.J. Tilleman à Coupang c.1822
colour collotype; 15.5 x 21.3 cm
Journal de Madame Rose de Saulces de Freycinet ... (Paris: Société d'Editions Géographiques, Maritimes et Coloniales, 1927), plate no. 12
Rex Nan Kivell Collection
National Library of Australia
Pictorial Collection (U8139l)

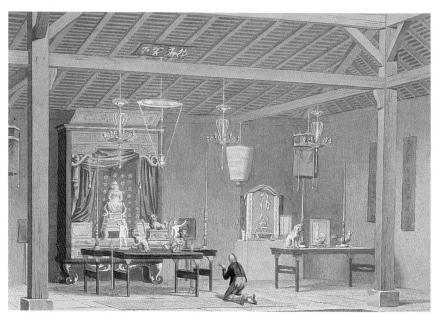

Chinese temple, Kupang,
Timor

Jean Nicolas Lerouge (b.1776)
*Vue de l'Intérieur du Temple
Chinois, à Coupang sur l'Ile
Timor* c.1822
hand-coloured stipple engraving;
23.3 x 32 cm
Louis-Claude de Freycinet, *Voyage
autour du Monde ... Exécuté sur les
Corvettes de S.M. l'Uranie et la
Physicienne ... : Atlas Historique* (Paris:
Chez Pillet Aîné, 1825), plate no. 26
Rex Nan Kivell Collection
National Library of Australia
Pictorial Collection (S7247)

of unpleasant local animals, especially a lizard which finds its way into
houses to bite you. It is called a gecko, because of the sound of its cry. Each
night, I heard one very close to our bedroom. For fear that it might creep in,
I always kept the light on. Irritated by its continuous cries which seemed so
near, I rose in the middle of the night and, carrying a light, I went looking
for it, only to find a large scorpion next to our bed.

The heat was unbearable. The Abbé, who was in poor health, came
ashore with us, and we did not know what to do to help him. Yet, the
houses were properly built to cope with the heat; their overhanging roofs
were sufficiently low to prevent the sun's rays from penetrating. They were
open on all sides so as to allow the air to circulate. One stormy day, we
suffered dreadfully; the air was oppressive and there was so little breeze
that, although we sat still, we sweated profusely. Fortunately a storm,
with thunder and rain, arrived and cooled the temperature down.

That night, we went to watch preparations for a Chinese festival for the
full moon. The temple remained lit up all night and twigs of sandalwood
were burnt before the idols. The priest gave Louis some candles and half-
burnt twigs, and assured him that, in the event of danger, these would
bring him luck.

At 4 a.m., we returned to attend the festival. The ceremony involves the
priests performing countless antics in front of the different idols; they kneel
four or five consecutive times with their faces against the ground, while
mumbling a few words in Chinese. They pour tea into small cups and place
these on the altar. In the middle of their temple, there is a tree planted in

a small square of soil reserved for it and, above it, the roof opens up so that it might enjoy the beneficial effects of the rain or sunlight. It is called the 'tree of life' and, near it, the Chinese burn pieces of golden paper, cut in thin strips. The altars were laden with chickens, roasted and boiled pork, pastries, jam and so on ..., which each person offers according to his means.

After the ceremony, we were asked to partake of all those dishes, as well as tea, but we declined. All those provisions are taken away by the high priest, inviting his friends to come and dine with him.

Louis revisited some Malays whom he had met during his first voyage. He also went to visit rajahs who offered him mangoes; in return, he gave them tools and equipment.

During Mme Tielman's soirées, Louis learnt a new game named tchonka which, aided by one of the servants, he played with the hostess.

Mme Tielman came to pay me a farewell visit, dressed in a black European dress. She gave me a bird of paradise. I sent her several bottles of syrup which she had tasted at my house and had enjoyed, as well as dry sweet biscuits.

We are leaving. Crossing the strait is tedious. We sail close to the coast of Timor which is lush and green. From time to time, towns and Dutch and Portuguese settlements come into view. Contrary winds and currents impede our progress. We meet a whaler and stay in sight of each other for several days. The captain comes to dine with us on a number of occasions. As he is about to head back to England in six months' time, he takes charge of a letter. Louis sends out a boat to the island of Ombai.

Chinese women playing tchonka, Timor

Jacques Arago (1790–1855)
Ile Timor: Chinoises Jouant au Jeu Appelé Tjonka c.1818
collotype; 14.4 x 19.2 cm
Journal de Madame Rose de Saulces de Freycinet ... (Paris: Société d'Editions Géographiques, Maritimes et Coloniales, 1927), plate no. 13
Rex Nan Kivell Collection
National Library of Australia
Pictorial Collection (U8139m)

57

Stopover in Dili – Official reception with the Governor – The Uranie sails through the Moluccas – Rawak and Waigeo Islands – Meeting and trading with Papuans – Widespread illness among the crew

November 1818 – The length and difficulties of our voyage during the last month or so, together with the number of sick crewmen and the fact that we had not been able to take on enough supplies at Kupang, all combined to persuade the Commander to call at Dili. The way we were received was a source of great amusement to me.

We anchored four days ago. Our salute was returned. Louis was also saluted by one special salvo when he landed from the boat which took him ashore. The Portuguese Governor, Don Jose Pinto Alcoforado d'Azevedo e Souza, welcomed the dear Commander and his crew with truly remarkable courtesy, and as soon as he learnt that I was on board, he sent me fruit and fresh bread together with an invitation to dine with him the next day. To this end, he announced to my husband that all the notable women of the colony would be gathered at his home to receive me. I did not possess suitable attire for such formal occasions; a light muslin dress alone, together with a hat decorated with a few feathers, was all the finery I had. The minute our boat landed, from a fortress nearby there was such a loud salute from so many guns, and such a large crowd had gathered on the beach that I needed Louis' arm to reach the end of the gangway without stumbling. The Governor was present with all his staff. When I stepped ashore, he gave me his hand and invited me to share with him the shade of a huge parasol carried by a Timorese slave dressed in strange clothes. A similar parasol was held over Louis' head.

In this way, we entered the palace, which had been pleasantly bedecked with foliage and flowers. To the sound of music, we crossed first a large planted yard which was surrounded on all sides by gardens. All the troops presented arms. The women, already assembled at the Governor's residence, came to greet me at the foot of the staircase. Don Jose Pinto introduced them to me. They were all rajahs' daughters who had married Portuguese officers, so that they had more or less swarthy complexions. One of them was a rather handsome woman. All were dressed lavishly in Portuguese

The reception awaiting the captain and officers of the *Uranie* upon landing at Dili, Portuguese Timor

Rose and Louis are shown being received by the Governor (bottom), however in the same scene in the official record (top) Rose does not appear.

(top)
Alphonse Pellion
Ile Timor: Vue de Notre Premier Débarquement à l'Etablissement Portugais de Dillé c.1822
watercolour; 23.7 x 32 cm
Louis-Claude de Freycinet, *Voyage autour du Monde ... Exécuté sur les Corvettes de S.M. l'Uranie et la Physicienne ... : Atlas Historique* (Paris: Chez Pillet Aîné, 1825), original of plate no. 30
Rex Nan Kivell Collection
National Library of Australia
Pictorial Collection (T228)

(bottom)
Jacques Arago (1790–1855)
Ile Timor: Réception à Diély c.1818
colour collotype; 16 x 21.5 cm
Journal de Madame Rose de Saulces de Freycinet ... (Paris: Société d'Editions Géographiques, Maritimes et Coloniales, 1927), plate no. 1
Rex Nan Kivell Collection
National Library of Australia
Pictorial Collection (U8139a)

clothes, in much the same way as French women dressed 40 or 50 years ago, with their hair worn straight on their foreheads, drawn back in a flowing chignon and fastened with gold pins. They also wore gold chains around their necks. But nothing seemed more ridiculous to me than the soldiers' costumes; imagine a big round camisole open at the chest; a loincloth typical of the country, worn as a skirt, which did not reach their knees. Over this, another cloth was thrown and tied at the waist. The sergeant wore it as a sash. He was also the only one to wear a large three-cornered hat, while the other soldiers wore multi-coloured handkerchiefs tied around their heads as hats, displaying a tuft of hair, in which they stuck some sort of bamboo comb to gather it in. All had bare legs and feet. The sergeant carried a long sabre in his hand and the soldiers bore rifles armed with bayonets.

The women, who went into the drawing room with us, seemed to pay a great deal of attention to me, but because they spoke Malay, Louis took charge of replying. I confined myself to thanking them for the obliging things they said about me, most of which I guessed. Each of the women had a slave crouched next to her, holding a handkerchief and a bag that contained betel-nut. You read what Péron said about the use of betel in these climes. Nearly all of the slaves were pretty, lavishly dressed in their own fashion and wearing gold chains and jewels.

The Governor offered me flowers and local saris, which I accepted. Some of the women noticed that I was examining the flowers carefully and, assuming that I liked them, asked their slaves to fetch more and offer them to me.

Judging from mine that their attire was a little old-fashioned, they seemed embarrassed, especially with regard to their shoes. They wore what, I think, used to be called mules, embroidered with sequins or coloured silk. Consequently, they hastened to tell me that large supplies of fashion items were due to reach them from Macao and that they awaited their arrival so eagerly that the sight of the *Uranie* had made their hearts beat faster, thinking it might be the long-awaited ship. They especially envied the advantage of my short curly hair in a hot climate; their husbands and the Governor urged them to cut their hair, which was very long and beautiful and which seemingly they held very dear. One of them seemed almost resolved to make the sacrifice; the Governor asked for scissors and pretended to want to cut it himself, but it was easy to see that the lady in question was not tempted. It was Dona Joachim, the wife of Don Francisco de Assis Durao, Captain Mor, that is, the second in command after the Governor.

The latter presented Louis with two young slaves from the interior of Timor, and he offered me two young indigenous girls from the same district.

Dona [Joana] Joachim, wife of Captain Mor, Dili, Timor

T. Choubard (fl.1807–1830)
Ile Timor: Dillie, Portraits: Dona Joana c.1822
coloured stipple engraving; 23.5 x 32 cm
Louis-Claude de Freycinet, *Voyage autour du Monde ... Exécuté sur les Corvettes de S.M. l'Uranie et la Physicienne ... : Atlas Historique* (Paris: Chez Pillet Aîné, 1825), plate no. 17
Rex Nan Kivell Collection
National Library of Australia
Pictorial Collection (S7238)

He wanted us to take them, but we begged to refuse. He insisted that we take at least one of each sex; what would I have done with a 6-year-old girl on board a ship? After explaining this to the Governor, while expressing our deepest gratitude so as not to hurt his feelings, we accepted one of the young boys who was 7 or 8 years old and whom I intend to leave at the first port where I can be satisfied he will be treated humanely.

The Governor offered us the spectacle of simulated combat between local natives in the traditional style, to display their agility and skill. First, the combatants appear armed with spears which they hurl at each other; during that exercise the men move constantly jumping, skipping, letting out horrible screams. Sometimes they almost crouch on the ground, then they jump into the air, and throw themselves this way and that, with a view to putting off the opponent who is taking aim, for the skill consists in adroitly catching the lance in the air and then hurling it back at the person who first threw it. These gestures are executed with such energy that the bodies of the poor men are covered in sweat. The combat with bows was conducted in a more sedate manner; the natives displayed their extraordinary skill for us. I saw them hit a very distant target, without missing once. Unlike the feigned combat which they put on for our entertainment, when they actually wage war they use bludgeons and a kris, a type of dagger which has a curved, poisoned blade. The natives in the Portuguese army sometimes use rifles.

A sumptuous dinner for 40 guests was organised in our honour, partly in the Portuguese and partly in the English manner. A great profusion of meat and stews made up the first two courses, which were followed by a fine dessert of various pastries, Chinese jam and fruit, which are superb and delicious in Timor. True to my word, I ate only mangoes and delicious pineapples. The china and the crystal which adorned the table were worthy of the rest; an air of luxury prevailed. Slaves of both sexes were present in large numbers and served the table very well. We drank a toast of Madeira wine to the kings and princes of Portugal and, with each toast, there was a salvo. Musicians played throughout almost the entire meal.

After dinner, the Governor, who is very kind and jovial, suggested that we should dance. The women seemed to welcome the idea; I took Don Jose's arm and we danced an English dance, but the heat was so intolerable that I begged to be allowed to rest. Then, the women of Dili set about performing charming Malayan dances, which I would have difficulty describing to you and which resembled the Russian dance I used to do in the old days. Judging by a minuet which the Governor danced with one of the ladies, he proved to us that he must have been an excellent dancer in his youth. It was late when we returned to the ship.

Joseph Antonio, a young Timor boy taken on board at Dili, Timor

Jean Nicolas Lerouge (b.1776)
Ile Timor: Joseph Antonio: Jeune Homme du Royaume de Failacor c.1822
hand-coloured stipple engraving; 32.2 x 23.7 cm
Louis-Claude de Freycinet, *Voyage autour du Monde ... Exécuté sur les Corvettes de S.M. l'Uranie et la Physicienne ... : Atlas Historique* (Paris: Chez Pillet Aîné, 1825), plate no. 31
Rex Nan Kivell Collection
National Library of Australia
Pictorial Collection (S7252)

Two days later, on 21 November, there was a similar grand dinner at the Governor's residence, after which he took us to a beautiful garden outside the town, where coffee and sugar cane are successfully grown. During the walk musicians who followed us played occasionally.

The terrain on which the town is built is damp and boggy, but the neighbouring areas are very picturesque. The Governor showed us a charming site on a hillside, which he had chosen for his country residence. The panorama is not as beautiful as that of Rio de Janeiro harbour, but the vegetation is quite lush in spite of the shortage of running water. Our walk ultimately ended up at the house of Captain Mor, who had invited us for tea. From what has already been erected of his house, one can tell that it will be quite attractive, even though it is built of wood and thatch in the local style.

We found the table set, and soon we were served, not with tea but with the most sumptuous dinner imaginable, where the silver service and the crystal rivalled anything one sees in Europe in the home of a wealthy man. It was 8 p.m. and we had already dined at 4 o'clock; you can imagine our inability to do justice to that beautiful meal. None of us could eat a lot, but toasts had to be proposed and were duly drunk, a little to the detriment of one of the guests who became excessively merry.

Captain Mor and his wife did the honours at their soirée with considerable social grace and affability. We danced after supper for so long that it was very late when we returned to the ship. When I bade farewell to Dona Joachim, she was most affectionate towards me and, in a most gracious fashion, she removed from around her neck a long gold chain made in Manila which she put around mine, beseeching me to accept it as a memento from her.

As we plan to sail tonight or tomorrow, I stayed on board today to recover from those festivities, while describing them for your benefit. The Governor has just sent an officer entrusted with the task of officially farewelling the Commander of the *Uranie* and his crew. He has sent me a number of things which he thought I would like to have, such as tea, fruit and so on. In return, Louis is going to send him several items which he thinks he will like; these gentlemen are vying with each other in polite behaviour, as is customary among well-bred people. Moreover, our good Governor has willingly undertaken to hand over this letter to the first ship bound for Europe. Louis' idea to call at this port was a good one, for not only have these four days of relaxation provided welcome relief from the tedium of a painful and monotonous voyage, but our officers have made fruitful observations of various types, and we have replenished all of our supplies exceedingly well.

9 December 1818, Pisang Island [north-west of New Guinea] – On account
of his poor state of health, the kind Abbé de Quélen was unable to go
ashore at Dili. Accordingly, only a few days after our departure he baptised
the young Timorese lad whom we had taken aboard. My husband and I
are his godparents and, in accordance with the wishes of the Portuguese
Governor, we gave him the name of Joseph, to which I have added that of
Antonio. Don Jose wanted the boy to have his name, so that, he said, we
would remember him. But we shall not forget his kindness towards us any
more than the happy events during this stopover.

Although our voyage was easier once we lost sight of Timor Island
because of a favourable fresh breeze, it was only after we emerged from
the strait that the heat, which had affected us badly ever since our arrival
at Kupang, became a little more bearable for those aboard who were in
good health. Our sick crewmen are suffering greatly; we fear that the Abbé
may have contracted scurvy; he has lost a lot of weight on account of
the heat. The Second Lieutenant, M. Labiche, suffers from dysentery;
several crewmen have already died from that disease. Such unfortunate
circumstances make our journey distressing. Otherwise, it would be so
enjoyable as we make our way through the Moluccan Archipelago, where
one comes across enchanting islands around every corner. The richness of
the soil is demonstrated by the luxurious natural forests which cover these
uncultivated lands. And what trees do we find in those forests? They are the
very ones which produce precious spices; their scent hangs heavy in the air
all around us. Thus, we have sailed past Amboina and closer still to Ceram,
two Dutch settlements which are famous for having contributed so much
to the wealth of that nation.

I sometimes recall that my mother wrote to me, when I was still in
Toulon, that a map of Paris and its surrounding districts was sufficient at
first for her to find each of the places where we lived, that thereafter she
needed a map of France and, finally, that she would only be able to follow
our progress on a world map. Now, a very detailed map of Oceania would
be required—if one existed—to know where we were. Even then, every day
I am told that Louis corrects geographical positions, erroneously recorded
until now, a fact which would not surprise anyone in this part of the world
where the Creator has sown islands 'as he sows dust in our fields'. Since
New Holland, we have not come across any land other than islands, and
it will be some time yet before we espy another continent.

Just as unfrequented dark streets in large towns favour bandits, so too
the numerous straits of these seas are infested with pirates, who usually join
forces to attack merchant ships. They put out to sea in long and narrow
boats similar to canoes with outriggers, and use small paddles which

require a different kind of handling to our oars, in that the paddles do not rest on the side of the canoe. The other day, about 15 of those boats, called *corocores*, appeared at nightfall heading towards us. Louis thought it wise to go on the defensive in case of an attack, but the pirates no doubt were deterred by the strength of the corvette and went on their way.

A few days after that insignificant event, we again encountered several armed *corocores*, but these belonged to the *Kimalaha* [chief] of the island of Gebe. I am not implying that they are not pirates. Louis believes they are when it suits their purpose, and that they were lying in wait for some ships when we saw them. But the chief, old sea wolf that he was, observing that we had the weapons to defend ourselves fiercely, came on board to start negotiations. Not only was he well received, but Louis invited him to lunch, which he accepted without waiting to be asked twice. He became very attached to one of our chairs, which was presented to him at once. In return for this present which pleased him greatly, he thought of nothing better than to remove his own hat and place it on Louis' head, who appeared to me quite comical wearing that type of straw parasol which is skilfully woven but with the same pointed shape as the lids of our saucepans.

The name of that strange character was Abdalaga-Fourou; he was fluent in Malay, so Louis was able to obtain a lot of information from him. The chiefs of the other *corocores* came to join him and, like him, stayed for dinner. The *Kimalaha*, better dressed than the others, was wearing trousers and some kind of open dressing-gown made of white calico, printed with stripes and red flowers. Under his hat, he wore a small red turban with a crown made of fine straw. He was bronzed and his face was lively and cheerful. These men endlessly chew betel and chalk, packed into pretty little boxes made of fine straw in various colours. They exchanged a lot of arrows, paddles and so on ... for mirrors, knives, clothes and so on ... When night fell, Abdalaga-Fourou went back to his boat, promising to return the next day. That prince had pressed Louis to go to Gebe and, while he was aboard our ship, in order to communicate more easily with his *corocores*, he had asked us to take them in tow. But as soon as the wind became fresh, they loosened the moorings and left us in order to return to Gebe. Consequently, Louis does not believe the *Kimalaha*'s promise that he will meet us at Waigeo, where we have to stop to take observations. To derive some advantage from several days' inactivity forced upon us by the calm weather, the Commander has sent naturalists to Pisang Island. As soon as they are back and the wind is fresh again, we will set sail.

A warrior from the island of Gebe

Barthélemy Roger (1767–1841) *Guerrier de l'Île Guébé* c.1822 hand-coloured stipple engraving; 32 x 23.6 cm Louis-Claude de Freycinet, *Voyage autour du Monde ... Exécuté sur les Corvettes de S.M. l'Uranie et la Physicienne ... : Atlas Historique* (Paris: Chez Pillet Aîné, 1825), plate no. 38 Rex Nan Kivell Collection National Library of Australia Pictorial Collection (S7259)

4 December 1818, Waigeo Island [north of New Guinea] – Our botanists had no sooner returned on board with rocks, shells and plants when a storm put an end to the calm and the *Uranie* set sail. Is it not a good enough reason to become reconciled with storms, that for some time we have been able to sail thanks only to the wind which they engender? Nevertheless, this almost constant succession of calms and squalls is often dangerous among a host of islands, whose coastlines for the most part bristle with sharp rocks. Eight or ten days ago, after a beautiful day's sailing, a dead calm befell us all of a sudden in the night. Fortunately, the moon was out and Louis was on watch. At 3 a.m., he noticed that the corvette was in shallow water; he had the depth sounded and found it was only nine fathoms deep. A boat sent out a little further found that it was no more than six fathoms deep and our ship draws almost three. The Commander wisely dropped a strait anchor.

We were surrounded by terrifying rocks onto which the currents were dragging us with the utmost fury. If the anchor had not held good, that would have been the end of us. Our poor ship would have been inevitably smashed against the rocks. The whole day was full of alarm, because we were threatened repeatedly by the calm and the currents. This lasted until a storm arrived to push us out of that terrible strait which runs between the islands of Waigeo and Balabalak.

The wind which remained fresh allowed us to steer an easterly course; the weather was superb, the sea beautiful and the moon at its most brilliant. As soon as the current had once more become favourable, we resumed our

Hat from the island of Gebe
Jean-Louis Denis Coutant
(b.1776)
Ile Guébé: Chapeaux, Armes et Ustensiles des Habitans c.1822
hand-coloured engraving; 32 x 23.6 cm
Louis-Claude de Freycinet, *Voyage autour du Monde ... Exécuté sur les Corvettes de S.M. l'Uranie et la Physicienne ... : Atlas Historique* (Paris: Chez Pillet Aîné, 1825), plate no. 40
Rex Nan Kivell Collection
National Library of Australia
Pictorial Collection (S7261)

The canoe of the Gebe chief, with Pisang Island in the background

Louis Garneray (1783–1857)
Caracore du Roi de Guébé c.1825
colour collotype; 14.5 x 21.4 cm
Journal de Madame Rose de Saulces de Freycinet ... (Paris: Société d'Editions Géographiques, Maritimes et Coloniales, 1927), plate no. 17
Rex Nan Kivell Collection
National Library of Australia
Pictorial Collection (U8139q)

The *Uranie* making its way
through the rocky outcrops
around Balabalak, near
New Guinea

Langlumé
*La Corvette l'Uranie Entraînée par
les Courans au milieu des Roches
de Boulaboula, près de la
Nouvelle-Guinée* c.1822
lithograph; 15 x 20 cm
Jacques Arago, *Promenade autour du
Monde pendant les Années 1817–1820*
(Paris: Leblanc, 1822), plate no. 10
Rex Nan Kivell Collection
National Library of Australia
Pictorial Collection (U5778)

journey, but soon with the wind disrupting our manoeuvres and with calm
weather returning, we found ourselves again in danger, surrounded on all
sides by reefs onto which we feared we would be dragged. At last, a violent
storm which came to buffet us in these circumstances enabled us to emerge
from the strait before nightfall and to approach Waigeo Island.

The maps show only one Waigeo Island but, in fact, it is an
archipelago of more than 50 islands or islets which, for the most part,
have extraordinary shapes. Imagine a base drawn in on all sides and
smaller than the upper part, as if the Creator's hand had deposited a large
island on top of a smaller one, which it overlaps by 6 or 7 feet all around
in the shape of a hat. Those islands would, accordingly, be inaccessible,
but for a few sandy bays in places. They don't seem to be inhabited,
although the vegetation is very lush and, even on the cliffs that jut out,
the soil is covered with trees.

As we sailed towards Boni harbour in Waigeo Island, we met a canoe
carrying eight natives. Only the chief was clothed, in an almost similar
fashion to the chiefs of Gebe, but the faces and especially the hairstyles
of the other natives seemed strange to me; they are of small stature, their
complexions are dark and their hair smooth, although the opposite has
been reported. What has possibly misled travellers, who have thought
their hair frizzy, is the fact that they crimp it or rather ruffle it in a manner
unknown to me so that their hair forms such a bushy mass and such
a huge one that one head is as large as four put together. But, imagine

the impression it creates, placed on top of bodies covered only with a strip of thin bark from the banyan fig tree, as wide as two hands, twisted around the loins and one end of which passes through the legs before it is twisted at the front into the belt. That cloth, both light and indispensable, is called a *langouti*. I think it goes back to a very ancient fashion, for it must have been the clothing worn by our ancestor after his original sin.

I would perhaps alarm you if I told you that these natives were Papuans or inhabitants of New Guinea, who are reputed to be cannibals, but Louis claims that even though this may be true of natives to the south, far from where we are now, the ones who live in this district are on the contrary sweet-tempered and witty. Indeed, we see a number each day and they appear far from fearsome.

Towards the evening of 15 December, as we were nearing Boni harbour, where we planned to stop to carry out observations, the colour of the water changed all of a sudden. The sounding line revealed the presence of an unknown coral bank which put us in some danger. Fortunately, there was a high wind and we were able to manoeuvre in such a way as to leave that spot and reach the open sea. Then Louis resolved to anchor between the small islands of Rawak and Waigeo. It was on the former that we set up a tent for the observatory.

Notice that we are exactly on the equator and that the sun beats straight down on us. However, although the heat is intense, it is less severe than at Kupang. These islands are very humid and covered in forests, which also means they are most unhealthy. Consequently, the Commander restricts the number of people who sleep on shore to a minimum. As for us, I hope that we shall continue to return on board each night, as we do now, once the observations have been carried out. As the corvette is not far from the shore, the crossing is short and easy.

A canoe carrying some Papuans, similar in every respect to the first one, arrived on 16 December, soon after we had anchored at Rawak. The natives offered us turtle eggs as well as turtles, but they wanted too much for them and, as it would have created a bad precedent, we bought nothing from them. Their chief spoke a mixture of Malay and Papuan. When he met the chief of the other canoe, they saluted each other by lifting their hands first to their heads, then to their hearts, then to each other's shoulders and finally by touching their noses.

Those islands have a pleasant appearance, but only because of their natural beauty, for there is no sign of any fixed settlement. A few

Native of Rawak Island
T. Choubard (fl.1807–1830)
Ile Rawak: Portrait c.1822
hand-coloured engraving; 23.5 x 31.7 cm
Louis-Claude de Freycinet, *Voyage autour du Monde ... Exécuté sur les Corvettes de S.M. l'Uranie et la Physicienne ... : Atlas Historique* (Paris: Chez Pillet Aîné, 1825), plate no. 41
Rex Nan Kivell Collection
National Library of Australia
Pictorial Collection (S7262)

ramshackle huts here and there are built on stilts near the seashore. Thus protected from snakes, these shacks seemed abandoned and are uninhabitable. We used the ship's sails to secure some of these derelict houses, which were to hold the equipment and the observatory. We were better off in a tent, but the ground was damp. The other day, I left a cushion on which I usually sit. The next day, wishing to sit elsewhere, I came to fetch that cushion; a snake which had curled up underneath it escaped. I ran out of the tent in terror. Do you believe that I have recovered from such a fright by now? I would rather sit under a tree to read or work, while our officers make their observations with the magnet or otherwise. Moreover, I do so only when I need to rest, for here more than during any other stopover, I devote a good deal of my time to my modest research into natural history: birds, insects, shells and even a few minerals ... You will see my valuable collection one day I hope, and what a lot of memories they will bring back for us!

My long walks are somewhat spoilt by ugly snakes which I sometimes come across and which I always dread. Our naturalists are more interested in them than I am; I would not relish adventures of this kind, but I would some others, such as their encounter yesterday with a living bird of paradise, or so they tell me! How I wish I could have admired for myself the graceful appearance and flight of this charming bird!

But let us speak of the Papuans, whom we see often. In return for small knives, mirrors and other such trifles, these natives bring us turtles, fresh fish, hands of bananas and beautiful crowned pigeons, bluish-grey in colour, one and a half feet high and delicious to eat; these are called *Mambrouk*. Coconut trees are plentiful here; in exchange for needles or pins, the natives climb them skilfully and collect nuts for us. Our sailors also climb them very well. When, however, their efforts are directed at obtaining the cabbage of the coconut itself, especially when they choose the youngest trees, they carefully hide from the natives because cutting the cabbage destroys the tree. After a big tree of that kind which was obstructing our observations had been felled, one of the natives came to complain angrily on behalf, or so he claimed, of the owner of the tree, and he asked for compensation. A handkerchief brought the dispute to an end. This man's name is Moro, a native of the island of Aju, not far from Rawak. He is more quick-witted and more intelligent than all the others and speaks Malay quite fluently. Despite his lack of manners and personal hygiene, Louis invites him to eat with us. Because he has acquired a liking for our cooking, he becomes quite entertaining. Among countless examples of his gluttony, which never cease to amaze us, he derives a great deal of pleasure from emptying the pepper shaker into his hand before inhaling the pure pepper, savouring it gleefully as a child would powdered sugar. He judges our pickles to be too sweet and eats them like jam. What do you think of the strength of this savage palate! At the end of each meal, he asks for, and is given, the plate, the glass and the bottle which he has used. He even wishes to have the napkin, but that item is denied him. Amiable, jovial and witty, he knows how to flatter cleverly, and even with a certain amount of subtlety, in order to get what he wants. When he arrived, he wore only a *langouti*. He intimated that he was too scantily dressed to appear at the table of a French lady and we gave him trousers and a shirt. Then, he asked for ribbons to wear as braces. In that get-up, Moro was the happiest man on earth. I cannot begin to describe his joyful countenance. This Papuan, by his amiability, would not be out of place in good company. And when I compare him to the inhabitants of our mountainous regions or even to our rough peasants, I wonder who is the real savage. But, to tell the truth, Moro is extremely greedy. He appointed himself chief of police to prevent other natives from coming aboard. He arranges all exchanges, and we notice that he always keeps a share for himself. In spite of this, he is useful to us, in that, by benefiting from such transactions, he obtains cheaper foodstuffs for us. His intelligence is comparable to that of the shrewdest dealer in Europe.

Unfortunately, the items which we have for exchange are not at all suitable to these natives. Instead of hardware, they would rather have cloth, handkerchiefs or clothes, and we have very little of these to offer. If I did not foresee that it would take us more than a year to replace the articles bartered, I would willingly give away more in order to have the refreshments we need, but we must think of the future.

Among the Papuans who come to barter there are a few who are horribly disfigured by a flaky leprosy, which is most disgusting, but which is said not to be contagious through touch. Just as well! Especially as these people are in the habit of shaking hands with all and sundry, just as the English do.

I had never seen charcoal being prepared and I thought the process very difficult. We were short of it on our arrival here, and Louis has just had some made. As I had fun watching the simple processes used for this purpose, I thought how useful it was for sailors to dabble in everything, especially during long voyages. My husband is never at a loss; there is no workman whom he does not try to advise in his work. His sharpness and quick eye, allied to his considerable composure, enable him to overcome all difficulties.

2 January 1819 – Yesterday I wanted to start the new year by wishing you a very happy one, I mean as happy as it can be for you in the absence of

The *Uranie* at anchor,
Rawak Island, Papua

Claude Niquet (b.1770)
*Iles des Papous: Vue du Mouillage
de l'Uranie sur l'Ile Rawak* 1822
engraving; 23.8 x 32.2 cm
Louis-Claude de Freycinet, *Voyage
autour du Monde ... Exécuté sur les
Corvettes de S.M. l'Uranie et la
Physicienne ... : Atlas Historique* (Paris:
Chez Pillet Aîné, 1825), plate no. 45
Rex Nan Kivell Collection
National Library of Australia
Pictorial Collection (S7266)

your beloved ones, who also love you. A most unexpected visit prevented
me from fulfilling that duty so dear to my heart and forced me to attend to
a large number of new guests. The sound of military music, which seemed
to come from behind the small island of Rawak, heralded the arrival
of *corocores* carrying those natives from Gebe whom we had met in the
Moluccan Archipelago. It was Abdalaga-Fourou, coming as he had
promised and accompanied by his seven brothers and a nephew. Louis,
who did not believe that he would keep his word, would have preferred
his arrival to have been postponed by one more day.

As we had completed the observations which we planned to make in
this spot, the Commander intended celebrating New Year's Day by giving
a dinner for the whole crew. Consequently, he explained clearly to the
Kimalaha that Europeans traditionally spend this day on ceremonies, which
would prevent him from entertaining his party. And to soften the blow,
Louis invited him to dine on board today with his entourage. They came.
But what strange guests they were! No sooner were they seated at the table
with us than all at once they got up and moved away in horror, and why,
good God! Because among the dishes they had spotted pork and turtle
meat. Reason could not prevail; we had to remove from the table the dishes
whose appearance alone offended their heathen beliefs. When Louis had
asked for a small morsel of one of the dishes, they were again on the verge
of leaving, unless the heretic agreed to move away and eat his morsel of
turtle at the dresser. As he did so, Louis laughed heartily at the prohibitive

and unsociable tenets of Mohammed. During this conflict, I thought to myself that the precepts of the Koran are far more rigorously adhered to by its followers than the Church's commandments are by Catholics. I have not forgotten the answer given by a great theologian in a similar situation, which you once quoted to me.

Although the natives of Gebe worship idols, their leaders are, as you can see, devout Mohammedans. More tolerant in other respects, they allowed other people present to drink wine, but to make up for this, they drank an enormous amount of coffee and, finding our cups generally too small, they fetched large bowls, which each one of them emptied several times. They

Map of the Moluccan Archipelago, showing the route of the *Uranie*

Louis-Claude de Freycinet (1779–1842)
Carte ... du Grand Archipel d'Asie
1823
Louis-Claude de Freycinet, *Voyage autour du Monde ... Exécuté sur les Corvettes de S.M. l'Uranie et la Physicienne ... : Atlas Historique* (Paris: Chez Pillet Aîné, 1825), plate no. 36
Rex Nan Kivell Collection
National Library of Australia
Pictorial Collection (S7257)

equally relished liqueurs from Martinique and ended up drinking arrack in large quantities. Their favourite dishes seem to be vegetables, jams and especially our bread, which is very much to their taste.

After dinner, they began to barter; it would be an understatement to say that they did so skilfully. I think that 'greedily' would be a more appropriate word. They brought with them a few birds and nutmeg and only gave us things in exchange for other items, in spite of Louis' kindness in showering them with gifts. Finally, they became so troublesome that we had to be rather cool towards them in order to convince them to go ashore to sleep. As they retired to Rawak to some of the decrepit houses on the shore, where Louis still had quite a lot of important dismantled equipment, as well as other things, the Commander took care to send ashore armed reinforcements to keep watch on the material, for there was quite a large group of them.

One of Abdalaga-Fourou's older brothers could remember seeing the envoys of M. Poivre at Gebe where they were sent to find spice trees, which have since thrived in our colonies. It would therefore seem that our compatriots have made a good and lasting impression in these islands.

5 January 1819 – Since the day before yesterday, when I interrupted this letter, I have thought that I would never be able to finish it. During a trip to Marouan Island, a fruit was found which bore some resemblance to an olive and which had a very tasty kernel. A number of people ate it, and I did so too with considerable pleasure. A little while later, I started vomiting violently and did so for 15 hours non-stop. I was treated for food poisoning and I thought that I was going to die. Thank God, all I feel now is extreme fatigue, no doubt the result of a setback caused by my feminine constitution, because among those who partook of the fruit only a few were slightly indisposed. The natives told us that the small fruit (from a plant called *Ximenia multiflora* by our naturalists, and *fofolaoui* by the Gebeans) is harmful only when it is not sufficiently ripe and that they eat it, when ripe, with no ill-effects.

12 January 1819 – It is a source of great happiness to me during this painful voyage, dear mother, to be able to chat with you, especially at difficult times when I need reassurance. Our stay in the humid islands of Rawak and Waigeo has increased the number of our invalids, and the health of those who were already sick has worsened: alarming fevers have broken out. Poor M. Labiche, the Second Lieutenant, perished on the 9th of this month; his death caused much distress, almost as though his long illness had not led us to expect this tragic outcome. He was a most pleasant young man and an officer well respected by all his colleagues. The state of the crew on board becomes more pitiful each day; 20 crewmen are in hospital and, with each passing moment, I dread to hear that more have fallen victim to this lethal climate. What grieves me most is that I have no more refreshments to offer our unfortunate patients. A few chickens are left which I have set aside for them, and which I will gladly offer them as Louis and I are in good health. Pray to God that afterwards, when we shall have exhausted all our supplies, Louis does not himself become sick. But what am I saying? No, I have complete faith in the Lord who will not forsake us. Has God ever abandoned his children in their hour of need?

Those who say that February is the shortest month of the year would have found it very long here, if they had spent it as we did. I thought it would never end! Without knowing what this month would bring by way of relief to our poor suffering invalids, it is a small blessing to see unhappy hours pass ... No doubt it is because we are always hopeful! 'Hope,' says one of our favourite authors, 'is the nursemaid of the wretched. Seated by Man's side, as is a mother beside a sick child, she rocks him in her arms, holds him to her inexhaustible breast and quenches his thirst with a milk which soothes his sufferings.' No-one has felt, more than we have, the truth of this comforting and accurate axiom! We who now depend for our survival solely on the milk of our kind mother Hope! Without sighting any other land since we left the humid islands of Rawak and Waigeo, where we contracted some of the illnesses which now afflict us, we see our ills worsening each day. You can well imagine how the lack of resources and my fears increase; I hide them as much as I can from my dear friend, who has enough worries of his own. Our health, which remains good in this wretched situation, sustains our hopes. It seems to me that this happy state of affairs is so miraculous that a wise and benevolent Providence watches over us and wishes only to put our courage to the test. Those grave thoughts will explain my prolonged silence to you; would I dare converse with you more often when all I can do is to bemoan our predicament?

Carved idol found on
Rawak Island

E. Forget
Idoles Trouvées sur l'Ile Rawak
c.1822
hand-coloured stipple engraving;
32 x 23.8 cm
Louis-Claude de Freycinet, *Voyage autour du Monde ... Exécuté sur les Corvettes de S.M. l'Uranie et la Physicienne ... : Atlas Historique* (Paris: Chez Pillet Aîné, 1825), plate no. 47
Rex Nan Kivell Collection
National Library of Australia
Pictorial Collection (S7268)

Health and Courage Restored

Caroline Islands – Mariana Islands: temperament of the natives – Guam stopover – Hospitality of the Governor

14 March 1819 – After having seen the small Anchorite and Admiralty Islands in the distance, we were still caught between storms and calm weather. The one event which temporarily aroused my interest was meeting a school of fish shaped like rays but of an enormous size, with big horns on their heads. By chance, I was the one who had a sufficiently good look at them to be able to make a sketch. I did so because it appeared that this species was unknown.

We reached the Caroline Islands on 12 March. We did not stop, hoping that within a few days we would reach the Mariana Islands where there is a Spanish settlement, while in the Carolines there are only natives; and yet how friendly they are!

No sooner had our corvette been sighted than a fleet of large and small canoes, remarkable for their shape and elegance, surrounded the ship, and a series of exchanges began. We obtained fresh fish, coconuts, saris, and so on ... It wasn't long before Caroline Islanders climbed aboard. They generally have handsome faces. Almost all are naked, except for a loincloth or belt, as is the case with other indigenous people. They have their arms and legs tattooed in blue. The chiefs wear a robe with an opening for their head, which makes it look like a chasuble. They all have their earlobes slit and hanging very low, and in that slit some of them place large yellow flowers and branches of greenery. They have bronzed complexions and the expression on their faces is lively, open and cheerful. Their gaiety is especially striking; they burst out laughing at the slightest thing and start dancing on any pretext. They displayed extreme honesty in their exchanges with us. What convinced us of their peaceful intentions was the fact that between them they had only one spear, which they agreed to surrender with a great deal of indifference. They handle their canoes with an extraordinary degree of skill and their workmanship is truly admirable. The canoes have a most attractive shape, and are painted and varnished red, with a black rim, rather like Chinese vases. Not only did they sail in the open sea in such frail boats without fear, but when a large number of them gathered around the corvette and there was such a mix-up that one canoe overturned, none of the natives appeared frightened. Through a rather skilful manoeuvre, they refloated the overturned canoe and its passengers were happy, as if nothing had happened.

Angela, a native of Guam
Nicolas Eustache Maurin
(1799–1850)
Angela, Femme de l'Ile de Guham c.1825
hand-coloured lithograph;
24 x 15.5 cm
Jacques Arago, *Souvenirs d'un Aveugle: Voyage autour du Monde* (Paris: Hortet et Ozanne, 1839), vol. 2, plate facing p. 283
Rex Nan Kivell Collection
National Library of Australia
Pictorial Collection (U5524)

The garden of the Governor's residence, Guam
Friedrich Schroeder
(1768–1839)
Ile Guam: Vue du Jardin et d'une Partie du Palais du Gouverneur c.1822
engraving; 23.8 x 32.3 cm
Louis-Claude de Freycinet, *Voyage autour du Monde ... Exécuté sur les Corvettes de S.M. l'Uranie et la Physicienne ... : Atlas Historique* (Paris: Chez Pillet Aîné, 1825), plate no. 67
Rex Nan Kivell Collection
National Library of Australia
Pictorial Collection (S7288)

Farming in Guam

Claude Joseph Pomel
(1781–1839)
Ile Guam: Travaux d'Agriculture
c.1822
hand-coloured engraving; 23.8 x
32.2 cm
Louis-Claude de Freycinet, *Voyage autour du Monde ... Exécuté sur les Corvettes de S.M. l'Uranie et la Physicienne ... : Atlas Historique* (Paris: Chez Pillet Aîné, 1825), plate no. 70
Rex Nan Kivell Collection
National Library of Australia
Pictorial Collection (S7291)

17 March 1819 – Praise the Lord! For the first time in the five months spent on board ship, we are about to reach a port. A stopover will no doubt help our sick crewmen to recover and will provide us with fresh supplies. We have a fair idea of the benefits we may derive from it by what we are experiencing now. We had not yet anchored when a boat tied up alongside the ship, carrying an officer sent by the Spanish Governor, Don Jose de Medinilla y Pineda, to ask who we were. Satisfied with our answer, he returned ashore allowing us to proceed.

Scarcely had we dropped anchor when another boat laden with fresh supplies arrived and immediately offered them to us. It brought meat, fish, vegetables, fruit and so on ... Manna in the desert was not received by the Israelites with more relish and gratitude! How thoughtful of the Governor to send us all this! Although I had not met him, this gesture alone led me to believe that he was a very fine man. And, as you will see, it was not long before he showed himself to be just that.

We finally anchored in the harbour last night and were very graciously received. At 7 o'clock this morning, Louis sent his First Lieutenant to the Governor to thank him, to discuss the salute and to announce that at midday the Commander would pay an official visit to His Excellency to present the officers of the *Uranie*. After M. Lamarche's return, the ship and the shore exchanged 21-gun salutes. Then, a little after 9 a.m., to our amazement, M. de Medinilla arrived accompanied by the Sergeant-Major, Don Luis de Torres.

The kind Governor enquired about our circumstances with keen interest; he promised to cater for our needs to the extent that the limited resources of his colony would allow, assuring us that everything he owned was at our disposal. Soon after the departure of Don Medinilla, Louis and his staff went to pay him a visit. My husband has just sent me word not to expect him for dinner. This does not surprise me. As a stay ashore will be the ideal remedy for our invalids after such a long voyage, Louis plans to find a building which will house the sick crewmen without delay. This mission and other similar tasks will probably keep him ashore for the rest of the day. As for me, I have begun to chat with you, but only after first savouring some bananas, figs and a jug of excellent milk, while also doing justice to a salad of tender purslane. Don't laugh at these objects of my desire; they acquire greater value because of our deprivations during such a long spell far from *terra firma*.

Umata Bay is neither deep nor enclosed. Judging from what I can see of it, the town does not appear to be large. Only a few stone buildings are visible, among them the Governor's palace and a church adjoining a convent. The language spoken here is Spanish; the little I know of Italian helps me to understand Spanish far more than I could ever have believed. Moreover, Provençal, with which I became familiar in Toulon and Marseilles, is equally useful to this end.

18 March 1819 – Louis came back early yesterday, happy to have found lodgings for his sick crewmen, namely in a former convent which used to belong to barefoot Augustinian monks. The invalids will be housed in healthy and comfortable quarters. However, this will be delayed by a few days because Umata is not the usual residence of the Governor—he only came here for our benefit. Besides, with the exception of water, which is fresh and easier to take on board here than at Agagna, we would have to acquire the rest of the supplies from the island's capital. That is why it was agreed with Don Medinilla that, as soon as enough water had been taken on board, the corvette would sail to the port of San Luis d'Apra, near Agagna, and that we would remain on board in the meantime, a decision which pleased me. When Louis and his staff paid a courtesy visit to the Governor yesterday, he invited them to dine with him, adding graciously that he wanted these gentlemen to look upon his house as their own, without standing on ceremony. Having gladly accepted such a kind offer, all the officers went off to wander round the town, and my husband, who was busy looking for lodgings, found some, as I indicated earlier. Overcome by fatigue and the heat, he returned to the Governor's residence; the table was set and covered with fruit and light pastries, in the middle of which were two large punch bowls. Seeing such a strange meal, Louis thought that perhaps it was a day

One of the shell specimens
collected by the expedition in
the Caroline Islands
Jean-Louis Denis Coutant
(b.1776)
*Iles Carolines: Divers Objets
à l'Usage des Habitans* c.1822
hand-coloured engraving; 32.2 x
23.8 cm
Louis-Claude de Freycinet, *Voyage
autour du Monde ... Exécuté sur les
Corvettes de S.M. l'Uranie et la
Physicienne ... : Atlas Historique* (Paris:
Chez Pillet Aîné, 1825), plate no. 58
Rex Nan Kivell Collection
National Library of Australia
Pictorial Collection (S7279)

A canoe of the Caroline
Islanders
Adrien Taunay (1803–1828)
Proh des Iles Carolines c.1822
colour collotype; 16.5 x 22 cm
*Journal de Madame Rose de Saulces de
Freycinet ...* (Paris: Société d'Editions
Géographiques, Maritimes et
Coloniales, 1927), plate no. 19
Rex Nan Kivell Collection
National Library of Australia
Pictorial Collection (U8139s)

of fasting in this country. What must have reinforced such a thought was
the fact that the meal, which he mistook for dinner, was eaten while
standing up. However, as one must always conform to the local customs
of the country in which one is a guest, Louis' only thought was to satisfy
his usual hearty appetite from the dishes offered to him. But soon there
was further cause for surprise; the table was cleared and on it was placed
a great variety of meats arranged in a thousand different ways; in brief, an
excellent dinner was served. The light meal which had preceded it is known
as *refresco*, its sole purpose being to whet the appetite. This is an ancient
custom adopted from Manila, and I wish our officers had been aware of it. I
shall certainly not forget this today when I dine at the Governor's residence.

20 March 1819 – All the sick crewmen were taken ashore early yesterday
morning. Palanquins are not used here to transport invalids; instead, one
relies on string hammocks, which are good substitutes. Louis accompanied
Abbé de Quélen in his hammock to the residence of the Governor, who
insisted on providing him with accommodation and taking care of him.
I also went ashore at the request of Don Medinilla. There were about 50
of us at dinner for, in addition to the *Uranie*'s officers and the country's
senior civil servants, the passengers and officers of the Spanish vessel
La Paz, which sails the day after tomorrow, were also present. I was the
only woman present. What a superb dinner, dear Lord! It would be fitting
to proclaim as do some travellers:

You who preside over dinners,
O Muse! Be kind to me;
Help me to describe all the dishes
Which appeared on that table.

But to describe it all would take far too long, for someone reportedly counted 44 meat dishes for each course, and there were three courses. The same observer declared that, to provide for this dinner, two cows and three large pigs were slaughtered, not counting the humble creatures which dwell in the forest, the farmyard and the sea. I don't think there has ever been such slaughter since the wedding of Gamaches. No doubt, the Governor believed that people who have suffered such deprivations at sea, as we have, should be feted sumptuously. The dessert was just as copious and varied but did not conclude the dinner. Its remnants were removed to make way for tea, coffee, cream and all kinds of liqueurs. And since the *refresco* had been served only an hour beforehand, in keeping with tradition, you will agree that certain food connoisseurs, known to us, in these circumstances could complain of nothing more than their stomachs' limited capacity. The Governor's birthday, which we are celebrating today, will bring us together again at his residence *in fiocchi* [dressed in full regalia].

Yesterday after dinner, I was taken on a tour of the town of Umata; this was a brief tour, as the town is neither large nor beautiful, nor very populated. What I liked most was a long, shady avenue, lined on both sides with orange and lemon trees, beyond which stood houses interspersed with coconut trees. Skirting the shore, this avenue runs from the residence or, if you prefer, the palace of the Governor, around to the busy fort of San Angelo, built on a hill. I took great delight in this shady evening walk before returning to the ship. During the walk, a request was conveyed to me, the substance of which you will never guess. It was such that I would only dare describe it to you in general terms in case, despite reading my narrative, you are not yet accustomed to such strange tales. The Sergeant's wife emerged from her home to greet the Governor. Then, she approached Louis' secretary, who spoke Spanish and sometimes interpreted for us, and after directing countless flattering remarks and exclamations to him concerning what she called my charming face and my curly hair, she begged to be permitted to come aboard ... to kill my head lice. Believe it or not, the poor woman could not be persuaded that my hair was free of them and fell over backwards when the person to whom she had spoken told her that her services were absolutely useless to me.

I think that within a few days we shall leave Umata to go and settle in the island's capital. There, I shall probably have the necessary leisure to converse with you about the natives of the Marianas, who are unlike any others I have seen.

4 April 1819, Agagna – We are in residence once more, and very well housed at that, here in the home of the Governor of Guam. He has provided us with a very pleasant and comfortable apartment in his palace, which is furnished simply but where we have everything we need.

12 April 1819 (Easter) – You may expect me to describe for you on more than one occasion the many religious ceremonies that took place during this stopover, which we have been forced to extend because of the medical attention required by our invalids. The natives of the Marianas do not observe the external rites of religion only because of Spanish repression; they do so for another reason. The Jesuits have in the past sent missionaries to these islands and met with considerable success; several of them suffered martyrdom here after leading very saintly lives. Their conduct must have convinced the natives to allow themselves to be converted, for if, according to Tertullian, the blood of martyrs fosters Christianity, the constant exemplary conduct of leaders is just as salutary for them. Religious festivals are very numerous here and processions are common. I have even noticed that all the locals, both men and women, wear a scapular over their clothes, and those who can afford them carry large rosary beads as well.

Last Thursday was Maundy Thursday, and important religious ceremonies were organised. The Governor fulfilled his Easter duties. At the end of mass and after the Blessed Sacrament had been placed at the shrine, the parish priest put around Louis' neck a gold-braided ribbon, to which was tied the key of the tabernacle. It was an honour bestowed on the Commander by Don Medinilla, which caused Louis a great deal of inconvenience, because he had the duty of carrying the cross at the head of the procession around the town in intense heat. Hence, the Governor felt obliged to apologise profusely to Louis for the trouble which he had caused him by bestowing on him the honours of the day. The crew of the *Uranie* joined the procession with great decorum.

This morning, a high mass and another procession were held, but all Louis had to do was to maintain a serious and contemplative bearing, which in my view set a very good example for his crew. The doctor had to give strict instructions to confine Abbé de Quélen to his quarters; he manages to drag himself around with the aid of a stick. He has been led to believe that he will be well enough to attend church next Sunday. I wish it with all my heart.

13 April 1819 – While I was enjoying having a quiet chat with you yesterday, I was suddenly snatched from this pleasant occupation by a terrifying earthquake, which lasted scarcely more than half a minute but which caused such creaking throughout the house that I thought the roof was going to come crashing down on our heads. Louis was meeting with the Governor at the time; we all scattered in different directions. Realising how frightened I would be, Louis rushed to my side but I had already taken refuge on a pretty terrace onto which our anteroom opened. Imagine tremors which make the earth undulate like choppy seas! There was such a clatter of tiles that one would have thought they had all been dislodged. Yet, there was no damage done. Such happenings appear to be commonplace in this country, for that same night we were awoken by new tremors, which were very short and were accompanied by a muffled hissing noise.

After dinner, we watched a cockfight. It is the most popular form of entertainment among the local inhabitants during feast days. It lasted from 5 p.m. until 7 p.m. when the angelus rang out, apparently to indicate that it was time to retire. I can well remember that, on the evening of our arrival in Agagna, the Governor said to Louis that he had prepared a salute for us but that it could not be fired because the angelus had sounded.

It is pitiable to see the manner in which cocks are trained to fight, even to the death; not content with the weapons which Nature has given them, men tie small sharp blades to their feet, by means of which one of these animals sometimes kills its opponent with a single blow.

The main interest in this sport lies in the bets laid for or against the combatants. This spectacle does not appeal to me in the slightest. We derived a great deal more enjoyment in the evening from an exhibition of Mexican dances, all of which appeared to refer to that country's history. They were performed by students from the town's college; their costumes, very ornate and made of silk, had been brought from New Spain by the Jesuits. These dances, quite similar to our pantomime ballets, were performed in front of the Governor's palace, in a square lit by torches and Chinese lanterns filled with tallow. The main character was the Emperor Montezuma, in ceremonial garb, with a crown on his head and a feather fan in his hand, accompanied by two lavishly dressed pages. Then came 12 dancers, all equally well dressed and wearing diadems, with whom the Emperor mingled at times. As they danced, they formed processions and various figures. Sometimes, the dancers carried one or two castanets each, at other times they carried only their feather fans. The last two acts of this five-act play were packed with war dances. Clowns entertained the audience during the intermissions, and even during the spectacle, by leaping about and performing countless capers, which had the children

Topographical map of Guam
Louis-Claude de Freycinet
(1779–1842)
Essai ... de l'Ile Guam 1819
Louis-Claude de Freycinet, *Voyage
autour du Monde ... Exécuté sur les
Corvettes de S.M. l'Uranie et la
Physicienne ... : Atlas Historique* (Paris:
Chez Pillet Aîné, 1825), plate no. 59
Rex Nan Kivell Collection
National Library of Australia
Pictorial Collection (S7280)

and everyone else in stitches. The clowns wore masks and grotesque costumes, and carried wooden swords with which they thrust about them. One had to be acquainted with the story of the unfortunate Montezuma in order to understand fully the allusions in various scenes. The plot ought to have been explained to the spectators who did not have such knowledge. Without wishing to challenge the supposed origin of these dances, Louis found that they bore a strange resemblance to dances known in Provence as *leis olivettos*, which were probably performed there long before the conquest of Mexico.

Be that as it may, after the Mexican dance, a Spanish dance was performed, called *el palo vestido y desnudo*, that is to say, the dressed and undressed pole. A pole is erected, to the top of which are attached 8 or 12 long, wide ribbons—some red, others yellow or blue. The colours vary roughly according to the number of dancers. Each person holds the end of a ribbon and dances backwards and forwards around the pole. As a result of the dancers' movements, a web or interlacing is formed as the ribbons are matted against the pole, which becomes very attractive with its multi-coloured and patterned design. To strip the pole, the dancers complete the same movements in reverse; the trick lies in doing and undoing the whole pattern without snarling the ribbons.

At the end of the dance, the same schoolchildren who had acted in the preceding scenes returned, several of them dressed as women. They all began to perform European dances which they executed as well as their earlier difficult roles.

We were seated in a covered gallery formed by a wide balcony on the first floor alongside the palace apartments. We would either go there in the evening to take a breath of fresh air, or else we would sit on the terrace of the garden, if indeed one could call a garden the rather long stretch of land, almost waste land, where orange and lemon trees grew, but where nothing else was planted except for tobacco. Louis set up in various locations all the instruments used for his observations. On Good Friday, we spent several hours of a splendid night on the terrace witnessing a total eclipse of the moon, which I saw clearly.

21 April 1819 – Having far more spare time here than my husband has, I can chat with you at length. Perhaps you will not think the detailed account of this stopover very entertaining, but you told me that you wished to accompany me everywhere. I therefore have no choice but to bore you a little whenever I myself am not having much fun. It is not, however, because our worthy Governor of Guam is not doing his best to lavish a great deal of care and attention on me. It is not his fault if the cockfights, which are held regularly on Sundays and on feast days, appal rather than entertain me. Nor is he to blame if the songs and dances of the Sandwich Islanders seem either monotonous or ridiculous to me.

How is it, you will no doubt ask, that natives of the Sandwich Islands are in Guam? It is because the Americans, having conceived a plan several years ago to found a settlement on Agrigan Island in the Marianas, brought indigenous people from the Sandwich Islands here as herdsmen. But the present Governor of Guam, claiming land in the name of his sovereign, the King of Spain, who is also ruler of the Marianas, sent troops without further ado to Agrigan. They abducted Sandwich Islanders and transported them to Guam, and since then the Governor has used them to work his lands and carry out domestic chores, in much the same way as natives are exploited in most of our colonies. These people are treated like slaves and are all in the service of the Governor; with a few exceptions, the women have very loose morals.

From what I have said above, namely that I have derived little enjoyment from the various forms of entertainment in Guam, please do not conclude that I am bored here. On the contrary, I enjoy the happy and peaceful existence I lead in this place; there are neither storms nor hurricanes to fear; the sky is almost always serene; the air is clear in spite of the heat. I have considerable peace of mind, because we are pampered at the Governor's residence and have no other worry but to decide at what time we would like our meals served. Don Medinilla is kind enough to vary the time according to my husband's occupations. For such poor travellers as us, isn't it sheer bliss to spend a month or two in this way? For a good part of the day I remain in our bedroom, which is fresh and healthy thanks to six casements along opposite walls. There, sometimes embroidering and sometimes writing or reading, I try to forget that we shall soon be forced to go back on board. *Correr dell'onde a cimentar los elgno.* [To skim across the waves to test the ship on better waters.]

What increases my peace of mind even further is the work of my travel companions, and the satisfaction my husband derives both from the recovery of our sick crewmen, and from the progress he has made in his observations and other work. We do not take a siesta as everyone else here does; the Governor goes to bed at noon, just as if it were night, and does not rise until 3 p.m. Each day, a little before dinnertime, when we go into the sitting room, we usually find there Don Medinilla and our good Abbé, whose apartment is very close to ours. Sometimes after dinner I play a game of piquet with the Abbé, while Louis talks with the Governor or the Major to obtain all available information from them concerning these islands and other matters of scientific interest. The Major in particular, being the most learned man in the country, is of great help to him. He combines sound judgement with an excellent memory and has developed a taste for empirical observation. Out of curiosity he has carried out research into the traditional customs and the identity of the original inhabitants of these islands. You can well imagine what benefits my husband derives from his conversations with Don Luis and with what care he records the information which he gathers. The keenness of one is matched only by the inexhaustible patience of the other.

Thus, living in the most beautiful house in town, I leave it only rarely. Yet, I can give you an idea of the kind of town Agagna is. Built on a very low plain by the sea, this town is flooded during the wet season by heavy rain and high tides. That is why the houses are built on pillars; a few have ground floors built of stone, but it is impossible to live there because of the dampness. Most of the streets are wide and quite well aligned. The majority of houses are well screened from each other and, in the space between them, people usually grow a little tobacco. That separation is useful, because in the event of a fire it prevents the flames jumping from cabin to cabin, almost all of which are built of wood, matting and straw.

However, there are a few impressive buildings such as the barracks, the hospital in which our sick crewmen are housed, and the general store which contains supplies and other goods belonging to the government. In addition, there are the college of St Jean de Latran, the former convent of the Jesuits, and the boys' school, both of which have wisely been placed at the opposite end of the town to where the cabin which serves as the girls' school is located. The house of Major Don Luis and a few others owned by the chief officers are quite spacious and well built. But without a doubt, the most elegant building is the residence which the Governor has put at the disposal of the crew of the *Uranie*, although he has earmarked one or two rooms in his own palace for the officers who may be slightly delayed by their observations. Throughout Agagna, there is not a single garden. Nor are there many trees, except for a few which grow near the river banks. Opposite the Governor's palace is an enclosed field where he grows maize; it is the only plantation, I think, which produces any crop other than tobacco. Thus, there are no flower beds and no flowers—how sad! Nor are there any of the vegetables which lend such delightful variety to our gardens. Whatever flowers one sees are on trees. Of the vegetables commonly known to us, here one finds only onions, purslane and tomatoes, which come from the country, where the Governor has some land under cultivation.

But if, judging from my description, you should deem the vegetable gardens of the Mariana natives to be quite limited, the surface of these islands is covered with trees and the roots of countless species, all of which contain nutritious substances, and which provide the inhabitants with an abundance of wholesome food. All they have to do is to collect it. What a wealth of natural resources one finds here, including breadfruit which is so plentiful in Guam and which we eat with such pleasure! I plan to take with me a large quantity for our consumption on board. I also intend to preserve some in a well-sealed tin so that you may taste it.

Moreover, the islanders live off their fishing expeditions in the surrounding seas, which yield more fish than anywhere else in the world. Hunting is always productive, whether it be deer, wild oxen or pigs, which roam beautiful vast forests. Such natural advantages explain why the inhabitants of the Marianas are generally reticent to cultivate the soil in a hot climate, which would make such work most arduous. Indeed, does it not appear as though the natives here are bound to work far less than people do in other countries?

I was astonished not to see a single shop in the town. I was told that everything is imported from Manila and is stored in government warehouses which supply the local inhabitants with whatever clothing and any other items they require. Manila, the capital of the Philippines, is the main trading centre for all Spanish colonies in these seas, a midway point between the Marianas and metropolitan Spain. Because there are no clothing manufacturers here, everything is imported from Manila. There is little demand for clothes, for I have never observed such a lack of luxury in any other town.

The men generally wear a type of small blouse which comes down to their waists and large breeches which hardly reach their knees; both are made of either plain or striped cloth. On their heads they wear leather or straw hats, and that is all. A large knife, called a *machetto*, hangs from their waists and has various functions. Camisoles worn by the women differ little from the men's tops; their only other piece of clothing is a rather long, rainbow-coloured skirt. Neither the men nor the women have shirts, stockings or shoes. Men who have acquired a few shirts, most probably from sailors, wear these hanging loosely over their breeches. I must confess that the first time I saw them serving us at dinner in this get-up, I found it hard not to burst into laughter.

You can only tell one woman from another by the rings and gold bracelets worn by the most elegant among them. Some also have shoes, and occasionally their blouses or camisoles are made of finer white cotton, but very few display such luxury. They all wear their hair long and straight, with a parting in the middle of the head and hanging free or tied at the back with a bow.

The European uniform of the military is in stark contrast to the general simplicity of the civilians. But a soldier, who at midday dons his uniform to keep watch, probably in the morning wears a sailor's outfit in the Governor's boat or is almost naked, that is, in his *langouti*, when engaged in some rustic occupation, for the natives who work in the fields are not dressed in the same way as the town dwellers; they would find town clothes cumbersome.

All the inhabitants have more or less swarthy complexions; being generally of average height, they are quite handsome. There are some real beauties here but, if perchance I have succeeded in conveying to you the way local women dress, you will acknowledge that their charms in such costumes are those of Nature herself; or, to put it simply, beauty triumphs against all odds. With the notions of simplicity which women in this town must have, what would one of them think if she were suddenly transported to Paris to witness a lady being outfitted? I am sure that the cost of a single fine cashmere would be enough to dress all the women of Agagna for ten years. Nevertheless, I have observed a certain elegance here, and you would never guess who displayed it. I am not sure that you would believe that the parish priest of Guam wears blue and white striped taffeta trousers under his black silk robe. And yet, nothing is more true. Moreover, this priest is a Creole from Manila. It may well be that the clergy in these countries have strange notions of how to dress and have obtained dispensations which our clergy have not.

Last night, we went with the Governor on a splendid outing to Mongmong, a village quite close to Agagna. On the way, we came across a number of natives returning to town from quite far away, some carrying firewood, and others the roots which they use as food. I was informed that these people rarely bring back more than the family's daily needs. From this I would conclude that they must spend a good part of their lives on the road. Each village has a chief who in some cases bears the name *governadorcillo* and in others that of *alcade*. Perhaps the latter is a soldier and the former a civilian, as are the mayors of our communes; I have not been able to ascertain this. I leave it to Louis to deal with this *ex professo* [as an expert]. But the fact remains that at Mongmong there is a *governadorcillo*. As soon as he saw the Governor, even before receiving us, he sent someone to fetch his staff which has a gold knob on top, the symbol of his status. His urgency, which I found amusing, was not amiss, for to see him in his short breeches made of blue cloth, his half-shirt thrown over it and the *machetto* at his side, it would not have occurred to any of us that this fine fellow was more important than the other villagers. Through the cracks in his cabin, we caught a glimpse of his wife, entirely naked, smoking a cigar and surrounded by her children. They took every precaution to remain hidden, but did their utmost to have a good look at us. We must, indeed, appear as strange to the natives as they are to us; this thought has often occurred to me. Our good *governadorcillo*, moreover, wanted his sons to escort us with torches, but it was such a fine night that we preferred to make our own way to the seashore by the light of the stars.

What I have omitted to tell you before this, however, is that here we have come across some natives of the Carolines, who had previously appeared to me so amiable when we sailed past their islands. No doubt, you have not forgotten what I said about them. Three of their charming canoes arrived here 15 days ago; in one of them were a 25-year-old woman and her little girl, about 6 years old. They were entirely naked, save for a *langouti*; they were forced to put on clothes after their arrival here. As these people came to see the Governor, I had an opportunity to take a close look at the woman and her daughter at leisure. They did not strike me as being any less extraordinary than the men; their pleasant faces displayed a sweetness which is far from typical of these natives, especially when compared to the natives of Rawak and Shark Bay. To these charming little faces add superb teeth, charming eyes and, what surprised us most, delightful feet and hands.

The Carolinians we encountered previously had only their arms and legs tattooed; several of the ones we have met here have tattoos all over their bodies, the drawings of which are as artistic as they are weird. In the wide slits in their dangling ears, they carry not only flowers and foliage as did the first ones we saw, but also any small object given to them, such as knives, cigars, fishing hooks, and so on. In brief, these act as their pockets, and I would even go so far as to call it their 'peculiar' way, if that word did not imply a judgement on my part. Indeed, where would one expect people who are almost naked to carry such small items? The Carolinians here do not differ in temperament from those we saw at sea; I believe them to be quite good-humoured. However, they show a keen interest in, and express surprise at, objects which are new to them. As they are very cheerful, they laugh a lot and, above all, they dance often. Their dances amuse me; in turn, they make fun of our civilities, which no doubt they take for antics. Whenever our officers meet and raise their hats to one another, the Carolinians laugh heartily. Nevertheless, they seem to us to be kind, sweet-tempered and even affectionate; they are the amiable offspring of Mother Nature, and if all indigenous people were like them, I would be tempted to forgive the inclination some people have to celebrate what they call the state of Nature. Nevertheless, I have learned, with deep regret, that on some of the Caroline Islands the natives are savage.

Not only did visits to Guam enable the officers to examine closely the canoes of the Carolinians, which are quite extraordinary, but I too was able to take a good look at them, having made a short trip in one of them. It happened thus: three members of the *Uranie's* staff, a naturalist, an artist and an officer, were sent by the Commander to the islands of Rota and Tinian to carry out various research and to make observations. Yet, as I have told you, crossing from one island to another is difficult in our boats. The Carolinians, on the other hand, are accustomed to these stretches of water and steer their light canoes so skilfully that Louis asked the Governor for permission to use some of them during the officers' short trip. This was agreed, but as the officers are not as familiar with this means of travel as the Carolinians, it would not have surprised us if they had hesitated to put themselves in the hands of the natives. As for me, I must confess that I felt uneasy to see them leave, and since their departure on 22 April, I have not stopped thinking of the risk they had taken. Hence, when news reached us an hour ago that they had returned safely, I was relieved; we heard that their trip had shed considerable light on the islands they visited.

It was on the occasion of the officers' departure that we travelled a short distance with them; a dinghy followed us and ferried us back, but the Governor, Louis and I climbed aboard the canoe of the chief pilot, Ouametaou, who was some sort of admiral of this small fleet. As we left, we witnessed a most unusual spectacle; it cannot be said that the Carolinians weigh anchor, because they don't have one; instead, they tie the ropes anchoring their canoes to rocks or coral. To tie and untie the moorings, one of them dives in like a fish. Until you see the sketches which we have drawn of these canoes, I shall tell you that the one which ferried us was 30 feet long, by 2$^1/_2$ feet wide. However, the outriggers give them an equilibrium which one would not expect from their proportions. Moreover, the sails of these canoes are surprisingly wide. The outriggers form a type of platform on which we sat. Louis' confidence rested on the acknowledged skills of Ouametaou who, though a Carolinian, has held the post of pilot for several years. He has even been baptised here.

10 May 1819 – Even though I cannot predict how the rest of my account of this stopover will reach you, I have derived far too much pleasure from recounting our story so far, in different circumstances, for me not to continue to take advantage of my leisure and chat with you. It's only since we have been parted that I have understood the value of this 'ingenious art of depicting speech and of speaking to the eyes'. I confess to having been unmoved when I first read these lines. Who would have thought then, when I was still under your wing, that one day the whole world would lie between us ...!

    This earth, at least that of Guam, shook once more yesterday and most violently! Yet, I was not the least bit frightened.

> Habit thus renders everything familiar to us.
> What once appeared dreadful and extraordinary
> Becomes less shocking under our gaze,
> When it occurs continually.

The fellow who wrote this was absolutely right; how many things have I not grown accustomed to during the last two years! For example, tobacco smoking; with the exception of Louis, everyone around me smokes, almost continuously. Even women have cigars in their mouths, like the men. This habit is far more widespread here than snuff is in France, and some people have become so accustomed to it that they carry a gold box. I might have been tempted to smoke if I had accepted all the gold smoking paraphernalia which Don Medinilla offered me one day, in the hope perhaps that he could thus persuade me to take up the habit. The jewels were so finely made that if the material had not been so precious, I might have accepted his gift without necessarily feeling under any obligation to follow his example.

    It occurs to me that, while speaking to you constantly of the Governor, I have not yet described him to you. He is in his fifties, of average build and quite handsome. Born in Spain, he has lively and intelligent eyes, a pleasant face with a distinguished air and considerable nobility in his deportment. Among his many attributes, the attention he gives to his grooming makes him good company; his hair is always well powdered and perfumed; his clothes are very becoming and his shoes polished. Because of the real concern he shows for the happiness of the people he governs, he is respected by all. He is as loved as his predecessors were disliked, and deservedly so, for they were far more intent on acquiring wealth for themselves than on helping the destitute.

Last week, a large group of us went on an outing to a charming little village called Simahagna. Travelling on elevated terrain to get there, one gains a splendid view of the town, the harbour and the countryside. On our return, we were all invited to take a glass of lemonade at the house of Major Don Luis, and the lemonade turned out to be a fine supper, both pleasant and well served.

For the last two days, the rain has come down in torrents. Louis took advantage of our forced confinement to corner Don Luis and obtain precious information from him on everything to do with the Marianas. Very little information is available about these islands in Europe, and yet they deserve to be better known. They will be one day, if Louis publishes his account of the voyage. The character of the islanders will provide food for thought for philosophers; cruel and fierce before the arrival of missionaries, they have been transformed by the teaching of Christian dogmas. Although they have had similar impact in other regions of the world, the missionaries appear to have had an extraordinarily strong influence here, which deserves to be analysed by far greater intellects than mine.

We have been loading our supplies on board for over three weeks now. Moreover, as our sick crewmen recover with each passing day, I think that before the end of the month our stay here, which has been indispensable to all of us, will come to an end.

Even though I may be abusing the privilege of travellers, I will tell you that one of my diversions here is to take some maize and handfeed a young calf which comes up to the sitting room to visit us. I would never have believed that such an animal could be so tame. In truth, its natural instincts show through occasionally, and when this happens I prudently back away. These animals are used to transport people and goods, and have become substitutes for horses, which are scarce here.

20 May 1819 – About three weeks ago, Don Medinilla proposed an outing to a spot made famous by the martyrdom of Padre Sanvitores, one of the first missionaries to arrive here and the true apostle of the Marianas. The

String hammocks, a mode of transport in Guam

Adrien Taunay (1803–1828)
Manière de Voyager par Terre à Guham 1819
collotype; 15.5 x 20.7 cm
Journal de Madame Rose de Saulces de Freycinet ... (Paris: Société d'Editions Géographiques, Maritimes et Coloniales, 1927), plate no. 23
Rex Nan Kivell Collection
National Library of Australia
Pictorial Collection (U8139w)

good Father was murdered in 1672 by Matapan, who then hurled himself into the sea. An altar has been erected at the very place where he was assassinated, and it is now a place of pilgrimage for devout Mariana Islanders. As the Governor no longer spoke of this outing, we thought that he had forgotten about it. We were all the less inclined to remind him of it because Louis was very busy with his work and the health of our dear Abbé was still uncertain, and yet he was to be in our party. On Sunday, Don Medinilla spoke once more of Padre Sanvitores, and yesterday was the day appointed for the trip. Several means of travel were proposed for the short journey of two leagues; some went by land on horseback; Louis and I preferred to join the Governor in his boat, and as he did not want us to miss dinner because of our devotions, another boat followed carrying his domestic staff and kitchen equipment. We set out very early in the morning; the weather was superb and our short voyage was incident-free. Along the shore, near a promontory, we had cause to admire the prodigious number of *federicos* which cover the coast; it is a tree whose fruit provides food for the locals. What surprised far more knowledgeable people than me was to see hordes of bats flying as high as other birds in broad daylight.

When we reached our destination, the silence observed by Don Medinilla for some time was finally explained. There are no houses in this spot; he had had the ground levelled for our benefit. Several huts had been erected and adorned with as much foliage as possible. One hut was to serve as our dining room and another as our sitting room; both of these were well sheltered from the sun. Others were destined to house the kitchen and the servants. An abundance of supplies had been brought, and we had everything we required.

After visiting the sacred site, which is revered because of the circumstances of the martyrdom of Padre Sanvitores, and after listening to the kind Governor's version of traditional tales on the subject, which perhaps fell on the incredulous ears of several in the audience, we went for a walk in the woods. Taking a very rough road, we headed towards a neighbouring village. With great interest I saw the *federico* being prepared; its fruit loses its poisonous quality through soaking. But we were struck by the small number of villagers, and especially by their poor state, considering the lush vegetation and the ease with which they could obtain wholesome food without too much exertion. We met fishermen who had been ordered by the Governor to provide part of our meal; we sent them off to the small camp where we ourselves returned without delay.

The dinner was in keeping with the customary lavishness of our host and satisfied our hearty appetites after our walk. We did justice to the meal. No sooner had we risen from the table than we saw a delegation arrive from neighbouring villages whose inhabitants had no doubt heard of the Governor's presence. As he was much loved, they came to pay homage to him with simple gifts. Each brought what he could; some offered chickens, others eggs. The *alcade* headed the delegation, in a great state of excitement. But when he shouted 'Music! Music!' to a poor violinist who was lagging behind, a peasant who carried a piglet around his neck moved suddenly and the poor animal's squeaks answered those of the *alcade*. It caused a general round of laughter among the members of our party and for a while confounded the poor villagers. However, the Governor received them most kindly; refusing their gifts, he distributed a few piastres and gave orders for the villagers to be fed. While the meal was being prepared, they began to dance in their traditional style, first in groups and in circles, gesticulating and contorting themselves to a rather slow tune. Then, two of them acted out some sort of interlude which was no more than an improvised song. One of them recounted to the other how the Virgin Mary had appeared to him; to this the other responded by singing: *mi allegre, mi allegre* [I rejoice! I rejoice!]. The first reported all the favourable things which the Virgin Mary had imparted to him and, after each detail, he stopped and the other incanted: *mi allegre*. And each time, both actors sang a refrain while dancing. Among the dancers we noticed two very pretty young girls aged about 14 and 17, whose extreme shyness surprised us in mulattos. The older girl blushed as soon as she noticed that we were watching her.

After the dance, a long mat was placed on the ground and the remnants of our dinner spread on it. The natives squatted on both sides of the mat and did not seem in the least embarrassed to satisfy their appetites. They especially drank a lot and we soon noticed the effect alcohol had on them, particularly when a matronly woman who had previously been silent began to prattle.

After these strange people left, we were shown how to extract sap from coconut trees. Depending on the various ways in which it is prepared, it can yield alcohol, vinegar and even sugar. As you can see, this tree which adorns the shoreline, where it flourishes, offers as many natural resources as the *federico* and the breadfruit tree.

We were then taken for a walk along the shore to see the *magnahac* being caught; it is a tiny fish which is delicious to eat and which the Mariana Islanders consume in large numbers. The local almanac indicates for each month the days of the full moon when the *magnahacs* are due, and they are plentiful. The locals arrive in hordes along the shore on the appointed day in order to stock up on fish. Among the fishermen, we recognised the people who had come to pay homage to Don Medinilla.

Looking around for our two pretty girls, we saw them, like the others, up to their waists in the sea, busy gathering this precious foodstuff. They had removed their camisoles which they wore as cravats around their necks. Their skirts were rolled up and did not cover them any more than would

a loincloth. Thus, when they emerged from the water, they were most embarrassed, but what amused us most was that in trying to put on their short-sleeved blouses, they seemed more concerned with hiding their backs than their breasts. Methinks the gentlemen were not tempted to take issue with them on this matter!

Night had fallen when we set out on our return journey to Agagna using the same means of transport as earlier in the day, the main difference being that a canoe preceded ours and carried big torches made of resinous wood, so that the pilot of our boat would avoid the reefs. I found it amusing to look at the bottom of the sea by the light of these torches and to watch amid the coral, over which we were passing, a school of fish, both large and small, which seemed to be sleeping.

> *Sereno é il cielo*   [Calm is the sky,
> *L'aura, l'onde son chiare.*   And the wind, and the waves are bright.]

Mariana Islanders dancing

Jacques Arago (1790–1855)
Danse d'Hommes Nus c.1819
colour collotype; 15.3 x 21.6 cm
Journal de Madame Rose de Saulces de Freycinet ... (Paris: Société d'Editions Géographiques, Maritimes et Coloniales, 1927), plate no. 21
Rex Nan Kivell Collection
National Library of Australia
Pictorial Collection (U8139u)

A traditional dance, Agagna, Guam, Mariana Islands

Jacques Arago (1790–1855)
Guham: Danses Exécutées à Agagna et Appelées dans le Pays 'Danses des Antiques' c.1819
colour collotype; 14 x 21.4 cm
Journal de Madame Rose de Saulces de Freycinet ... (Paris: Société d'Editions Géographiques, Maritimes et Coloniales, 1927), plate no. 22
Rex Nan Kivell Collection
National Library of Australia
Pictorial Collection (U8139v)

In the course of a day which had been so well spent and which had provided us with such pleasant entertainment, I can assure you that nothing touched us more than the contented look of the Governor. He derived such enjoyment from pleasing others that his face visibly lit up whenever he saw that something interested or amused his guests. One could truly say of him that he shared in the happiness of others.

24 May 1819 – Only now do I have a precise idea of when we shall go back on board. It has been decided to send our invalids on board tomorrow; their lengthy convalescence has prolonged our stay on this island. The natural history collections, and so many other precious items which have been gathered, prove that our staff has turned this extended stopover to good effect. As for me, I have tried to restore my health and courage. In some respects, I have lived here, as I do on board, largely in the company of men; the mother and the wife of Major Don Luis de Torres were the only members of my sex whom I encountered. We paid each other a few reciprocal visits, but as these women are no more fluent in French than I am in Spanish, we naturally experienced little pleasure in each other's company.

What occupies us most at present are our preparations to be underway. As for our supplies, we have been stocking up for some time. Don Medinilla wanted to personally take charge of the supplies for our private table, and certainly nothing that is available in Guam will be lacking, thanks to his generosity.

1 June 1819 – Yesterday in Agagna there occurred what can only be described as a dual festival, for besides being Whit Sunday celebrated by the Church, it was also the birthday of the King of Spain, Ferdinand VII. The whole town rejoiced; to celebrate his sovereign, the Governor gave a dinner for 50 people, including all of the country's officers and our crew. The portrait of His Majesty was exhibited in one of the palace galleries which opens out onto the square. Soldiers kept watch over the portrait in this gallery. The *Uranie* joined in the celebrations; it was decked out with flags and gave the usual gun salute.

But what was more surprising and more unusual than any other festival elsewhere was the conduct of the Governor of Guam towards us. After a stay of more than two months in his home, marked by his extraordinary attention toward us and generous offers to assist us in our work, not only did he refuse to let us thank him as it was our duty to do, but when it came to working out the cost of daily supplies for the crew since our arrival in the Marianas, together with the even more considerable provisions to replenish the ship, he refused to even discuss the subject. The purser, who had gone to settle the account, as is usual, returned to report to the Commander on the Governor's extraordinary generosity. In vain, Louis wrote insisting on payment, while expressing to Don Medinilla both our deepest gratitude and his surprise; in his reply, this peerless gentleman apologised for not being able to do as much as he wanted, because of the scarcity of foodstuffs caused by the six-month drought which had devastated this island. He also expressed a keen interest in the success of the expedition and professed his personal esteem for the Captain.

All morning, we have been actively looking through our possessions for anything which, in our view, might please the kind Governor, deploring the meagreness of our resources. You will agree that one would willingly travel around the world in order to find two men like M. Smith and Don Medinilla.

My heart told me to write these words to you before leaving these shores. I can now go back to packing my trunks and to making ready for our departure. My letter will go with me on board, for it is rare to find ships here which are about to leave for Europe.

8 June 1819 – You will see by my shaky handwriting that I have got out of the habit of writing at sea; but I shall soon become accustomed to it again. On 4 June, with all our possessions already on board, we ourselves boarded, ferried out to the ship in the boat of the Governor who accompanied us, as did Major Don Luis, the parish priest of Agagna and Don Justo de la Cruz, the college principal, who all insisted on seeing us off. It was 2.30 p.m. when we climbed aboard the *Uranie*. We had taken steps to invite our guests to dinner, with the officers of the corvette. It was our turn to entertain them and we did so wholeheartedly; the toasts and the gun salutes were well synchronised, the latter being answered by a fort on the island. By the time our guests rose from the table, it was too late to go ashore. Accordingly, they slept on board, except for Major Don Luis who, being close to his country residence located next to the anchorage, went to spend the night there.

The following day, we intended sailing past Agagna to drop off the Governor and his retinue. A boat was reserved for this purpose, but a contrary wind prevented us from executing our plan until early on the morning of 6 June. Thus, we bade our friends farewell the day before yesterday.

Rubbing Shoulders with Royalty

Chapter 8

*The Uranie visits the Sandwich Islands [Hawaii] — Rose Island —
Arrival at Port Jackson*

8 August 1819, Owhyhee, Sandwich Islands – I cannot recall which
author has said that the names of places and men should be short to make
them easier to pronounce and remember. The names of localities in the
Sandwich Islands are not the greatest curiosities offered to the traveller.
We have been anchored since this morning just off a village named
Kayakakoa; no doubt this is one name which I won't remember, especially
as it is highly unlikely that I shall set foot ashore if my migraine continues
to torment me. It has prevented me thus far from seeing the natives whose
canoes have come alongside our ship each day since we neared land.
However, yesterday we invited to dinner the chief of Koknassi village
adjacent to where we were moored. This man who goes by the name of
Poui is about 45 years old, tall and well built. He has a noble air for a
native but looks a little fierce. His arms, shoulders and chest were bare
but he wore draped around his body a piece of white local cloth which
had turned yellowish. On his head, he had a straw hat with a pointed
shape and a wide brim. With that, he had a *langouti* made of the same
cloth, while the rest of his body was naked and covered in scars. On one
of his arms were inscribed quite distinctly the following words:

Poe died 5 May 1819
Tamaahamaha
Died 8 May 1819

As he knew a few words of English, he confirmed the news, which Louis had
already heard, of the death of old King Tamaahamaha and added that the
King's son, Hourio-Rio, had succeeded him.

On arriving, Poui presented the Commander with a pig, coconuts,
onions and bananas, in exchange for which he received more than those
items were worth. Then, he gladly accepted our invitation to lunch, as did
another man who was with him and who asked for permission to go and
fetch his wife, who had stayed behind in the canoe. Oumaye, Poui's wife,
was wearing a sari rolled around her waist which acted as a skirt. She wore
another, sometimes on her shoulders but more often below them when she
needed to use her arms to eat. It would be more precise to say 'devour', for

Jack, the pilot (also known by
the name Kaike-Koukoui)
Barthélemy Roger (1767–1841)
*Keïhé-Koukoüi, surnommé Jack,
Pilote Royal* c.1822
hand-coloured stipple engraving;
23.8 x 32.2 cm
Louis-Claude de Freycinet, *Voyage
autour du Monde ... Exécuté sur les
Corvettes de S.M. l'Uranie et la
Physicienne ... : Atlas Historique* (Paris:
Chez Pillet Aîné, 1825), plate no. 84
Rex Nan Kivell Collection
National Library of Australia
Pictorial Collection (S7305)

Baptism of the King's Prime
Minister, 'William Pitt', aboard
the *Uranie*, Sandwich Islands
Jean Nicolas Lerouge (b.1776)
*Iles Sandwich: Baptême du
Premier Ministre du Roi à bord
de l'Uranie* 1822
hand-coloured stipple engraving;
23.5 x 32 cm
Louis-Claude de Freycinet, *Voyage
autour du Monde ... Exécuté sur les
Corvettes de S.M. l'Uranie et la
Physicienne ... : Atlas Historique* (Paris:
Chez Pillet Aîné, 1825), plate no. 89
Rex Nan Kivell Collection
National Library of Australia
Pictorial Collection (S7310)

97

had I not encountered the Rawak natives, I would have been horrified by the voracity of our guests; they swallowed what they were given so quickly that one would have thought they were famished or being hunted. That's not all; for the sake of peace, we were forced to give them the glass, plate, bottle and even the napkin which they had used. Far from seeming satisfied, Poui became even more grasping. He wanted to have the Commander's coat; in return for four coconuts he demanded a rifle, gunpowder, cloth—what did he not ask for? Finally we made it clear to him that he would receive nothing more unless in exchange for pigs, which are so vital to the ship's supplies. He went off promising that he would bring back a large number, but to this day he has done nothing about it. I noticed at dinner that in spite of Oumaye's enormous appetite, she refused pork, saying that it was taboo, that is, forbidden for women.

However much of a savage Poui might be, he seems to be accustomed to giving orders and to being served. Louis told me that, when Poui was on deck with him, the chief, observing some of the officers, had asked if those gentlemen were *eri*, that is to say noblemen, and that upon receiving an affirmative answer, he had touched their hands. But seeing a crewman next to them, he had presented his foot to him in a scornful manner, as if to say: Be gone! This gesture, which did not amuse the sailor, provoked mockery among his mates.

The chief of Kayakakoa came on board this morning, accompanied by a single officer and a young child who carried a fly-swat made of feathers. This chief is one of the most powerful lords of the Sandwich Islands; the son of a former king of Maui Island and the brother-in-law of King Tamaahamaha, he was previously known by the name Kaioura (Kouakini), but has now adopted the English name John Adams. He seems to be about 30 years old; his obesity matches his excessive height, for he is at least 6 feet 3 inches and a real colossus. I have never seen such a tall, fat man. He speaks English fluently and asked Louis a question suggesting a knowledge of geography which one would not expect from a native, not even from a prince. Further conversations with him will provide much useful information.

10 August 1819 – The day before yesterday Louis went ashore with Prince John Adams, and he has returned each day. While doing everything possible to gain an audience with the King for the purpose of obtaining the necessary supplies to restock the corvette, he continues to make scientific observations with his staff and learns countless curious details about these people and their customs. Each night I hear interesting tales relating to all this, but apart from the fact that I like to describe to you only what I have witnessed at first hand, I must confess that my illness makes me loath to go into details. Be patient; if God brings us home safely and if my husband publishes an account of this expedition, you will become acquainted with all the people he has met, with places which I never suspected existed and with customs which bear no resemblance whatsoever to ours.

Today, Louis brought John Adams to dinner, with the intention of offering him gifts in return for the diverse foodstuffs which the islander has provided. We were seated at dinner when, to our great surprise, Keohoua, the prince's wife, arrived with one of her friends. Her size was as unexpected as her presence; imagine a woman in her thirties, 5 feet 10 inches tall, fat not in proportion to her height, but out of all proportion—in short, enormous. But imagine what such obesity must have looked like when completely naked; it's true that she had a sari wrapped around her from her waist down, but from the waist up one saw nothing but bare flesh. At times, she wears a second sari draped a little over one shoulder, but not always. Louis had met her at Kayakakoa, but what he had described of her did not prepare me for the shock of seeing her. Her companion was equally as enormous. Both wore earrings and necklaces made of very pretty beads, from plants unknown to me, and of various shapes. They also brought gifts and fine local cloths. They gleefully accepted a few lengths of gauze, mirrors and other trifles. Both said *ocowa* to greet me; this means 'how are you?'—a somewhat briefer utterance than the names of localities here. The prince, his fat wife and her friend returned ashore before nightfall.

This morning, a pilot named Jack and another man came as envoys from the King to invite the Commander to go and anchor in the bay of Kawaihae. The King promised us that we would find everything we needed there. We will thus leave this anchorage tomorrow for another to which Jack, the pilot, will take us. Despite his English name and his English costume, Jack is a native of these islands; he previously bore the name Kaike-kou-koui. While we are waiting to change anchorage, Jack has become our table companion. Although he has given up his native name, he has kept his native ways, and I find that his half-European clothes make them all the more shocking. For example, if he is inconvenienced by the heat, while at dinner with us, without further ado he removes his clothes and throws them on the floor next to him. At other times, he blows his nose in his napkin and, without any inkling of the disgust which he inspires in us, as soon as he has greedily satisfied his voracious appetite, which is no less amazing than that of his compatriots, he rises from the table as they do, slapping his stomach and exclaiming: *mahoha*, that is: 'My stomach is full'. Then he rushes out for a walk on deck.

12 August 1819, Bay of Kawaihae, Owhyhee – I cannot imagine a more
arid and horrible scene than the part of Owhyhee Island which we can see
now. Not a tree grows here, nor the smallest bush. It is as if the area has
been consumed by fire. Yet, it is in these parts that the King has chosen
to reside. This morning, Louis received a delegation from His Majesty the
King of the Sandwich Islands, which told my husband that their master
impatiently expected him ashore. One of the envoys was a prince, a brother
of John Adams, and as gigantic as he is. The other was a Frenchman from
Gascony who has become important here probably because of this and who
seems to curry favour with the court. Louis went ashore with them; if I am
able, I shall give you an account of his audience.

During the last part of our voyage, I took the trouble, as I usually do,
of reading the narrative of Vancouver's voyage where reference is often
made to the Sandwich Islands. It was there that I had, so to speak, become
acquainted with old King Tamaahamaha. It is a pity that he has died;
Louis fears that his death might make it difficult for us to obtain supplies.
He will find out today.

13 August 1819 – How peculiar the court of the King of the Sandwich
Islands is! However, Louis found that, in the midst of primitive living,
an air of grandeur reigns, no doubt instilled by the deceased King who
instigated so many innovations among his people. The King, dressed in the
ceremonial uniform of an English captain, waited for Louis on the beach
adjacent to his house; the whole court stood some distance behind him.
His wives were not far away, under a shelter built near the beach. The King

Portraits of Sandwich Islanders
(left to right) Cox, the chief of
Maui Island (also known as
Kiaimoku); one of the chiefs
of Owhyhi Island; and Cox's
chief officer

Adrian Migneret (1786–1840)
Iles Sandwich: Portraits c.1822
hand-coloured stipple engraving;
23.6 x 32 cm
Louis-Claude de Freycinet, *Voyage
autour du Monde ... Exécuté sur les
Corvettes de S.M. l'Uranie et la
Physicienne ... : Atlas Historique* (Paris:
Chez Pillet Aîné, 1825), plate no. 82
Rex Nan Kivell Collection
National Library of Australia
Pictorial Collection (S7303)

himself gave the order for a gun salute in honour of his visitor. After this order had been carried out, he nodded slightly to Louis and invited him to come and rest in his residence. Louis followed only after having paid his respects to the Queens who, without ceremony, held out their hands to him. The King's residence is no more than a straw hut 10 to 12 feet long and a little less in width; the floor was covered with mats on which His Majesty reclined and he invited my husband to sit beside him, with the interpreter seated opposite. The chiefs squatted randomly around the hut. Next to the door, just inside the hut, stood an officer carrying a long wooden lance, apparently as His Majesty's bodyguard. The chiefs' costumes were varied. Some wore long coats made of red woollen cloth, which had been presented to them some time ago by Cook and Vancouver; others were dressed in coats of red and yellow feathers; and some of them just wore capes made of the same material. The soldiers did not have a uniform and each held his gun as he pleased; many were naked; that is, they wore nothing but a *langouti*. In general, one could say that the soldiers looked rather grotesque. Moreover, instead of a drum, it was a bell that signalled the arrival of the troops.

After Louis informed the King of our need for supplies, which His Majesty promised to provide, the King, who had stared constantly at the Commander's sword and had had an animated discussion with his chiefs about it, finally expressed the wish to acquire it. He asked Louis if he had another like it. Reading the King's mind, Louis returned it at once to its sheath and presented it to the King, begging him to accept it. The King hesitated a moment, saying that to do so would be to disarm the Commander, who did not fail to reply at once that 'one had no need of weapons in the company of friends'. The King raised no further objections but thought it proper to offer Louis the attractive lance of his bodyguard in exchange for the sword. He then offered Louis a glass of wine, which was duly accepted, but which had to be drunk in another hut some distance away. This was undoubtedly the dining room, for it is customary in this country to have a separate hut for each purpose. Two armchairs were ready for Louis and for his First Lieutenant, who accompanied him. They sat down but the King and his chiefs reclined on mats.

From there, Louis went to visit the elderly Queens, widows of King Tamaahamaha. Except for Kaoumanou, mentioned by Vancouver who had reconciled her with the late King, all the others were old or ugly. Louis found them all lying flat on their stomachs, with their chins resting on small cushions, in keeping with local custom, and surrounded by servants armed with feather fly-swats. Kaoumanou claimed to be sick and liked to inspire a lot more pity than one was inclined to feel for her, seeing how well she looked. Corpulence seems to be the distinguishing feature of women of noble birth in the Sandwich Islands.

Louis also went to visit old and venerable M. Young, friend and adviser to the late King Tamaahamaha. Regrettably I am not in a position to describe that visit. Later, Louis met the Prime Minister of the present King and invited him to come aboard. He was invited, in turn, to dinner without ceremony. After taking his leave of the King, my husband returned to the house of the Minister near the seashore, as it had been agreed that he would take him back to the ship. Louis thought that he had gone home to dress, but found him wearing only his *langouti* and a European shirt, which was more dirty than clean. It was in this elegant costume that Kaimokou (Kalanimoku), known as William Pitt, Prime Minister to the King of the Sandwich Islands, came to dine with us. He had asked Louis' permission to bring with him his favourite wife, Rikeriki, a request which was granted at once. But the poor creature did not benefit at all from the visit, for on the pretext that she was tabooed, her husband forced her to remain on deck where she was sent some jams which she gladly ate. When her husband had risen from the table, she came to take her place and made up for having missed dinner by downing several glasses of brandy with an extraordinary look of delight on her face.

This woman is quite young and has a rather pleasant face; she is less corpulent than the other women I have encountered, and the scantiness of her clothing is less shocking. As soon as night had fallen, Pitt pressed us to launch a few rockets; these aroused the admiration of the Sandwich Islanders who shouted at the top of their voices: *metei, metei*—'very beautiful, very beautiful'.

Prime Minister Pitt, three other chiefs, the pilot Jack, the Gascon interpreter, Pitt's wife, Rikeriki, and the wife of one of the chiefs came to dine on board today. One of the three chiefs is no more than 24 or 25 years old; his face is very pleasant and he looks very distinguished. He is known as Kioravaya and is yet another brother of John Adams. After dinner, during a stroll on deck, Pitt met Abbé de Quélen and questioned him about his function on board. Having heard the reply, he told the Abbé through an interpreter that he had set his mind on becoming a Christian for some time, and consequently he begged him to baptise him. He added that on her deathbed his mother had herself asked to be baptised, the ceremony being conducted by an Englishman or an American present in the islands at the time. Following a few remarks from the Abbé, tomorrow was the day appointed for the ceremony, which is to take place on the corvette. I probably won't attend, for in an hour's time I shall be bled in the foot for persistent migraines, for which our surgeon can see no other remedy and of which I wish to be free. Louis, who felt unwell this morning, went ashore tonight to pay his respects to the King. He has just returned aboard with an enormous pig which His Majesty gave him.

16 August 1819, Anchorage of Reina (Lahaina) – The ceremony which was performed the day before yesterday attracted a lot more spectators than we expected. Louis had returned ashore in the morning to attend the King's council, which was to debate the question of the supplies we needed. After finishing his business satisfactorily and taking his leave of the King, he was about to return to the ship, intending to weigh anchor today and proceed to Maui, where we are to take on water and other supplies, when the King informed him that he and his whole court wished to be present at the Prime Minister's baptism. He asked for the boat to be sent back as soon as it had ferried Pitt to the corvette. This was done at once; soon after, we saw the King, his wives, the dowager Queen Kaoumanou, a young prince, brother of the King, and a large number of double and single canoes crowded with chiefs and the principal courtiers, both men and women. We fired an 11-gun salute for the King. The quarterdeck was adorned with flags and the whole deck covered with matting for the fine company to sit on. The altar had been erected near the poop. Two seats had been placed beside it for His Majesty and his favourite Queen, Kamahamarou. Do you have the impression that you are reading *A Thousand and One Nights*?

Still weak after having been bled, I remained confined to my husband's quarters, where the window opens onto the deck. From there I had a perfect view of the ceremony and the spectators. Abbé de Quélen baptised Pitt, who appeared quite moved during the entire ceremony. The Commander was his godfather and Pitt was christened Louis. The ceremony was followed by a light meal for the King, his wife and his entourage. It was extraordinary to see all the refreshments disappear so quickly, especially the wine and the brandy. We began to fear that the King might not be in a fit state to return ashore. Fortunately, the light was failing and our guests were thinking of leaving. But first, we had to present the King with a few bottles of brandy from which he wanted, so he said, to drink to the health of the Commander and to the successful completion of his voyage. The dowager Queen received the same, and all the chief courtiers were far too loyal not to follow the example of their leaders. You could say that in just two hours our intrepid guests drank or took away with them the equivalent of more than three months' supplies of wine for our table.

The King's favourite, young Kamahamarou, is both his wife and his half-sister. She is tall and pretty; she has two other sisters among the five wives of the King and they bear the official title of Queens. One of these,

Kaourohi, was also one of his father's wives. I thought that all these women knew how to drape their saris with a great deal of elegance and grace and that, despite their bronzed complexions, the young ones in particular could well be regarded as beautiful. They are all chieftains' daughters, and we have already noted that these chieftains are generally taller and more corpulent than the common people. The way they wear their hair varies a great deal; the most original shape, in my opinion, is when they have it close-cropped over the temples and allow it to grow from the forehead to the back of the neck, so that it is ruffled and resembles a helmet. The King's favourite was the only woman who wore her hair loose around her face; the others had it more or less cut in strips or in various shapes.

On the night of the baptism, there came on board one of the chiefs who rule Maui Island, off the coast of which we have been anchored since midday. He was yet another colossus who had relinquished the name Kiaimoku (Keeaumoku) for that of Cox, as he is now known. The King wanted us to visit his island, from which he had been absent for a while. Louis went ashore with M. Lamarche, the chief and his entourage, to look for high land with a view to finding a suitable site for the observatory. He told me that as he walked on the beach, he was followed by several old women who were lamenting and snivelling. Louis was informed that these antics were customary and that the women were expressing their joy at the return of the Governor. The latter remained very dignified but the mourners smiled when they saw how surprised the officers were. This scene reminds me of another witnessed by Louis at Kayakakoa, which he described to me and which involved the pilot Jack and Prince John Adams. After the customary greeting of touching each other's noses, the two chiefs, who had not seen each other for some time, began to weep and utter loud cries while rolling on the ground and showing all the signs of the deepest grief. Watching such a scene, the French officers were touched, unaware of what they have since learned, namely that it is the custom in this country and that one must not take such behaviour any more seriously than the expression 'yours faithfully' which closes letters in France. In my opinion, a similar tradition is the native chiefs' habit of breaking off one or two of their front teeth as a sign of mourning for the death of someone they revere. So too is the custom of inflicting on their bodies a large number of scars which vary according to the degree of respect and affection they have for the dead person. Likewise, some native chiefs, like Poui, have had tattooed on one of their arms the name of Tamaahamaha and the date of his death.

The Commander has just obtained proof that Rives, the Gascon who served as his interpreter at Kawaihae, is a blaggard and a rascal.

Utensils used by Sandwich Islanders

Jean-Louis Denis Coutant (b.1776)
Iles Sandwich: Armes et Objets Divers à l'Usage des Habitans
c.1822
hand-coloured stipple engraving;
32 x 23.8 cm
Louis-Claude de Freycinet, *Voyage autour du Monde ... Exécuté sur les Corvettes de S.M. l'Uranie et la Physicienne ... : Atlas Historique* (Paris: Chez Pillet Aîné, 1825), plate no. 90
Rex Nan Kivell Collection
National Library of Australia
Pictorial Collection (S7305)

Fortunately, he had not been paid in advance for the pigs which he boasted he would be able to deliver to us from his alleged properties in Maui, where it turns out that he does not possess an inch of ground nor anything whatsoever, except a well-deserved reputation as a villain.

21 August 1819 – At last I set foot on Maui Island a few days ago, because I was feeling a lot better. The whole week has been taken up with magnetic and other scientific observations which require my husband's almost continuous presence. However, each day we have returned on board to dine and sleep.

We found it quite interesting to observe the manufacture of the strange cloth which is worn here. Louis has learned all the details of which I have only a general idea. The cloth is made from the bark of a tree, the paper-mulberry tree, which is softened by being macerated in water and is then separated into various layers. These are then repeatedly beaten until they become as thin as paper. There are thicker layers which serve as cruder material, as well as finer ones which at the end of the process are of a beautiful white colour and can take printed patterns. Yellow is the colour most preferred by the natives; elegant women wear yellow saris with red and black patterns. In my opinion, this material which closely resembles paper is probably not strong enough to be sewn up like the cloth we use, but worn loosely, as local men and women do here, it is sufficiently soft to be draped most gracefully around the body. This explains why natives here are not entirely naked; even little girls wear their saris wrapped around them. It is only when they bathe that men and women are seen intermingling unashamedly and completely naked.

26 August 1819, Port of Honorouro, Woahoo Island (Wahoo) – No sooner had we dropped anchor today than Louis went ashore to visit Boki, the island's Governor. He is Pitt's brother but is reported to be less intelligent than Pitt. As he landed, my husband was greeted by Boki and by two other dignitaries who accompanied him, MM. Davis and Marini. The former, an American, is a captain, a landowner and the owner of several ships which trade in furs on the north-west coast of America. M. Marini is a Spaniard, born at Xeres in Andalusia. He came to the Sandwich Islands at a young age and has been successful in agriculture and in cattle breeding. He has been a resident here for more than 26 years and has successfully planted most of the vegetables and fruits from Europe. Experience has taught him that the soil in these islands is highly suitable for the cultivation of vines, and he offered Louis wine produced from his vines, which my husband found to be fairly good. M. Marini is fluent in the local dialect and is in a position to provide Louis

with much useful information. My husband greatly regrets that he did not
come to Woahoo in the first place; he would have saved a lot of time and
would have avoided quite a few thorny problems concerning our supplies;
changing anchorages is so time-consuming!

The objective of our present stopover was to purchase rice and biscuits
which M. Wildes, the captain of the *Paragon*, had for sale; this has been
achieved. The purser went ashore with the Commander, struck a bargain
and Captain Wildes has been gracious enough to have the supplies ferried to
our ship in his own boats. Moreover, the generous M. Marini has intervened
to provide us with firewood. Boki, who had to be stirred from his indolence,
sent 150 of his men at once to cut firewood in the forests. Louis went to
dinner at the residence of Captain Davis who gave him a guided tour of
the European cemetery and of other sites on the island, after which they
returned to the Governor's residence. Having learnt from M. Davis that his
brother Pitt had been baptised on board our ship, the Governor declared that
he wished to imitate his brother. Consequently he entrusted Captain Davis
with the task of negotiating this with Louis who promised that, provided the
Abbé did not have any objection, the ceremony would take place tomorrow.

From the Governor's residence, these gentlemen went on board the
Paragon to visit Captain Wildes, whom Louis invited to dine with us
tomorrow, together with a few other Americans. M. Marini, who is on a strict
diet for health reasons, declined an invitation to be in the party. He plans to
spend the time in a way which would be most beneficial to the expedition.
I am to accompany Louis ashore tomorrow morning; we have been invited
to lunch by Captain Davis.

29 August 1819 – During my visit to Woahoo on
Thursday, what interested me most was the home of
M. Davis, who has resided here for a few months. His
wealth and manners have earned him a lot of respect
in the community. Moreover, he is the nephew of
General Amosa Davis, the Governor of the State of
Massachusetts in the United States of America. His
house is spacious and, although built in the same style
as those of the Sandwich Islanders, it differs from theirs
in many respects, especially the furniture, as one sits
on chairs and even on a settee. Moreover, in his home
one eats at a table, a practice unknown among the
people here, who prefer to sprawl on matting. The
most ornate hut which Louis visited at Kayakakoa
(belonging to a princess) had as furniture just one
wooden bed in the European style on which were
spread a few mats and around which hung a curtain
of printed calico. I visited a few houses at Woahoo and
saw nothing else but matting.

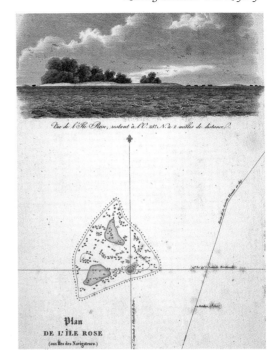

M. Davis is married, according to local custom, to the daughter of an
American, his neighbour, who has lived in Woahoo for 26 to 28 years and
who would be very wealthy if the value of property in this country could
be guaranteed. The large family of M. Hume [Holmes], that is the name of
M. Davis' father-in-law, caught our attention; the youngest of his daughters
is the most pleasant child I have ever seen. We did our utmost to take her
away with us, but her parents, and especially her mother, would not give
their consent.

We ferried back the Governor, who had just been baptised; he was
accompanied by his only wife. Boki is taller and stouter than his brother
Pitt; but his legs are covered in so many ulcers and are so tangled up in
cloth that he has great difficulty in walking. Accordingly, he does not look
as intelligent as the Minister and the other chiefs whom we have met to
date. I truly believe that he asked to be baptised only to imitate his brother.
Perhaps, too, his apathy is caused by his poor health.

Because the entrance to the harbour is difficult to negotiate, our hosts took
their leave immediately after dinner. I must confess that I was glad, and the
next day I pretended to be too indisposed to go ashore, when in reality I was
unwilling to do so. Louis visited Captain Davis with several officers of the
Uranie. We were due to set sail the next day but were delayed on account of
the lackadaisical manner in which Boki proceeded to deliver the promised
firewood. As a result, we were forced to postpone our departure. This morning,

Rose Island, named after Rose
de Freycinet by her husband
Louis-Isidore Duperrey
(1786–1865)
(top) *Vue de l'Ile Rose* 1819
(bottom) *Plan de l'Ile Rose* 1819
Louis-Claude de Freycinet, *Voyage
autour du Monde ... Exécuté sur les
Corvettes de S.M. l'Uranie et la
Physicienne ... : Atlas* (Paris: Chez
Pillet Aîné, 1825), plate no. 19
Rex Nan Kivell Collection
National Library of Australia Map
Collection (RA 260)

after returning ashore once more to see to the wretched firewood, Louis went with Abbé de Quélen and several other officers to dine on board the *Paragon*. They were well received and lavishly entertained by Captain Wildes, who had organised for their benefit the amusing spectacle of a dance performed by a native of the Marquesas Islands who was a member of his crew.

I much preferred to stay on board and chat with you. I am beginning to tire of these natives and their conduct which at first can cause surprise, but which soon inspires more disgust than amusement. However, the latest island we visited, where we have just spent four days, is less primitive than the first ones we encountered. This is no doubt due to the large number of Americans who reside here or who land here quite regularly. Despite that, the natives are still far from civilised.

Among the Sandwich Islanders who came to the corvette each day, their chief priest ventured out on several occasions, but he never went any further than the edge of the ship because he claimed that his religion forbade him to pass under ropes of any sort. For him to do so appears to be taboo. I have used the word on several occasions without explaining it to you; it conveys some sort of prohibition or ban which most certainly originates from religious beliefs and which is always strictly observed. For example, when Louis asked to use a site, either for his observatory or to set up his meteorological or other instruments, and expressed his fear that curious people or thieves might turn up, the chief who chose the spot immediately declared it taboo. This is done by driving a stick into the ground, at the top of which is tied a piece of white cloth. That is sufficient to deter anyone from drawing near on pain of death. Louis has recorded countless strange details on the subject.

I am not certain yet whether we will be able to weigh anchor tomorrow; today has been an important festival in Honorouro. Games presided over by Boki were organised. Despite Louis' repeated pleas, Boki could not be persuaded to leave the celebrations for a short while to give the necessary orders. Such delays are frustrating.

12 September 1819 – With all the necessary supplies finally loaded on board—supplies which are more plentiful than they are of good quality, we set sail and it is now six days since we lost sight of the Sandwich Islands. About a hundred pigs, a few goats and a fair number of kids constitute all the livestock we were able to obtain. I would have wished for a large number of chickens, but we acquired very few. The natives in these islands don't know how to breed chickens. The few fresh vegetables which we found will not go very far. We ought to be on our way to Port Jackson but, to my deep regret, this part of the voyage will be greatly prolonged by the fact that we have changed course radically to the east, a decision which the dear Commander has taken in order to collect data on the magnetic equator. However much I respect science, I am not fond of it, nor am I likely to be reconciled to it by Louis' prolonging of the voyage, which holds nothing terribly exciting for me. It is true that this work is one of the main objectives of the voyage, that the weather is favourable and that we are sailing on an ocean which has been aptly named Pacific. If only, like so many travellers, we were fortunate enough to discover some new island! Louis has promised me that if he finds one that is new and still unknown, he will name it after me. Until then, *per poco mi consolo* [I gain much consolation from so little]. I try to imagine what awaits us at the end of this part of the voyage. The account published by Louis of his previous expedition, which took him to Port Jackson, has made me sufficiently familiar with that colony to whet my appetite further. We will no doubt meet there some of the people with whom he became acquainted 18 years ago.

1 October 1819 – I shudder when I see on maps how far away science has taken us; it would make you shudder for different reasons if, upon consulting the world map on which I know that you are following our progress, you were to realise the present location of the *Uranie*. The fact is that we would have far less distance to cover to reach California than the east coast of New Holland, towards which we are heading—most certainly by the longest possible route. When I complain about this, others do not fail to praise the calm ocean on which this long voyage is taking place. But I find that the Pacific Ocean resembles extremely placid people who always share your views; while they please at first, in the long run they become insipid, and one would much rather have a few quarrels to liven up the conversation.

During the limited free time which continuous work and supervision allow Louis, our favourite pastime is to make plans. Since news reached us that, upon our return, nothing will stand in the way of the joy of living with you, we spend each day building, alas perhaps, castles in the air! ... at least, in all of them, you have your place reserved and, as in our hearts, it is not the least important one! A country retreat often suggests itself to us as the promised land and, in this respect, your taste, which is well known to us, guides our choice. What flights of fantasy occupy us in our utopian world? We plant, we design, we water; we dream up all kinds of follies, but when I awake from these beautiful dreams to see the whole world lying between you and us, the spell is broken, and all I can look forward to are the precious letters which hopefully await us on our arrival in Port Jackson, the first ones I will have received from you in two years!

21 October 1819 – I am pleased to inform you, Madam, that the corvette *Uranie* has discovered, to the east of the Navigators Archipelago, a small island which does not appear on the most recent charts of these seas and which the Commander of the above-mentioned corvette has named Rose Island. It is done; my name has been linked with a small corner of the world; a very small one, indeed, for envious people will perhaps deign to call it only an islet. Such as it is, if met by night, it could well have been fatal to us. Instead, it has now been marked on the charts of the expedition. Future travellers will beware of it and no-one, I hope, will fall victim to the perils which surround Rose Island.

31 October 1819 – By dint of travelling and living from one day to the next, one comes to the end of the longest months and the most painful crossings. Thus, we have reached the end of this particular one. And as it is a long while since we exhausted all our precious supplies for this voyage, I cannot wait for the next stopover to replenish our stocks. Our expenses in Toulon on this count were enormous; if the voyage had lasted only two years, the supplies would have been sufficient. Besides, most of the provisions have not been replaced adequately in the last few ports where we have stopped.

Sailors are often criticised for eating excessively when they go ashore; should this surprise anyone? The numerous deprivations they endure at sea must inevitably have such an effect. As for me, once so indifferent to gastronomic pleasures, I find myself at times dreaming of the pleasure I would derive from a nice fat chicken, or just eggs, or even fresh milk. Another of my favourite fantasies is to pick a rose or a carnation; a fresh flower would be a real joy to me. Do not conclude from what I have said that I have become greedy, but imagine our diet at sea over so many months: salted beef or boiled pork, cold roast pork, dried fish, rice and beans, that is the vicious gastronomic circle in which we are caught, without any variety except for what those dishes afford. Luckily, I eat very little and our cook knows how to prepare quite good soups; a piece of chocolate and some jam—such are my remedies against a diet of which my stomach and my taste buds are equally weary.

The small number of chickens we were able to obtain in the Sandwich Islands, though of poor quality, are preciously reserved in case of illness, and the invaluable tins provided by dear M. Appert have been put aside for the long, and equally painful, crossing which will take us from Port Jackson to Cape Horn.

It seems like a miracle to me that, in spite of all this, we continue to enjoy good health. Louis has not had a bad cold since we set off, and neither have I. Being bled in the foot has made my headaches tolerable; we are heartened by this.

17 November 1819 – I cannot comprehend by what stroke of bad luck, after Port Jackson had been signalled to us as early as 13 November, a violent storm which lasted two days kept us out at sea.

Scherza il nocchier tallora	[Sometimes the helmsman laughs
Coll'aura che si desta;	With the awakening breeze;
Ma poi divien tempesta	But then it turns into a storm
Che impallidir lo fa.	Which makes him grow pale.]

We are still off the coast, now delayed by calm weather, almost in sight of that land which we long to set foot on. We have yearned for it long enough without this double hitch which has further increased our craving. What a fine opportunity to be taught a lesson in patience, if I were in the mood for it! But I must confess that I have never been less inclined than I am today. However,

Si stanca la fortuna,	[Fortune grows tired,
Resiste la costanza,	But constancy keeps fighting
E si triomfa al fin.	And we triumph at the end.]

You will note, I think, that our favourite author has entertained me during this long voyage. Indeed, on more than one occasion, the gentle harmony of Metastasio has relieved my boredom. I believe that at times he has also helped you to forget our absence.

— ⇥⧫⧉ —

[**Editor's Note:** Rose's letters to her mother leave us off the coast outside Port Jackson, and three weeks elapse before Rose's journal resumes—three weeks in which the initial reactions of the *Uranie*'s officers and crew to Sydney Cove and its surroundings, and to the extraordinary hospitality extended towards the French ship, would have been recorded. To fill this period, I have selected three letters written by the expedition's official artist, Jacques Arago, to a 'friend of my boyish days' and inserted them at the beginning of the next chapter. Written to an intimate friend in the same way as Rose recorded her experiences for her special friend, Caroline, Arago's letters document in the most delightfully descriptive way his first impressions of Sydney. These letters are from Arago's *Narrative of a Voyage round the World in the Uranie and Physicienne Corvettes ...* (London: Treuttel and Wurtz, Treuttel Jun. and Richter, 1823).]

Sydney and environs — Hospitality enjoyed — A visit to Government
House — A dinner on board the Uranie — Farewell visits and gifts —
Heading for Cape Horn — Iceberg sighted — Stormy weather — Stopover
in the Falklands — The Uranie runs aground

November 1819
Arago Letter CXXXVI   *Sydney (New Holland)*

The entrance of Port Jackson may be at most a league across. A few reefs,
and two or three rocks even with the water's edge, nearly touch the north
point of the river, and are consequently little to be dreaded by ships. As
we advance, the passage imperceptibly widens, and offers to the mariner
a considerable number of little creeks, that are well sheltered, and a sure
protection against bad weather.

The coast that borders the spacious harbour of Port Jackson, is a curious
spectacle; a novel and vigorous vegetation is there intermixed with small
houses, the European architecture of which strikes our eyes, and excites our
admiration. We see only the advanced posts of a city, and are struck with
astonishment: we are scarcely arrived, and ask how many ages this colony
has existed.

An edifice equally useful and majestic first presents itself to the view
of the traveller. At the south entrance of the river rises a magnificent
lighthouse, equally solid and elegant in its structure; the light is visible at
a distance, is revolving, and shows itself only at equal intervals, that ships
may not confound it with fires kindled on other parts of the mountains.
A telegraph is added to this building, and corresponds, through two
intermediate posts, with that placed on the governor's palace at Sydney.
Farther on we see country houses, that remind us of the elegant seats in
the environs of Bordeaux. Large, useless plants and weeds have given place
to the fruit-trees of Europe and regular odoriferous hedges; and amid a
prodigal and sportive nature appear, as if by enchantment, long and
spacious avenues, terminated by country boxes, carefully embellished by
the ingenious hand of art.

On the left of the river, a handsome dwelling, seated on the slope
of a hill, shaded by light casuarinas, elegant Norfolk pines, and lofty

View from the observatory
set up by the *Uranie*'s crew
at Port Jackson

Jacques Arago (1790–1855)
Port-Jackson: Vue de
l'Observatoire de l'Uranie c.1819
colour collotype; 13.7 x 38.5 cm
Journal de Madame Rose de Saulces de
Freycinet ... (Paris: Société d'Editions
Géographiques, Maritimes et
Coloniales, 1927), plate no. 25
Rex Nan Kivell Collection
National Library of Australia
Pictorial Collection (U8139y)

The gardens surrounding
Government House, Sydney

Louis Philippe Alphonse
Bichebois (1801–1850)
Vue Prise dans les Jardins du
Gouvernement à Sidney c.1830
lithograph; 19.3 x 26.2 cm
Hyacinthe de Bougainville, *Journal*
de la Navigation autour du Globe de
la frégate la Thétis et de la corvette
l'Espérance pendant les Années
1824–1826 (Paris: Arthus Bertrand,
1837), plate no. 12
National Library of Australia
Pictorial Collection (S3633)

eucalyptuses, particularly claims our attention. The grape, the peach, and the apple, enrich it alternately. Little terraces are intersected by trenches filled with cool and limpid water: huts are reserved for the stores: a noble building denotes the abode of the master. Every thing is turned to advantage, every thing is rendered useful, round this superb habitation: and M. Piper, the harbour master, who built it, seems to have embellished it only the better to entertain strangers.

He was the first person who came on board us; he welcomed us in the most flattering manner; and it was impossible for any one to show more readiness to serve us. Shall we find every one here equally obliging?

... A new fort, regular and of little elevation, but built like the ancient towers, is also capable of protecting or preventing a landing; and seems placed there more particularly to defend the stores and residence of the governor, whose stables appear to me to be built with a view to render them capable of being fortified in case of need. Their architecture is so whimsical, that I cannot find terms to describe it.

It was near this last fort, that we dropped anchor the first day; and thence also the landscape appears in all its majesty.

Arago Letter CXXXVIII   *Sydney*

Our staff went ashore to-day, and were introduced to the principal officers of government by M. Piper, whose obliging attentions never slackened for a moment. General Macquarie, governor of all the English possessions in New Holland, received us with extreme kindness, and assured us, that whatever the country afforded was at our service. The judge-advocate, M. Wylde, a person of great merit, and the judge, M. Field, were emulous to convince us, that we were among friends. The storekeeper-general of the colony expressed in the most flattering terms, the happiness he should feel in doing any thing to serve us: in a word, we were loaded with civilities; and when these visits were concluded, the officers of the garrison, the colonel in particular, joined us, would be our guides in our different walks, and shewed that they also set some value on our friendship.

I will not give you a description of the town, which I have just gone through: I am enchanted, and I had rather give my admiration some respite. Magnificent hotels, majestic mansions, houses of extraordinary taste and elegance, fountains ornamented with sculptures worthy of the chisel of our best artists, spacious and airy apartments, rich furniture, horses, carriages, and one-horse chaises of the greatest elegance, immense storehouses—would you expect to find all these, four thousand leagues from Europe? I assure you, my friend, I fancied myself transported into one of our handsomest cities.

The English garden that embellishes the Government House, particularly fixed my attention; I spent two hours there in one evening; and beneath a Norfolk pine, whose horizontal and graceful branches agreeably sheltered me from the heat of the sun, I sat down to meditate on my native land. The shrill cry of the yellow-crested white cockatoo occasionally struck my ear; and while I pursued with my eye, and could stroke with my hand, the silky plumage and rounded bodies of several black swans, that stalked sedately through the walks, my attention was distracted by the irregular noise of the swift kangaroo, which, resting on its tail and long hind feet, leaped over hedges and bushes, without any object in view. Every thing was new to me, trees and animals; and I cannot express to you the magic charm I felt, as my memory dwelt on the dearest objects of my own country, from which every thing in nature told me I was far away.

A single instant had produced this metamorphosis, a single step had caused these new emotions. In the town, I beheld Europe, for European hands had raised it: here nature was not altered, and not a form, scarcely a leaf, resembled the productions of our countries; I was alone with myself, I was a stranger to every thing ...

Arago Letter CXXXIX   *Sydney*

M. Wollstonecraft, one of the principal merchants here, and whose name has acquired a certain degree of celebrity in England, has given us some accounts of this colony (which one of his partners has made very dangerous scientific excursions to explore) that strongly excite our curiosity. M. Scott, private secretary to the storekeeper-general, and a man of great erudition, particularly captivated our attention, even on subjects of little importance, by his agreeable and original powers of description. M. Oxley, the surveyor-general, whose skill and courage have had the guidance of expeditions to the interior of New Holland, that have shared with him their honourable dangers, has also given us an interesting account of his adventurous excursions; and already makes us sensible, that we shall hereafter be indebted to his zeal and courage for the knowledge of a vast portion of this fifth quarter of the globe. M. de Mestre, and one of his friends, whose name I am sorry I have forgotten, offered themselves as our guides in the different excursions we wished to make. The officers of the garrison have proposed to join us in shooting parties, in which we shall find both an instructive and useful recreation. We have engagements for a fortnight, and all the inhabitants of Port Jackson rival each other in their attentions to us.

The town of Sydney-Cove, the capital of Cumberland county, is built partly in a plain, partly on a little hill, that overlooks the south side of the river, so as to display an amphitheatre, and form a delightful prospect.

The principal buildings exhibit themselves in a very original manner over the old wooden houses, which are gradually disappearing, and have their places supplied by structures of hewn stone, ornamented with pleasing sculptures, and embellished by balconies, in a style truly remarkable. You would imagine that our best architects had deserted Europe, and repaired to New Holland, to re-produce their most elegant designs.

You see at first, on the left, the spacious residence of the Governor, surrounded by a magnificent English garden. The apartments are remarkable for their distribution, richness, and for the pictures they contain of combats between the savages of New Holland. The Governor, who resides a part of the year in his palace at Parramatta, has not had the bad taste to overload this fine dwelling with too many sculptures or other ornaments, which are almost always detrimental to the general appearance, and spoil the effect.

To the right of the palace, but at a great distance, appears the regular front of the superb barracks, built of brick and stone. Still farther on is an hospital of elegant design, ornamented with a fine colonnade, where the patients may breathe a pure and salubrious air at all hours of the day. At a less distance is distinguished a spacious building, which is the house of prayer; and still nearer, on the harbour itself, we perceive immense magazines, in which are deposited the goods kept in store. Fronting this storehouse, on the other side of the cove, is a quay not yet finished, where ships may be laid down to careen, without incurring the least danger. A great number of other public buildings and private houses embellish this truly magnificent prospect; and nothing indicates that this town, already so beautiful, is the work but of a few years.

In the new quarter, the streets are wide, straight, but not carefully paved; which renders them difficult of access, and disagreeable in the rainy season. As to the old quarter, built on the slope of a steep hill, foot passengers alone can make use of the paths close to the houses; and it is easy to foresee, that in a little time it will be destroyed, unless the ground be levelled, which in certain places would require infinite labour.

The environs of the town are not very luxuriant, though tolerably well cultivated. A few country-houses however, built with elegance, and embellished with gardens loaded with the fruits of Europe, fix the attention. Of the trees transferred from our climates, the peach and the oak have succeeded best. The former produces excellent fruit, and grows without trouble; the latter is as beautiful as in our finest countries; and, if I may credit our botanist, even acquires here more valuable qualities for building. The other trees that shade the ground, are the fig, the pear, the apple, and the orange; all useful, all furnishing resources in time of scarcity.

When the sun is setting, and the observer from the top of a lofty building turns his eyes towards the country, he enjoys a prospect truly interesting. From the midst of those deep forests that lately were trodden by the feet of savages alone, arise immense columns of smoke, impelled by the wind, amid which burns a bright flame, illumining the distant horizon. All the new grants are cleared by burning; ... but, as these burnings must be frequently repeated, and the proprietor of a piece of ground must guarantee the adjacent property, he begins by circumscribing with the axe, the space he means to cultivate. The fire, arriving at this boundary, as it ceases to find aliment, stops, dies away, and its beneficent ashes give life to the land it has thus cleared.

[Rose de Freycinet's journal resumes]

In Sydney we received several invitations which we were forced to decline. On 28 November Captain Piper gave a party at his country residence, situated in a very picturesque spot on a headland overlooking the harbour. The house is not quite finished; it is going to be most attractive and well appointed. There was a rustic ball after the meal and everyone had a lot of fun. M. Carling, a lawyer, gave a reception and MM. Piper and Wylde organised dinners. As I am unwell, Louis attended these functions alone. A few days later, M. Wylde gave a ball, but I was still so sick that I could not be present; Louis once more went by himself. The ball was magnificent and splendid.

Having recovered slightly, I went with M. and Mme Field to visit the lighthouse [on South Head]. Mme Macquarie had promised to take me, but a serious illness confined the Governor to bed and prevented him from travelling to Sydney. Mme Field lent us her carriage; M. Field, his wife and young Macquarie travelled on horseback. The road struck me as extraordinary both on account of the care with which it was maintained, and because of the difficulties which had to be overcome to make it less steep, as the lighthouse is built on top of quite a high mountain. The sides of the road are surrounded by wild vegetation just two miles out of town, this area being less fertile than Parramatta. The view from the mountaintop is splendid. The building which houses the lighthouse is made of stone and contains several rooms. The lighthouse itself was brought out from England.

M. Field had organised quite a substantial meal and, while it was being prepared, we went for a walk to enjoy one of the beautiful panoramas of the harbour. We climbed down a hill along a gentle slope which led us to a small fishing bay. There, we noticed a tree so large and whose shade was so dense and so extensive that a table could be laid out underneath it with

20 place settings and be as sheltered as if it were under a roof. Feeling hungry and hot, we returned to the lighthouse. After resting there awhile, we headed back to the town.

As M. Macquarie was still very ill, his wife invited me to lunch at Government House so that we might be able to tour the building and its gardens at leisure. As she had remained in Parramatta, her nephew came to fetch us from our ship where we had gone to hear mass. Major Antill, his wife and young Macquarie acted as our hosts. We toured the gardens and the building, which is unattractive because of its irregularities. The interior looks better and there are two splendid sitting rooms.

The same day, we went to see the Botanical Garden and the strange building erected to serve as stables to Government House. It looks just like an old fortress, with towers, battlements and so on ... no-one could tell us what the Governor had in mind when he had it built. I personally think that it was to add to the beauty of the harbour from which one can see this building on top of a hill close to the town.

The building which houses the hospital is magnificent; the barracks, the officers' quarters which adjoin them and the convicts' quarters form very fine monuments which would not be out of place in our capital cities, nor would some of the individual houses here.

M. Wylde, who was sorry that I had been unable to attend his ball and wished to give another party, invited us to a ball on 6 December. The room was attractive, bedecked with flowers and paintings; it was emblazoned with the coats of arms of France and England as well as those of Louis' family. On the parquet had been painted Cook's ship, the *Adventure* [the *Endeavour*], M. King's *Mermaid* and the *Uranie*. All the paintings in the room had been commissioned for the ball and related more or less to France and to us.

A lavish supper capped the splendid occasion; the toasts lasted a little too long and each gave rise to a speech. Although I was not familiar with English dances, I was unable to avoid them. I did rather poorly. But what seemed horrible to me was the heat which was far too oppressive for dancing.

Deprived, after a long voyage, of many items which are necessary for an official function, we resolved nevertheless to organise a dinner on board for all the people from whom we had received such hospitality. It was a very modest affair but we counted on the fact that our guests would understand our difficult situation. The deck was cleared of everything that crowded it, including the top mast. This provided two separate reception areas, decorated with flags and garlands of foliage and flowers. Regimental music was played throughout the meal.

A young crewman, who was a good artist, designed two watercolour portraits on transparent material—one representing the King of England, the other the King of France. They remained out of sight until the moment when Louis proposed a toast to King George, which was accompanied by a 21-gun salute. The portrait of Louis XVIII was unveiled when the Governor drank a further toast to his health. There was more noise and uproar than you could possibly imagine.

Nor could you imagine the distress of our chef who, 15 minutes before serving dinner, sent me word that all was lost, and ruined. The deck space set aside for the kitchen was so limited that the poor man had encroached on a cannon, placing a plank on it and thus making a table on which he had placed all the prepared dishes. When the order came to prepare for the salute during the dessert, gunners had removed a little too abruptly all the monuments raised to the glory of our chef, their arrangement being thus rather disrupted. Imagine the anger of that haughty man who, a few days earlier, had refused to be taught by an English cook how to make puddings because he claimed that a French cook had nothing to learn from English cooks.

On 14 December, we went to spend two days at the country residence of M. Macarthur. His oldest daughter is 26 or 27 years old, witty, well educated and very kind. I wish I could have become better acquainted with her, but her ill-health and my short stay prevented it. She came to fetch us in her father's carriage.

We arrived at Parramatta at dinner time. M. Macarthur was waiting for us with another of his daughters, a younger one. His house has a simple exterior but is well furnished with every luxury which affluence and elegant

Church in Parramatta

Friedrich Schroeder
(1768–1839)
Nouvelle-Hollande: Port Jackson: Vue de l'Eglise de Parramatta
1823
engraving; 32 x 23.6 cm
Louis-Claude de Freycinet, *Voyage autour du Monde ... Exécuté sur les Corvettes de S.M. l'Uranie et la Physicienne ... : Atlas Historique* (Paris: Chez Pillet Aîné, 1825), plate no. 95
Rex Nan Kivell Collection
National Library of Australia
Pictorial Collection (S7314)

simplicity can offer. He has another younger daughter who stayed in town with her mother, while two of his sons arrived soon after us. They had returned from a magnificent farm near the Nepean River, where M. Macarthur has a flock of 6636 merino sheep, more than half of which are pedigreed merinos.

M. Macarthur's gardens are well kept and very beautiful. Many European plants and trees in particular flourish there, among them olive trees.

During my stay at Parramatta, I wanted to bid farewell to M. Macarthur [Macquarie]. The Governor, however, was far too ill to receive us; his wife did so with extreme courtesy. She told Louis that she had been asked by the Governor to offer him replacement pieces for the silverware which had been stolen from us or to compensate him in cash. We declined both offers, despite her strong pleas. Among arguments which she put forward to persuade us to accept was her claim that it was the fault of the police and therefore the responsibility of the government to make good the loss. We did not give in, but thanked them anyway.

We went to visit Mme King and Mme Hannibal Macarthur, with whom we had dined the previous evening. She is the daughter of M. King, the former Governor. She assured Louis that her brother, Lieutenant King, the Commander of the cutter *Mermaid*, which had set off to explore the coast of New Holland, would have liked to have met and thanked him for all the obliging remarks Louis had written in his reports about his father.

I saw Mme Field on numerous occasions. She was extremely courteous towards me and a fortnight ago sent me the first ripe apricot of the season. I had not tasted one since leaving France! We spent the last few days together and we dined at her house frequently. She has a charming disposition, is very well educated and has a good knowledge of French literature. Her appearance is equally agreeable; she is very pretty, with a ravishing ankle, or so Louis noticed. I must say that I spent some delightful moments in her company.

On the day we were due to return on board, I went to have lunch with her and felt a pang of anguish when it was time to bid her farewell. She gave me a little cornelian ring on which was written *Remember*. I did not need this inscription to remember all her friendly and kind deeds towards me.

We returned on board on 24 December but only set sail on the 25th, on Christmas morning, after the Abbé had said mass. All the English sailors were unhappy to see us leave on a Friday because they claimed it was unlucky!

My sadness on leaving this land where I had been so well received was diminished only by the thought that, from that moment on, we would be heading back to France.

The wind was fresh and we quickly drew away from the coastline. The next day, we were far out at sea when we noticed the presence of ten convicts who had stowed away. To avoid further delays, and because the season was already advanced, Louis decided to keep them on board and employ them in various functions.

I omitted to say that on 20 December M. Macarthur wrote to Louis asking him to send out a boat to collect a pair of merino sheep, which he presented to us together with a cassowary. We had already taken on board two other young cassowaries, eight black swans and a cassican, which sang very well and which had been given to me by Captain Piper. M. Macarthur sent me two she-goats on behalf of his young son. To this the Governor added a cow, a calf and a dozen beautiful sheep. All these cluttered up the ship a little but provided useful additional supplies. We therefore hastened to express our thanks to the Governor.

I was extremely sad to be leaving Sydney. The thought of rounding Cape Horn frightened me and I had to remind myself of the fact that we were sailing towards France, in order to rekindle my courage, weakened somewhat by such a long absence from my homeland.

The sea was rough as we sailed past Bass Strait. The ship laboured and developed a leak which nearly forced us to put in at Van Diemen's Land or New Zealand for repairs. This would have delayed us further and consequently we would have rounded Cape Horn during the bad season. Fortunately, the damage did not get worse; it was sufficient to use a pump for a short while each day and we were able to continue on our way. We sailed past Campbell Island which seemed bleak to us; the trees were dark green and the rocks black; in brief, it looked sinister. We felt very sorry for the fishermen who, for the sake of a pittance, exiled themselves to this ugly outpost. We had the wind astern and it drove us towards America, without rough seas or bad weather.

January 1820 – On 21 January, we sighted an iceberg of average height which resembled a badly shaped cone. Its estimated height was 90 to 100 feet. Of a dull white colour, it stood out against the deep grey sea under an overcast sky.

On 7 February, land was sighted. The coastline was spiked with black rocks, devoid of trees and covered with dark vegetation. The next day, we at last rounded the notorious Cape Horn, which is itself made up of an arid rock. The weather was very fine; the wind had abated and had become variable. We had to tack in order to round the Cape and the breeze was so light that we had all the time in the world to observe it. The sun was shining and the sea was calm. Was this really the notorious Cape, so dreaded and so fatal to the fleet of Admiral Anson? It treated us like friends and we shall proclaim far and wide that it is not as diabolical as it is black.

We were at last sailing in the ocean which washes the shores of France and we thought that we were already home. As we steered a course towards the north, the sky darkened and, although the sea had become a little choppier, it allowed us to make for Le Maire Strait where we were to stop briefly. We caught sight of the Bay of Bon Succès and, as we sailed into it, we marvelled at the different appearance of this land compared to the extreme tip of America. The whole coast was covered with woods and the vegetation was very lush. Each one of us was making plans: the hunters eyed with envy the beautiful geese and all the wildlife which was so abundant in these woods; the naturalists longed to go and collect the treasures which they expected to find in a country so rarely visited by travellers.

The skies darkened further still; the wind became fresher, but we paid no attention to all this. Having dropped anchor, we believed ourselves to be safe from any perils. However, my husband, mindful of the safety of the ship, was apprehensive, and his only thought was to protect it from the hurricane which he saw looming. Suddenly, I heard the following words ring through the ship: 'Cut the cable!' And he ordered the sails to be hoisted. Engrossed in this new country which so impressed me, those words roused me from my daydream. I observed the position of the ship and saw that it was moving. But if the sails which we hoisted had not kept the ship moving in the right direction, we would inevitably have been dragged onto the rocks which lined the coast and which we scraped against. The anchor had dragged and the tempestuous wind was driving the *Uranie* violently towards the coast. In very little time, we emerged from the bay and were in the strait. Land lay on both sides and it seemed to me that at any moment the increasingly violent squalls would smash us against the rocks. I shall never forget it as long as I live.

The last sail had just torn and the ship could no longer be steered. 'Land ahead!' someone shouted. I thought we were doomed. I commended my soul into God's keeping and I was distraught at the thought of the horrible death which awaited all of us. I wished only that my head would be smashed against something, to put an end to the uncertainty of life or death. We then realised that the imaginary land was nothing more than an enormous wave which stood out against the horizon.

For at least two nights and two days, we suffered this dreadful torment; the wind, gusting from the south, drove us northward and convinced Louis to call at the Malouines, in the vicinity of which we found ourselves, rather than sail all the way back to the Bay of Bon Succès, which would have delayed us considerably. Louis thus steered a course to reach these islands as speedily as possible. We sighted them on 12 February but only for a short while because thick fog had formed, which forced us to move very slowly towards the anchorage.

On 14 February, the weather improved and we made for French Bay where we were to stop. The ship was about to round the last cape which concealed the entrance to the harbour when it struck a rock. It stopped in its wake for a moment, then started again. A first inspection of the hull revealed nothing abnormal. During a second inspection, it was discovered that water was leaking into the hold with sufficient force to suggest that a piece of the rock struck by the *Uranie* had remained embedded in the hull and had then been dislodged by the ship's movement.

The spot where we intended to anchor was still some distance away and the entire shoreline around us was steep and bristled with sharp rocks. The ship could have been completely destroyed. Soon Louis ordered the whole crew to man the pumps and resolved that, if the pumps could keep the vessel afloat, he would make for a sandy beach to try at least to salvage the *Uranie*'s contents, that is, the equipment and the collections assembled during the expedition. What a cruel blow it would be for us to witness the disappearance of two long years of painstaking labour!

However, the ship was still taking water; the breeze was light and the strength of the men, who had not eaten for a long time, was failing. We were overtaken by nightfall in this cruel predicament!

Having retired to my apartment, overcome by the horror of our situation, I was unable to make any useful contribution to the safety of the crew! I was deep in thought, as I considered the likely disastrous consequences of the tragedy which had befallen us; perhaps the ship would sink and we would only be able to save the crew with the greatest difficulty. What then would become of us? Shipwrecked without any resources on this desert island! I was roused from my daydream by the Abbé who, weary of pumping, came to be at my side and attempted to comfort me in my solitude. We both prayed to God that He might take pity on us.

The water continued to fill the hold despite the crew's valiant efforts. The biscuits were brought up to the poop to save them from being soaked. It was 1 a.m. and the weather was now perfectly calm.

The sailors kept up their courage in a strange fashion; the officers who were working with them encouraged them to sing, so much so that the poor *Uranie*, by now half-submerged, resounded with songs and shouts which were hardly in keeping with the crew's state of mind in such dire straits.

Shipwrecked Chapter 10

Equipment and documents salvaged – Setting up camp – Topography of the country – Means and difficulties of finding supplies – A foreign ship is sighted – Negotiations regarding safe passage

February 1820 – God took pity on us! He sent us a light breeze which drove us towards a beach where we hoped to find a sandy bottom.

Louis sent a boat with an officer to seek the most convenient place to run the ship aground. In accordance with his instructions, the ship was driven almost imperceptibly onto the sand at 3 a.m. Although this is the most horrific situation for a ship to be in, there was no alternative and the manoeuvre was carried out just in time to save us, for the crew were exhausted. Yet they still had to toil further and provide support for the ship, to prevent it from listing onto its side. As they were unable to move fast enough, the corvette tilted slightly on its side, which made life on board quite unpleasant, for we had to walk continually on a sloping deck.

Each member of the crew was allowed to sleep for a few hours. Our awakening was dreadful; daylight revealed to us the nature of the coastline on which we had run aground. It looked barren and sandy; not a single tree broke the monotony of endless sand dunes covered with dry grass. There was little likelihood of sufficient natural resources for one hundred men, who would be obliged to search for food, perhaps for several months!

An officer was sent out in a boat to choose a suitable site to pitch the tents in which the salvaged supplies would be stored. The weather remained fine all day, making possible the transportation of everything required to set up camp. Moreover, the hunters were given the task of providing us with wildlife as food, for whatever supplies had been salvaged from the ship were religiously kept for the time when we would put to sea again.

16 February 1820 – Louis is going ashore with some of the expedition's records and equipment; he has given orders for the camp to be pitched and for the hunters to supply us with meat.

18 February 1820 – A boat was sent to the site of a former French settlement, the remains of which might have been of great assistance

The *Uranie* shipwrecked in French Bay, Falkland Islands

Nicolas Eustache Maurin (1799–1850)
Naufrage de l'Uranie c.1825
hand-coloured lithograph; 10.2 x 19.4 cm
Jacques Arago, *Souvenirs d'un Aveugle: Voyage autour du Monde* (Paris: Hortet et Ozanne, 1839), vol. 4, plate facing p. 248
Rex Nan Kivell Collection
National Library of Australia
Pictorial Collection (U5553)

to us. The officers returned the following day, having found nothing but ruins. The walls of the houses have survived but not one of them is roofed. They spent the night in a large fireplace.

We are still on board, as Louis does not wish to abandon the ship before the most essential items have been removed from it. The weather is getting worse. It appears that there are squalls out at sea. We see enormous waves lifting the ship and dropping it with great force. Each time this happens, we feel that the *Uranie* is going to split into two.

20 February 1820 – The weather is horrible; it is raining, it is cold and waves are still lifting the corvette. The rolls are so violent that I am constantly ready to abandon ship for fear that some catastrophe may befall us, forcing us to make a quick escape. I would then have to go through a window, for the door to my room is on the side which is submerged, and I would be unable to get out that way. Such thoughts prey on my mind and only pangs of hunger make me forget them. Out of necessity and for want of anything better, I am obliged to eat meat without bread. It is like eating sand, for however much water I swallow, the meat sticks in my throat. It is impossible to add any seasoning to the meat, as all our salt and our remaining spices are underwater. What will be left of them after such treatment? We are reduced to eating boiled goose or seal!

The sea has been so rough that those who went ashore were unable to send us our dinner. It finally arrived around 7 p.m.

22 February 1820 – The night has been frightening, and there are such fears for the safety of the people on board that Louis has resolved to remove all the remaining precious goods and to get everyone ashore. I can assure you that I was one of those who welcomed this development; the last four days have seemed to me like years of torment.

My first night on land was not sufficiently pleasant to compensate me for all the uncomfortable ones spent on board. Our tent had not been pitched and, as it rained all night, we were soaked in our bed. At last, day broke. We arranged our house of canvas a little better and were more comfortable during the days that followed, especially after the marquee had been set up. But whether it rained or not, because of the damp nights and the dew from which we were protected only by canvas, our sheets were constantly damp. We shall be most fortunate if we are not afflicted with rheumatism in our old age. Yet, I shall console myself with the thought that I might have perished on that very rock which we struck ...

Louis has checked the longboat, which he plans to send to Montevideo to seek help.

29 February 1820 – The longboat has been taken ashore; a tent has been pitched for the carpenters and another for the blacksmiths. Our camp looks like a small village; there is a tent for Louis, one for the equipment and the records where we will also take our meals, one for the staff, one for the midshipmen and one for the volunteers. Three other tents have been pitched, for the hospital, the sailors' barracks and the masters respectively. There are also small tents for the cooks and the supplies. At some distance from the camp is the powder magazine where arms and ammunition are kept under lock and key. The crew are still busy salvaging anything they can from the ship. We go on walks with the Abbé to look for wild celery which we eat in salads. The hunters ventured further inland and found wild horses, several of which have been killed. This will be a great help to us, for geese are becoming scarcer and seal flesh does not appeal to the crew. Not surprisingly, for it tastes quite unpleasant.

4 March 1820 – Louis goes aboard each day to supervise the salvage operations. We are eating all the perishables, while everything that can be preserved has been placed in the stores. The swell is very heavy and the sea continues to lash the coast with such fury that boats moored in a small bay have been driven onto the shore. The smallest one has been smashed to pieces; Louis' boat, which was damaged, was repaired at once.

7 March 1820 – Two horses have been killed, to the delight of the crew.

8 March 1820 – I rose early today to take advantage of the fine weather. I went for a short walk with the Abbé and as he had to speak with Louis, who was near the longboat, we headed towards it. I had not visited that spot for a few days; I found the work on the longboat well advanced, so much so that it is beginning to look like a small vessel. Louis presses ahead with the installation of the observatory.

High tides have prevented any salvage operations in the *Uranie*, as the top of the battery is permanently underwater. I spend all day tidying up our tent; I sort out things in our trunks where they were hastily thrown. Today I found a little salt in a barrel used for salting. What a find!

9 March 1820 – The weather is overcast. After lunch, a boat is sent out to hunt penguins on the island of that name because the hunters are tired and need a rest. Moreover, game is becoming scarcer in the vicinity of our camp.

The weather fined up today around midday. This allowed me to open boxes of wet biscuits and put them out to dry. In one of the boxes, the biscuits were nothing more than a veritable salty and bitter paste. However, in our predicament, we eat it in soup after rinsing it in fresh water. I also keep an eye on my dear potatoes and observe with a great deal of sadness that almost all are rotting. I have decided that they should be eaten at once, for in a few days' time they will be fit only for the dustbin.

Tonight, as he climbed one of the high mountains that surround us, a volunteer saw very thick smoke rising about seven leagues away. Could there possibly be other human beings in this wretched country? It would require a very long trip to investigate this, and perhaps it would be in vain ...

We think that the smoke probably indicates the presence of seal hunters who are busy extracting oil from the animals they have killed. But of what use can they be to us? As a rule, those people are left behind for six to eight months to fish, and at the end of their stay a ship comes to collect them. In that case, they might be of some use to us ... But, to travel 14 leagues for a little smoke which may perhaps be nothing more than a cloud! ...

Once more, we have attempted to produce salt, and at last we have succeeded. Though not white nor fine, it salts and that is something at least.

10 March 1820 – Louis is feeling unwell; he is unable to work. As the weather is fine, we have resolved to send the hunters to set up camp three leagues from here, in order to surprise oxen and horses which are extremely difficult to approach. Four hunters and 11 men left at 1 p.m. to carry the necessary equipment to the new camp.

11 March 1820 – One of the hunters returned this morning at 6 o'clock to announce that three horses had been killed last night, and as this occurred near the shore, a boat has been sent out to fetch them. The joy with which this news has been greeted in the camp is unbelievable. Louis went aboard to fetch a number of items essential for the fitting-out of our small vessel. He brought back several things which we did not have time to take with us. The Lieutenant dragged the sea with a net to try to vary our diet a little. But either because the sea was too rough on this coast, or because there was a dearth of fish near the beach, he brought back only a few small, albeit delicious, gudgeons. The boat sent out to fetch the horses has not yet returned. As it was a beautiful evening, we went for a walk to a spot where we imagined there would be a lot more fish, but stones and rocks tore the net's mesh. M. Lamarche, who went hunting tonight, sent me a snipe, which provided a delicious meal.

12 March 1820 – Today, Sunday, the weather has been fine enough for mass to be said, and we all attended. The work is not so urgent that the crew cannot spend half an hour on such a worthwhile activity. I must admit that I am gratified, for religion is my only source of consolation. The thought that God will compensate me in heaven for the sufferings which He inflicts on me in this life, if I endure them steadfastly, eases my hardship and sustains my courage.

The longboat came back with three fine horses. The new moon has brought back the high tide, and the men have seized the opportunity to go on board today.

13 March 1820 – Louis is still unwell and is confined to bed. The strain of the last two months has been too much for him. When I woke this morning, I noticed that everyone was concerned with a large fire visible on Penguin Island. As it had not been seen again since the hunters last visited the island, it was attributed to inhabitants of this land, and a boat was speedily sent out. But M. Raillard, who was in command of the boat, reported that no-one had been spotted and that the fire had probably been lit in the first place by our hunting party and had been rekindled by the wind. The low tide made it possible for a large number of items to be salvaged from our poor *Uranie*. The search party managed to reach a hold containing biscuits and removed a large number which will be an invaluable ingredient for the crew's soup, for they are now reduced to eating only meat. The men even refuse to drink broth when there is nothing in it; they claim that it is not nourishing.

14 March 1820 – I spent a peaceful night in my bed, which consists of a plank, two chairs and a long cushion by way of a mattress. It is on such occasions that my kimono works wonders; the thickness of its cloth makes it remarkably warm, so much so that when I am in bed fully dressed and wrapped in it alone, I do not feel the cold one bit. Louis is extremely weak.

Today I experienced a pleasure which could only be understood fully if one takes our circumstances into account. We have been deprived of any sort of bread for a month. The crew's cook, who is a baker by trade, built a small oven yesterday in order to roast the meat better and prevent it from smelling of smoke, as has been the case until now as a result of making fires with heather. In Guam we came across a type of flour made from the fruit of a tree which we deemed useful for several purposes. The Governor gave a large sack of it to the Abbé, because the latter discovered that it powdered hair better than starch and wanted to take some back with him to France. This sack was salvaged and brought ashore; it fell into the hands of the cook during the construction of his oven. Today he kneaded this flour. The Abbé sent me a bun which I found delicious. After checking that it was really made from Gago flour, I quickly gathered several other sacks which had been taken on board in Guam as pigfeed. Thus, we are all happy; the Abbé is delighted to be eating his curling powder, while I am pleased to share my piglets' dinner!

Today has been most eventful and, as I have some free time, I can have a long chat with you. Everyone is asleep in the camp, with the exception of the sentinel who has just turned his hourglass and is sounding midnight before retiring to bed. The only sound that disturbs me, and will torment me for a long time to come, is the noise of the waves crashing against the rocks on the shore, close to our tent. And, when this tempestuous ocean holds back its frothy waves for a few moments, my attention is drawn to the noise made by a portion of chicken which is boiling beside me on the table, where I write by the glow of my lamp. The chicken is to make broth for my poor Louis. Weary of soup from stock cubes, I decided tonight to kill one of the five or six chickens saved from the shipwreck, which I was keeping for an occasion such as this.

You see, dear Caroline, that I am prepared to use up both my time and paper to record such trivia. But perhaps when you know that I am safely back in my beloved homeland, you will read of my misfortunes with interest. In a situation like this, the slightest occurrence takes on major significance; I can only speak from my own experience, of course.

Today many other items have been salvaged. But what made me praise the Lord far more than I had done previously was that the Lieutenant, noticing a large piece of wood at the bottom of the sea, almost directly under the corvette, dredged it and recognised it as a plank from the *Uranie*. It contained a gash at least 7 feet long. The plank comes from the section of the ship which struck the rock, and the rolling of the sea has loosened it. The sailors, who are experienced in such matters, deem it a miracle that we had time to reach the coast, for with damage of such magnitude the *Uranie* ought to have sunk soon after the collision! Well, at least we are on firm land, albeit a miserable stretch of land. May God watch over our return to France ... my gratitude will know no bounds if He allows me to hold my mother and my friend in my arms once more.

15 March 1820 – At 8 a.m. we saw an eclipse of the sun which held our attention for several hours. We recorded many observations which will no doubt be useful. Louis is feeling a little better today.

16 March 1820 – Word has reached us from the hunters' camp that four horses and two foals, as well as a pig, have been killed. You can well imagine the joy in the camp. As for me, I was particularly glad to hear of the pig, which will taste so much better than horsemeat. Even if one overlooks any instinctive aversion to it, horsemeat is tough and does not make good broths. In stews and casseroles, it is tolerable. In the absence of potatoes, I bake Gago buns, which are not as good as those of the Abbé. Moreover, I had previously tasted them hot; when cold, they become very hard. Mine are so hard that one must break them up with a hammer. They taste reasonably good, but the darkest bread of our French peasants would seem like cake compared to everything we eat.

17 March 1820 – The fire lit by the hunting party a long time ago is spreading each day. It now worries us a little, as it appears to be drawing nearer. Fortunately, the wind is in our favour and will at least prevent it from gaining too much ground. I have made use of essence of hops bought in Port Jackson, with which one can make beer by adding sugar. I followed the instructions given to me and I bottled the beer, which we tasted today. It is all the more agreeable because for the last month we have been drinking wine mixed with saltwater or just fresh water.

18 March 1820 – Again the weather is very fine today and my husband has decided to take a walk to the makeshift shipyard. We found work on the longboat to be well advanced; it will be ready to go to sea within two or three days. Her masts and gear are finished. Yesterday the crew salvaged from the ship something very precious for the longboat: a barrel of pitch. They also removed a box containing 66 cheeses in good condition. Today the pork has been distributed; each table had its fair share, albeit a small portion. However, it tasted delicious to us, for it has been a long time since we have eaten something familiar.

19 March 1820 – Today, Sunday, we had to rise early to attend mass. I found it difficult, as I am in some pain. After lunch, the weather was fine and Louis, the Abbé and I decided to go for a long walk in search of a sandy beach suitable for fishing. On the way, we went to take a look at the longboat which has been painted and looks really charming. We were continuing on our walk when we heard extraordinary shouting coming from the camp. Everyone climbed up the sand dune on the edge of the sea; we saw nothing, but our gaze was fixed on the entrance to the bay.

A gunner was sent to inform us that a ship had been sighted. Indeed, Louis soon noticed a cutter manoeuvring to enter the harbour.

The longboat was not there; unfortunately, it had been sent to fetch two horses killed the day before. Louis' boat, though in a poor state, was fitted out; three guns were fired and a white flag raised at the highest point. With favourable winds, the boat drew alongside within a few hours. At about the same time, the longboat returned and was sent to offer whatever meagre refreshments we could spare. Imagine our joy at the thought that our exile would soon be over!

At 5.30 p.m., the boat that had taken supplies to the small vessel returned and the volunteer in command informed us that the vessel was a sloop which belonged to a whaler anchored 20 leagues along the west coast of the Malouines. It had been hunting seals for 18 months and was only due to complete its loading after another 10 months. The sloop had not yet dropped anchor when the boat left, but an hour later the captain himself came to visit Louis and confirmed the earlier news. He seemed reluctant to grant Louis' request, that he should return at once to his ship with an officer who would ask the Commander to come and fetch us and our effects and take us to Rio de Janeiro. Louis promised to compensate him for his losses. He replied that he still had another eight days' fishing before he could go back and that he did not dare take it upon himself to return without his small cargo. This did not suit Louis. Nevertheless, Louis, who had not given up all hope of persuading him, invited him into his tent, offered him a small glass of rum and showed him the United States passport which enjoined all ships to render assistance to the *Uranie* during her voyage. He read and re-read this document, which had more impact on him than anything that he had been told until then.

After Louis had written to the Commander and had given verbal orders and issued written instructions to the officer [Dubaut] who was to accompany the captain of the sloop, my husband reiterated his pleas, although he did not insist too much. It was agreed that they were to return at once to the whaler. Indeed, the officer left immediately with the captain who intended, if the wind were favourable, to put to sea that same night.

I need not explain to you the effect this news had on me. I am still in a daze and I am over the moon at the thought that our wait will not be as long as we feared. Although I am not yet certain that the whaler will want to transport us, I am delighted at the prospect that this may happen. At least, even if this does not eventuate, these few days of self-delusion will have been less painful than the others. I have started the letters which I planned to send by the longboat; I shall leave them unfinished until further notice, because I would much rather write to you from a place where we are safe than from a country where you would think us more unhappy than we really are.

20 March 1820 – The first noise I heard upon waking this morning was very agreeable both to me and to the whole camp. It was a messenger from the hunters, bringing word that three oxen had been killed. Imagine what pleasure this has given to people who have eaten little but horsemeat for the last month!

Light winds did not allow the sloop to set out until approximately 6 p.m. We watched it tacking all day, attempting to get out of the bay. Louis and I went on a long walk toward the summit of the mountains which line the southern part of the plain where we are camped. It was a fine day and we enjoyed a magnificent view from the mountaintops, from where we could see a large part of the island. At 7 p.m., a boat from the sloop came to the camp with a message that they had been forced to call at a neighbouring bay because of strong gales out to sea. This boat carried only a boatswain and some sailors, and returned to the sloop after a short stay at the camp. The hunters' fire, which is still burning and whose smoke we saw from afar, has flared up again tonight with quite a lot of intensity on the mountain slopes which line the plain where we are camped. Pray God that it does not come any nearer to torment us, for it would be very vexatious to have to transport all our equipment elsewhere. The seashore which is sandy would be our sanctuary, but the fire would also destroy all the heather which we cook with, in the absence of firewood.

21 March 1820 – Tormented by the thought that the fire could reach us, I did not get a wink of sleep all night. I imagined the awkward position that this would put us in; I could not prevent myself from being distressed at the prospect that the little we had salvaged from the fury of the waves would be destroyed by the flames! At last, submitting to the will of God, I begged Him to spare us. The kind Lord took pity on His poor castaways and did not seek to afflict them with this final blow. Heavy rain finally put an end to all our fears.

Work on the longboat is complete. It has been launched this morning but its planned voyage has been postponed because of the arrival of the small American vessel. M. Duperrey will use it to complete a detailed chart of the bay. High winds have prevented the crew from working on board the *Uranie*. They will have to wait for the full moon to make further attempts to salvage the goods left in her hold. The beef arrived in time for today's soup. I do not need to describe to you the pleasurable sensation we experienced; it was an old, tough bull which nevertheless seemed delicious to us.

I was delighted to welcome the rain which put out the fire raging on the mountains, but it lasted the whole day and, being accompanied by squalls, it caused us great inconvenience. Our tents are generally badly pitched, and the cold caused by the wind cannot be kept out by walls of wet canvas. As soon as night falls, we choose to go to bed; only there are we safe and warm.

22 March 1820 – Bad weather has persisted all day, although it did not rain as much as yesterday, and the strong squalls have continued, which has made work on board impossible. The crew are busy tidying up the rigging and the various items salvaged from the *Uranie*. And the longboat cannot be launched. I spend many peaceful hours reading or working in my tent while blowing on my fingers to warm them up. Louis is busy transcribing various completed observations and at the same time oversees the setting up of his observatory.

22 and 23 March 1820 – We cannot explain the large number of sick crewmen. If one excludes the four or five men who are out in the longboat and six others sent out in the boat to hunt penguins, there are scarcely ten men fit enough to work. A large number suffer from colic and diarrhoea; others have pains or wounds. The Lieutenant himself, who has just recovered from a fall on board, resulting in the bruising of several ribs, has now pulled a muscle.

Yesterday and today the weather has been superb. I took advantage of the sun to dry out a number of items in our tents which got wet during the heavy rain. My clothes especially are all mildewed. That's all we needed after the accident at Rawak and the thefts at Port Jackson.

The hunters have again been successful; they are sending us a bull, a cow and a horse. As for me, I enjoy eating snipes, for our good doctor, having learnt that these wild birds appealed to me, has been kind enough to shoot several for me. Louis' health continues to be quite good, but I can see that he is still weak, for observations which previously he carried out with ease, now tire him out. He presses on with the building of his observatory and intends to set up the equipment tomorrow. My husband has just revealed to me how he will force the ship to take us, if the captain refuses to do so of his own accord. I must admit that the idea fills me with apprehension. I would much rather things were settled amicably. He would capture the sloop upon its return and man it with his own crew. He would then set out with the sloop, the longboat, ammunition and arms, leaving behind in the camp only the Lieutenant and enough men to guard it, entrusting me to the care of the Abbé. Louis would then lead the attack.

All this would be inconvenient, even if not a single shot were fired, for it would greatly prolong our stay here. May God preserve us and bring back the sloop bearing good news!

26 March 1820 – Today Louis is again in a lot of pain and is obliged to stay in bed. The weather has been dreadful all night. It was windy; there was thunder and lightning, and it poured. Although today is Palm Sunday, the Abbé cannot say mass because of the foul weather.

27 March 1820 – I was not surprised this morning to see ice when I went out early; I found the night very cold and felt most uncomfortable on my two chairs. While requesting assistance today to move their camp because they can no longer find any wildlife, the hunters have shot a rabbit. Though long in the tooth, it will not fail to please us because it is so rare. It is now a few days since the sloop left with the officer from the *Uranie*; it must have reached the ship, and perhaps at this very minute the officer is pleading the cause of his companions in misfortune. We wonder whether he has found someone who sympathises with our views, or whether he has come up against a person with a heart of stone who cannot be moved to pity. Although we are hopeful that the captain will grant our request, especially as we pledged to compensate him for everything, so many factors could lead him to refuse that our fears are probably well founded. In general, Americans care only about their own commercial interests, and they are a little uncouth. But the captain of the *General Knox* has been to France, he speaks our language and perhaps, when he visited our country, some of our polish may have smoothed a little of the roughness which is common among whalers from the New World.

28 March 1820 – The whole morning has been taken up with a whale washed ashore three miles from the camp. The men tried to kill it; after ten shots, it appeared dead, but when an attempt was made to tie it to the rocks to prevent it from being dragged out to sea, the whale began to splash about, managing to refloat itself. I did not witness the spectacle for myself, and I regret this all the more as it is now gone forever and I shall perhaps never have another chance to observe one in such propitious circumstances.

The longboat, which has been at work out in the bay, moored near us around 3 p.m. At about the same time, we sighted a three-master entering the bay and reproached ourselves for having doubts about the whaler's goodwill. Instead, he seems to have responded very promptly. He could not have deliberated long, as it is only nine days since the sloop left the bay and the boatswain thought then that we might have an answer in 10 days. The wind was contrary and our saviour, not wishing to tack all night, lay at anchor in the middle of the harbour.

M. Duperrey left in the longboat at 8 p.m. to go on board the vessel. He came back at 1 a.m. and reported to Louis that the three-master was not the whaler we were expecting, but an American ship, the *Mercury*, which was en route to the Pacific and had already rounded Cape Horn when a leak forced her to head back to the bay for repairs. The captain heard of our misfortune with a great deal of sympathy and sent a message to Louis that he was ready to render assistance and take us, our crew and our baggage to Rio de Janeiro. You see, dear friend, that God has not forsaken us; He has provided a solution at a time when we least expected it. The cold is becoming intense and affecting me badly, especially my feet. This will be the case so long as we remain here because the sand we walk on is often damp.

29 March 1820 – M. Duperrey left again this morning to go on board the *Mercury*, because a persisting contrary wind has prevented it from anchoring at the far end of the bay. Its crew is too weak to tack any further. Louis has sent 12 of his best sailors to their assistance and, as soon as it is lying at anchor, our workers, who excel in all kinds of repairs, will check its leak and fix it promptly. The fine weather of the last two days, which made it possible for the crew to board the *Uranie*, has not kept up and nothing could be salvaged, even though high tides arrived with the full moon. The recent bad weather has heeled the *Uranie* over much more, and the battery is now permanently submerged. We have no choice but to abandon the rest of the goods left on board.

The *Mercury* set sail around 7 a.m. and dropped anchor around midday. At 3 p.m., the American captain came to pay his respects to Louis, accompanied by one of the passengers. Although still in bed, Louis felt a little better. The American informed us that he was flying the flag of rebels in whose service he was and that the purpose of his voyage was to transport cannons to Valparaiso. Whether he had not explained his good intentions towards us clearly enough, or whether the officer [Duperrey] had misunderstood what he had said, the fact is that he was more than willing to offer us passage to Chile, but would be persuaded only with great difficulty to take us anywhere else. He argued that he was not rich enough to miss out on his commercial deals, and despite Louis' pledge to compensate him for the losses he would incur, he did not wish to commit himself at this stage. Nevertheless, my husband undertook to send master carpenters and caulkers to his ship to check out the leak and repair it. He also lent him a boat to return on board because his own boat was about to undergo repairs, as it was in a poor condition. The captain was kind enough to bring me raisins, nuts, almonds, butter and cheese, thinking that I would be gratified to receive these. In exchange, Louis sent him some magnificent geese.

30 March 1820 – Our diet is very poor; during the last few days, the hunters have sent us nothing and geese have become so rare in the surrounding district that we are reduced to eating dreadful seagulls. The cold has been most unpleasant every day and it never stops raining. I am truly frozen to the bone; my feet especially ache continually. It is not surprising that I should feel the cold so much; during the last two years we have visited some very warm countries. The limited shelter which our tents provide in such a cold and wet climate is very trying. Finally, I am always hungry and this does not help to keep me warm. I eat only to keep my strength up, as I am weary of our diet. As for the small Gago buns, not only do they taste unpleasant, but they are not nutritious because the flour comes, not from wheat, but from a root.

31 March 1820 – Today we had a visit from the American captain. Louis learnt from his master carpenters of the poor state of the vessel whose boards are coming apart due to the heavy weight of the cargo of cannons in the hold. Urgent repairs are required but cannot be carried out without our assistance, as the American does not possess a spare plank nor any rigging nor even a single workman capable of fixing the slightest damage. Thus, our two unfortunate vessels will be of use to each other.

The damage to the American ship is so extensive that all our master carpenters can hope to achieve is to patch her sufficiently to allow her to sail for one more month on calm seas. Therefore, it is vital that she put into port for repairs before she rounds Cape Horn.

Even if Louis had not been given these details, he might have guessed from the way in which the captain spoke to him. His manner of speech was quite different from the tone he had adopted two days before; one could see clearly that he needed us more than we needed him. He spent most of the time asking for what was required to repair his ship and discussing the arrangements to accommodate us on board. This will be easy because the steerage is superb, and we can even easily store everything salvaged from our poor *Uranie*.

The captain has gone on board the American ship with the Lieutenant to find out what is needed; Louis has given orders for anchors, rigging, pumps, timber, etc. to be sent out to him, together with all the carpenters fit for work and some other sailors to help manoeuvre the ship.

We have such a dearth of supplies that we had to apologise for being unable to invite them to dinner. We can only offer wine, which they drink with great pleasure, finding it all the more delicious because they have run out of it.

The captain has asked us for some rum for his passengers. They are very short of supplies and are obliged to feed the crew on wildlife and to deprive them of biscuits, just as we have done for the last month and a half, so as to conserve the scant provisions left for the sea voyage. You will be surprised to hear that they left the Rio de la Plata on 16 February. But this is typical of Americans; they always carry just enough supplies for one crossing so that, whenever there is a delay, they are short of everything. This is precisely what has happened to our visitors, who should by now have reached Valparaiso. Nevertheless, with the precautions we have taken and in view of the short voyage from here to Buenos Aires, lasting between 12 to 15 days, we will have ample supplies. The captain returned to his ship around 5 p.m., taking several carpenters with him.

1 April 1820 – We have been very busy all day packing our books, and have hastily prepared crates for all our effects. Louis, who is not yet well enough to make observations, has asked officers to stand in for him and measure the earth's declination with the compass.

2 April 1820 – Today the Abbé said mass for Easter and I was moved when I compared our modest service to the customary magnificent ones in our poor country. May God allow me to celebrate this feast in my homeland in 1821!

The weather is reasonably fine today; we took the opportunity to go and see a stranded whale, which is beginning to smell. I shall not describe this enormous animal for you. You will find suitable descriptions of it in books, as it is a known species (the whale with the pointed snout of Lacépède). This one is 54 feet long.

M. Duperrey has returned to the camp. He continues to busy himself with hydrography. The hunters still send us nothing. A party has been sent out to hunt penguins; they brought back enough for two days' supplies. Louis has given orders for the hunters' camp to be relocated and has increased their numbers. Thanks to the generosity of the American captain, we have received some medicine, which we had not been able to salvage from the *Uranie*. How fortunate it is to fall ill in these circumstances!

The weather has been quite good and Louis has made a few observations which have tired him a little. I kept busy all day packing our crates.

Around 4 p.m., a ship was seen entering the bay and it was thought to be a schooner. Fog rolled in and prevented us from seeing whether it was anchoring or continuing to tack. We believed that it had been sent by the whaler, for in addition to his small sloop he had a schooner to help with the fishing. It is most likely that the captain did not wish to come all this way and has sent us just this small vessel.

4 April 1820 – Louis left early this morning to go on board the *Mercury*. M. Lamarche accompanied him. They are both going to inspect the alterations which need to be made to provide accommodation for all of us, if not in a lot of space, at least under shelter. The captain has been good enough to agree to everything Louis has asked for; he has put his own room at our disposal and is content to occupy another so small that there will not be enough space beside his bed to undress.

The two captains have agreed that we will eat together by combining our supplies and that meals will be served in the large room occupied by the four passengers, who will dine with us. Large quarters are being prepared for our officers, who will take their meals with their counterparts on the American ship; another will be set aside for the midshipmen and the volunteers, and finally there will be an area reserved for the masters.

Louis went on board the schooner which was sighted the day before and which had anchored next to the *Mercury*. This morning he met M. Dubaut who informed him that the schooner belonged to a whaler, the *General Knox*; the ship's captain came to tell him that he was prepared to accept his proposition, to make arrangements for compensation to be paid to him and to discuss other such matters. His ship, anchored in the harbour, has unloaded all its cargo and has been unrigged during the fishing season; the captain did not want to rig it without being sure that it would be to his advantage. You can see what generous souls they are!

His terms were a little harsh; he demanded no less than 50 000 piastres as compensation for the voyage. By bargaining a great deal and allowing him to pillage the *Uranie*, Louis reduced the sum by 10 000 piastres, which was a considerable saving. However, he was glad that we had another offer, because he wanted to press on with his fishing which, he claimed, was quite lucrative. It is a cruel occupation; they eat nothing but meat and drink only water, and they live in small vessels where they suffer from the cold and dampness without firewood. They burn the flesh of seals to melt their fat and turn it into oil. The sloop's captain showed M. Dubaut six spots where ships had been wrecked recently. These wretched islands are surrounded by uncharted rocks, and the captain told Louis that there were perhaps 50 wrecks in this area. He knew the rock which we had struck and maintained that if we had sailed closer to shore, we would have dodged it. But who could have foreseen this? So it is that one meets one's destiny on the very path taken to avoid it.

Louis was absent most of the day, having taken the opportunity to visit the former French establishment. I was busy all day packing our books in boxes.

5 April 1820 – Louis made magnetic observations throughout the morning. The captain of the *General Knox* came to visit him. He gave him notes and details on the Malouines, but he urged Louis to hasten his departure, because at the end of the month the weather would worsen and in our tents we would suffer from the cold. The carpenters work tirelessly on the ship and Louis sends them whatever they need. The officer who is on board the ship believes he overheard the passengers talking to the captain, urging him to leave without us as soon as the repairs are completed. What do you think of such selfishness? However, as this young man does not understand English very well, Louis has not mentioned it in case he was mistaken.

After lengthy discussions with the captain of the *General Knox*, Louis has offered him items which were likely to appeal to him, and he for his part has demanded gunpowder, lead, flints, sail thread, canvas, etc ... Louis promised that, with regard to these, he would be as generous as our difficult position allowed. His relocation until now has not cost him dearly because he has fished along the whole coast on the way here, and he will do the same on the return journey. Two passengers came to the camp to ask for leadshot. Louis gave them some for the third time in four days. I continue to supervise the packing of our boxes.

6 April 1820 – Magnetic observations continued to be made this morning. Louis supervised them with M. Lamarche for part of the day, while in the afternoon the latter took over with midshipmen. Carpenters have been sent on board to press on with the work and to find out whether the captain had unloaded his cannons, as agreed with Louis.

Tonight a letter dispatched by M. Guérin confirmed that the captain had admitted to him his passengers' request to sail without us. He is a kind and weak man; he allows himself to be dictated to. That is why I have pleaded with Louis to send men on board immediately to hasten the loading of all our goods and even to dispatch some of our effects. Meanwhile, the captain of the *General Knox* has assured the captain of the *Mercury* that if he wanted to go to the harbour where his own ship was anchored, he would carry out the repairs. These are false arguments which the passengers have put forward, in order to convince him to refuse us passage. To put an end to this and to secure the ship, Louis intends sending the Lieutenant with about 20 men; as the other crew comprises 12 or 16 men at the most, we would have the upper hand if it came to a dispute.

The captain of the *General Knox*, who was planning to sail today with his schooner, has decided to remain here but to send the schooner taking his orders back to the ship anchored in the harbour. He is staying behind at our infirmary to take care of one of his crew who has cut an artery.

The captain has taken delivery of another 50 kilos of gunpowder, together with all the items he has asked for. It is almost as if all these nasty foreigners are plotting to rob us before abandoning us. But we are stronger than they are and we remain on our guard.

7 April 1820 – In his letter yesterday, M. Guérin stated that the captain had asked Louis to send his belongings and those of the crew as soon as possible, but he seems to have forgotten that the workmen are still busy on the ship and there would not be enough room to store all of it. Louis therefore left at 5 o'clock this morning to speak to the captain. The blacksmiths have worked all night to make large pins which will fasten the pieces of wood used to strengthen the bottom of the ship.

Louis has admonished the *Mercury*'s captain, by pointing out how ungenerous it would be of him to leave us behind after all we have done for him; that, with the number of boats at our disposal, the loading of our belongings would hardly delay him at all; and that his passengers had no right to complain, because until now we had worked only for their benefit. It would seem that one of them is inciting the others; he is a young captain in the Chilean navy who appears to be either conceited or irresponsible. He asked Louis to have coffee with him this morning and paid him a lot of compliments. We shall invite all of them to dinner in two days' time.

Louis came back around 10 a.m. and spent the rest of the day making magnetic observations, while I continued to oversee the packing of my crates. You will not be surprised to learn that I shall be busy with this work for a few more days, as all the books, maps, etc of the expedition need to be packed, in addition to all our personal effects. Today I have numbered the twenty-second box and I still have about another ten to do.

8 April 1820 – The captain of the *General Knox* has not dispatched his schooner today, as he intended to do. He has rendered assistance to the captain of the *Mercury* by taking on board some of his guns, with the intention of throwing them overboard at sea. This work is already well advanced and will allow us at last to send our baggage on board. Today Louis received a letter from the captain of the whaler who has heard that we planned to burn the remains of the *Uranie*. He asked for permission to remove everything that might be useful to him beforehand. But Louis does not wish to burn anything nor allow anything to be taken, not knowing whether the government will send a rescue party to salvage all those objects, many of which, such as anchors, cannons, masts, etc, are very valuable. He is going to reply that unless he wishes to pay for it, the captain has no right to take away this material. I believe that he has no intention of purchasing anything whatsoever and his conscience will be lax enough for him to return after our departure and brazenly take what has been refused him.

The hunters, who have sent us horses for a few days, have forced us by their prolonged silence to resort to eating penguins, but the flesh of these amphibians is not as nutritious as horsemeat and a lot of it is needed to feed 12 people.

A few days ago, a party was sent out to cast nets in a spot where fish had been observed, but they brought back only 30 pounds of fish, and small ones at that. Today the captain of the *Mercury*, who had sent his men to fish elsewhere, was much more successful. He sent me six splendid fish, which tasted delicious and which we thoroughly enjoyed. Several boats have been required to load our baggage. Louis sent word to M. Duperrey to return to the camp, and his rowboat anchored in the bay near us at around 4 p.m. Fortunately, he had almost completed a detailed geographical chart of this wide bay, finding that previous charts were fairly inaccurate. As it was foggy, Louis busied himself with magnetic observations which do not require sunshine. I am making good progress with our boxes and I think that I shall be just about finished tomorrow.

8 April 1820 – Yesterday was Saturday, 8 April, and so is today, because by going round the world, we have gained one day. But in order to have the same Sunday as the people who have not accompanied us, and so as not to lose two days in one week by celebrating our Sunday on a different day to the crew of the *Mercury*, we have resolved to have a week with two Saturdays.

I was wrong to assume that I could finish my packing today; it would seem that the objects are multiplying in spite of the number I have decided to discard. And yet, we are taking with us only what is indispensable! Louis, for his part, is still busy with his magnetic observations. A number of barrels have been sent on board. The captain had asked for a cable and, when it had not been sent immediately, he wrote to Louis insisting that unless he received it within three days, he would sail without us. It was nothing more than a tantrum, for without the help of our crew he would not be in a position to leave within eight days. Nevertheless, Louis will send him what he wants tomorrow morning. Today, we are taking advantage of the fine weather to transport the biscuits aboard.

9 April 1820 – The Abbé said mass for us today, Low Sunday [the next Sunday after Easter].

I have been unable to continue packing my boxes today, for not only is it Sunday, but I have also been busy getting a thousand things ready to receive, as best we can, the strangers we have invited to dinner.

By 3 p.m. I was ready to receive them and, without boasting, I can honestly say that I offered them a dinner which was quite tolerable for castaways. I will describe the menu in detail for you so that you can judge for yourself: soup, then boiled goose and ham occupied the table in turn. The latter even stayed on the table for the rest of the dinner. I had prepared four entrées: one was a hot pâté of snipe and fish; another was a ragoût of goose and the last two were made with pork, one being pork shoulders which I had boned and stuffed. Next came two roasts, one of goose, the other of pork, two dishes of small fresh fish, one with peas and the other with M. Appert's green beans. There were two sweets as well, but as all I had to offer was plums and cheese, these were added to the desserts, which consisted of a cherry tart and a meringue cream. You see that it was thanks to M. Appert's jars that the dinner was tolerable, for, without these, it consisted entirely of pork and goose. By an unusual stroke of good fortune, the chickens which were left, having grown a little stronger because they had been allowed to roam freely, had laid eggs and, thanks to some milk and M. Appert's cherries, I was able to add a little luxury to my dessert. The meal ended with coffee, tea and liqueur, of which I still had ... one last bottle. In brief, our guests, who had hearty appetites, found the whole meal delicious.

This was accompanied by a small morsel of good bread; and here is how we managed it. Each day, a pinch of flour dampened with saltwater was allocated to each member of the crew of the *Uranie* for soup. Having saved this for a few days, we collected enough to make bread for all our guests. It is only since we ran out of damp biscuits that flour has been distributed.

The dinner went on until nightfall and, as the weather turned nasty, it was decided that our dinner guests should spend the night in our camp. We managed as best we could, collecting cushions and blankets in sufficient numbers for our guests, who spread out into different tents.

This morning, thanks to the ham left over from last night, some goose and M. Appert's vegetables, I was able to offer them a tolerable lunch.

They all set off around 11 a.m. to return on board the *Mercury*. The captain of the ship apologised for not staying longer, because of the weather, which indeed had worsened, as well as a number of jobs which required his supervision. He had a good excuse, but perhaps he was still a little upset with the delay in sending the cable. The repairs are progressing very slowly on his ship and Louis has sent M. Lamarche on board to supervise the work and to speed things up.

A dog given to us by the whaler's captain is truly wonderful. It has tracked down some pigs which the hunters have sent us over the last few days.

11 April 1820 – As it is promising to be fine today, Louis is taking the opportunity to set up a pendulum. The captain arrived in the camp but he was unable to speak to Louis who is still busy with his pendulum. He came to discuss the terms of our passage. We wanted to invite him to dinner, but the officers forestalled us by doing so soon after his arrival.

12 April 1820 – This morning we offered breakfast to the captain, who had been unable to return to his ship. He left us around 11 a.m. Louis then went back to his magnetic observations, as the weather is not fine enough for observations involving the pendulum. We learned that the hunting party had killed a bull and a horse; a boat has gone to fetch these although they are some distance away. How I long to go on board, for I am suffering a great deal from the cold, which intensifies each day, and our stay under canvas is becoming increasingly unpleasant. I can hardly walk because my feet hurt so much from the cold; the dampness and rain which persist each day are becoming intolerable. All our clothes are wet and the bedclothes are also damp, and consequently unhealthy. I am afraid that all this will give me aches and pains at a young age and I think I shall be afflicted with nothing less than scores of rheumatisms in my twenties. Tonight, Louis received a letter from the captain on the same matter which had brought him to the camp previously. But as it is easier to discuss such matters face to face, Louis plans to go on board tomorrow morning to talk to him. All day, our boxes have been transported to the ship; 25 or 26 have already been loaded.

13 April 1820 – Louis left soon after lunch, accompanied by M. Requin, *Uranie*'s purser, to negotiate our passage. They returned in the afternoon with the captain, but without a decision having been made because the latter refused to make arrangements in front of his passengers. Louis invited him to stay for dinner, after which these gentlemen talked business until 10 p.m. The conference was very unpleasant; the captain's demands were excessive and our officers refused to accede to them. He wanted 10 000 piastres to transport us to Buenos Aires. After much discussion, our officers decided that it would be more advantageous to proceed to Rio de Janeiro, because of the resources which we would find there (this country is not in the grip of a revolution as is Buenos Aires), and the presence of a Consul and a French Ambassador. To take us there, the captain is demanding 15 000 piastres and wants to think on the matter until tomorrow morning. We offered him hospitality under our tents so that this matter could be resolved once and for all. He is refusing to unload anything from his ship until a decision has been reached. For eight days now, he has been promising us that the room which we are to occupy would be cleared, as well as the quarters for the officers, and yet nothing has been done about it.

14 April 1820 – Fresh negotiations began quite early. But having thought about it, our Jew is still not inclined to make any concession; instead of 15 000 piastres, he now wants 18 000. This is an enormous price to pay for the minor inconvenience we shall cause him. But he is a rogue who is trying to profit from our present predicament. Discussions resumed after lunch and Louis, wishing to safeguard the interests of his government, highlighted the assistance which the crew of the *Uranie* had rendered the *Mercury* since its arrival, for without our help it is unlikely that the captain would have been able to carry out the repairs. Nothing could sway our miser. Finally, caught between the dreadful alternatives of being stranded here or of accepting his outrageous conditions, our officers decided to write down the terms of the agreement, having been unable to knock a penny off the price. The captain is refusing to let one person or one item of baggage go on board until payment has been made. Louis rejected this clause out of hand, very hurt that the captain had proposed it. Contrite, the latter assured Louis that he had expressed himself badly and meant to say that all the baggage ought to be brought on board within eight days so as not to delay the departure.

The conference continued until around 4 p.m. The captain needed to return to his ship and has agreed that tomorrow morning he will sign the duplicate copies of the agreement which are to be drafted.

At last, almost all my boxes have been transported on board and I think that tomorrow we will be in a position to join them. We are short of all kinds of supplies; penguins are becoming so scarce that they no longer constitute a resource for us. Not one goose has been sighted and tomorrow no-one, from the Commander to the ship's boy, will have a morsel of meat to eat. To start using the supplies set aside for the voyage would be imprudent, especially as nothing else can be salvaged from the *Uranie* and we have just enough for the voyage, which could be long and made more difficult by unfavourable winds. At last, it is time to leave a country where we would most probably have died of hunger and thirst. God knows how a hundred men would behave in such a dreadful predicament! This is what our Jew is fully conscious of and what makes him so demanding.

15 April 1820 – It is now two months since the *Uranie* ran aground on the sand of the Malouines, never to rise again. This reflection makes us all the sadder because disaster struck toward the end of our mission, just before we were due to return to our homeland and after two and a half years of an incident-free and peaceful voyage. Such are the decrees of Providence and we must submit to them. Will I be able at least, after so many trials and tribulations, to see my friends and my native land once more? That is my only wish. I would spurn wealth and long only for a cottage where I could live happily with my mother and my dear friend! What a happy day it will be when I can hold you against my heart!

This morning, M. Requin and Louis, after conferring with MM. Duperrey and Lamarche, have thought fit to appeal to the captain against the decisions taken yesterday. Louis was reluctant to do so, being of the view that the captain would not consent to our officers' wishes not to sign any agreement here, but to refer the price to experts who would be nominated on our arrival in a Christian country. But Louis' duty to his government demanded that he should accept the views of the majority and, as all the others were of a contrary opinion to his, it was agreed that their proposal would be put to the captain, who arrived at the camp while deliberations were still in progress. He declared that they ought not to break off negotiations with him and said many unpleasant things. The officers put forward contrary arguments. Fortunately, the interpreter, who was one of the passengers, and Louis, who understood perfectly what was being said by both parties, moderated their expressions a little and succeeded in pacifying both sides.

The captain said that he would offer us passage as a humane gesture but that he would stick to his original destination, Valparaiso, because the repairs which we had carried out had been so successful that his ship was now in a fit state to round Cape Horn, etc. Then, our officers asked to meet in private to discuss this.

Meanwhile, I chatted with the captain and offered him something to eat and drink and, after half an hour, he was recalled to the meeting. All the arguments of our officers became void and they agreed unanimously to revert to last night's conditions, happy that he had not stipulated new ones. However, that is precisely what he proceeded to do! He declared that he was not the one who broke off negotiations but that, as this had happened, he had given more thought to the losses he would incur, and that he would not be able to transport us for less than 20 000 piastres. Louis and our officers stressed all the assistance we had offered him and what he had already received, in order to induce him to abide by the previous terms. Finally, he consented, adding one further proviso that we would be leaving in five days and that anything not transported on board by then would be left behind.

To speed things up, the committee agreed to announce that we had only three days left and, as an incentive, the men were given double rations.

16 April 1820, On board the Mercury – At last, here I am on board a foreign ship, but not the one which will take me back to my beloved France. *Uranie*! Poor *Uranie*! You who were my abode for so long, you who transported us over such vast expanses, you in whom I had hoped to return to France, we must now forsake you forever!

May you, dear Caroline, read these lines and pity the dear friend who has penned them! Her heart is full of anguish, and her own life is a burden to her after months of suffering and misery. But all will be forgotten if she returns home safely.

The conference had delayed the loading of various items which Louis wished to take charge of personally, so that midday was upon us and there was still a great deal to do. Our bed had been transported on board in the morning and we could not, therefore, go back on our decision.

The hunters, who had killed a horse at some distance from the camp, led us to believe that we would have meat for dinner. It was 2 p.m. and the boat had brought nothing. In the circumstances, unable to go aboard until nightfall, I resolved to have a cow slaughtered for us and the crew.

The captain was detained in the camp by our officers, who pressed him to have dinner with them, and he left to return to his ship soon afterwards. It was night when we reached the vessel.

It took us a long time to get there. As the night was very dark, we sailed a little too close to a promontory and ran aground, but only for a short while. We were made very welcome by the captain and the passengers, and while some of our effects were being carried to our small room, we took tea with a little bread and butter. I slept like a log, though only for a short time; the substitution of a well-protected room for a tent, and a thousand thoughts, both sad and comforting, made me restless and kept me awake during part of the night.

Louis returned to the camp to give orders and to bring back various objects which could not be transported in the dark.

We are to eat our meals with the captain and the passengers in the large quarters occupied by the latter, where they have their bunks. Louis did not return until around 6 o'clock.

17 April 1820 – I slept very little tonight because of the worries which the wind caused me. Louis, who is too tired to go back to the camp, has had our bedroom tidied up. However spacious it may be in proportion to the ship, it has to hold so many objects that there is hardly enough space left for us to sit beside our beds. The only natural light comes in through a small round piece of glass, and each time someone steps on it, we are left in darkness. Our hunters have shot some geese at one end of the bay where they are plentiful and each day they send us a sufficient number to feed everyone.

18 April 1820 – Early this morning, Louis returned ashore to supervise part of the camp being packed up. Our room is still being tidied, so that we might be tolerably comfortable, but we cannot be given an inch more of space and that is what we need most.

To have a better idea of its size, imagine two narrow couches facing the same way, and between them there is barely enough space for a chair. These couches are about five and a half feet long. At the end of one is a small wardrobe and at the end of the other a small narrow door. Men must be insane to go to sea in such matchboxes, but I can assure you that I would gladly give up half again of my quarters to shorten the length of the voyage that lies ahead of us and to find myself back in France much earlier.

Around 4 p.m., a small brig was sighted sailing into the bay; fog prevented us from seeing its flag. We guessed that it was a Scottish brig, engaged in hunting seals around the islands, which had been anchored for a while in a northern port of the large island. Louis came back from the camp quite early and brought back our last few remaining belongings. The officers also arrived and took up their posts. The midshipmen have been on board for two days.

19 April 1820 – The ship sighted yesterday is not a brig, but a three-master, the *Andrew Hammond*, which has been whaling in the South Seas with extraordinary success. The cargo, which was scheduled to have been completed in three years, had been taken on in only two years, so that the captain was in a position to give us some biscuits in exchange for rigging. The captain joined us on board for lunch. He seemed so elated with his success that he almost lost his head over it.

20 April 1820 – We are still not ready to cast off; all the fresh water has not been taken on board, but Louis is so unwell that he has been unable to leave his bed. As the whaler is going directly to London where it plans to arrive in 60 days' time, I am busily writing a few letters to my mother, to you and to my father-in-law. How I wish I could travel in one of these letters and reach France in two months! It seems to me that the day I set foot on French soil will be the day of my resurrection, for I am truly almost dead from pain. I feel that all my courage is deserting me and I cannot stop crying day and night. I am so agitated and tormented that I cannot sleep a wink. As a result, I suffer from dreadful headaches. Louis is continually in pain, a sight which is not likely to comfort me. I find it all the more difficult to take my meals with these strangers because I have never been in the habit of doing so. As well, I have the added worry of being in charge of providing food for the table, as the captain's resources are limited. The hunters no longer supply us with game, and they are running out of leadshot. I had no alternative but to have one of the pigs slaughtered, but their condition is not what it used to be. During our stay on land, they were fed to a large extent on penguin flesh and have begun to smell so strongly of those animals that I who loathe penguin flesh cannot bring myself to eat the pork. However, our famished passengers have devoured it as though it were delicious. I intend taking charge of distributing the food, for I do not want the four of us to contribute more than the six of them. Today, they are short of coffee; I don't mind providing them with some. It is the coffee which was soaked during the shipwreck, although I have had it washed and dried and it is quite fit for drinking.

21 April 1820 – I am still very perturbed and I don't quite know where this will end; I am afraid that I may become ill. I fell asleep at 2 a.m. but by 4 a.m. I was wide awake. I resort to prayer to try to recover my courage; it deserts me every time I compare our present circumstances with what they were three months ago. Then we were well housed, well fed, about to complete a voyage which up to that point had been entirely successful, and here we are now in a miserable foreign vessel, in a room where we cannot both sit down without touching either the walls or the bed, eating indescribable food with strangers to whom one has to be pleasant and whom I would often like to send packing, one because of his bad manners, another because of his pride, and still others because of their pretentiousness and silly self-centredness. To list all their foibles for you would be an endless task!

I am most distressed to see Louis suffering continually. This saddens me and troubles me so much that I cannot stop crying.

22 April 1820 – This morning Louis received a letter from Captain Galvin informing him that for a number of reasons, because we had not loaded all the baggage of the *Uranie* on board in five days as agreed, and because he had not received a copy of the contract, again as had been promised (all this was stated verbally and was thus not binding), he, Captain Galvin, believed that the signed contract had been breached and he felt under no obligation to offer us passage to Rio de Janeiro, etc. Although in his sick bed, Louis asked the captain to come and see him; he proved that his allegations were unsubstantiated and assured him that the agreement was still valid, that he would provide further explanation in a letter as soon as his health permitted him to do so. Our poor Jew did not know what to reply and looked very silly. It seems that the news of our passage to Rio has been leaked and his passengers have threatened to summon him to appear before the Spanish Consul and to make him pay enormous compensation. Hence his letter to Louis. My poor husband is worn out after that distressing conversation.

23 April 1820 – Louis has given orders for the hunters to be fetched and for their camp to be packed up. The other boats have been dispatched to bring back the remaining equipment and the crew.

24 April 1820 – I continue to see to the correspondence. Still unwell, Louis dictated to me part of his letter to the Minister. The weather is foul; the tempestuous gales make us fear for the safety of several boats out at sea. This does not prevent the captain and the passengers from dining on board the English whaler. They returned very late at night, and I think that they must have drunk too much of his wine, which is very good and which they have been deprived of for some time. M. Lamarche went on board our poor wrecked vessel to remove various small items and found that everything was smashed or damaged and that several things had been stolen, including a beautiful mirror which used to stand in the poop-deck. He had no doubt that the culprit was Captain Orne who, believing that no-one would go back to the *Uranie*, had taken what he wanted. M. Lamarche headed straight for our old camp, where he knew he would find the captain, to accuse him of the theft, hoping at least to recover the mirror. Orne was lost for words but assured us that his sailors had gone on board the *Uranie* without his consent, and that he believed the mirror was in the sloop and he would send it to the *Mercury* the following morning.

25 April 1820 – The correspondence was completed this morning; Louis is sending his mail via the English whaler. Although he feels a little better, he is still not out of bed. Our captain has raised more difficulties concerning some topmasts which M. Lamarche had brought on board and placed on the deck. He arrived in a huff to tell Louis that the weight was excessive and that this endangered his ship. After some discussion regarding the fact that the ship was overloaded, it was agreed to jettison half of the goods at sea. It is a great loss, since these masts would have been most useful on the ship which we plan to purchase in Rio, where wood from the north is very expensive. My husband has received a most obliging letter from the Scottish captain whose brig is anchored 20 leagues from here. Although his offer arrived too late, it seems to have been made in good faith. Captain Hales, to whom Louis offered a medal when he entrusted him with some packages for France, has sent my husband six beautiful whale's teeth and two samples of spermaceti oil. Tonight the Scottish captain came to visit Louis who offered him his rigged rowboat; as we cannot take it with us, Louis thought that it would be useful to the captain for fishing. He appeared to be very grateful and told us that, out of greed, Captain Orne had concealed the tragedy which had befallen the *Uranie*, and that he had heard about it from that American rogue only after he arrived in the bay with his schooner. He asked for an official document stating that the rowboat has been presented to him, fearing probably that Captain Orne would challenge his ownership of it. I have heard that he asked what my name was and has called this small sloop *The Rose*.

26 April 1820 – We are preparing to sail. But the wind is so strong that the captain has been forced to postpone weighing anchor. Louis is vexed, for with the breeze being fresh, albeit contrary, we should be taking advantage of it. To all the fine qualities displayed by our captain should be added his cowardice!

Back at sea – Purchase of rescue ship, renamed the Physicienne –
Montevideo – Reception ashore (dinners, balls and parties) –
Farewells – Stopover in Rio de Janeiro – Arrival in Cherbourg

April 1820 – On 27 April, as the wind had abated a little, we decided to
weigh anchor and at 9 a.m. we were under sail. We faced into the wind for
four hours to load the boats and although our captain tried to speed things
up a little, the manoeuvres were not, for all that, any better executed.
What took four hours in the *Mercury* would have been completed in just
half an hour by the crew of the *Uranie*. Louis received a letter from Captain
Hales asking him not to believe the rumours circulating that he was
staying behind, after our departure, to pillage the *Uranie*. My husband
replied in a very courteous letter that he had too high an opinion of
Captain Hales to believe him capable of such unworthy conduct. The
master caulker has reported that the ship is letting in only two inches
of water per hour, which is a big improvement on the 120 inches it was
taking in on its arrival. Around 4 p.m. we sailed out of the bay. The sea
is choppy and the ship is labouring to such an extent that everyone on
board feels sick. Even I am seasick; fortunately, the nausea goes away
when I lie down.

28 April 1820 – The wind and the sea are tempestuous. I stay in bed
for fear of being seasick. We lie to all day, that is to say that we use only
one or two sails to steer the ship. It labours excessively and is shipping
water from many waves. During dinner, I heard a loud noise coming from
the main quarters, as if water had gushed in. A sudden fear came over
me when, stepping down to see what might have caused the noise, I
felt water under my feet. As I opened the door, I saw only one or two
Englishmen in the area; the rest of the passengers and Louis had gone on
deck. I anxiously enquired what was happening; someone reassured me
and told me that it was nothing more than two or three waves which had
removed one of the rear windows and had flooded the main quarters.
As my first thought had been of the ship sinking, this explanation was
a welcome relief.

The Church of Notre Dame
de Bon Voyage, overlooking
Rio de Janeiro harbour

Jean Desaulx
Vue de Notre-Dame de Bon
Voyage (Rade de Rio de Janeiro)
c.1822
engraving; plate mark 23.7 x
32.4 cm
Louis-Claude de Freycinet, *Voyage*
autour du Monde ... Exécuté sur les
Corvettes de S.M. l'Uranie et la
Physicienne pendant les Années
1817–1820: Atlas Historique (Paris:
Chez Pillet Aîné, 1825), plate no. 4
Rex Nan Kivell Collection
National Library of Australia
Pictorial Collection (S7225)

29 April 1820 – The wind is abating, but the sea remains rough and the ship is still labouring. Once again I spend a good part of the day in bed. I am not bored because the passengers have lent me English books which I find easy to read, although I am far from being able to speak the language fluently. I become more and more adventurous, but I realise how difficult the English language is. One may understand a conversation quite well, and especially something one reads, while being at a loss to say the slightest thing. Among other works, I have read a book by Fielding which is quite inferior to *Tom Jones*. It is written in the same style as *Roderick Random*, also by Fielding.

Louis, who is now completely recovered, is busy replying to the captain's letter. He points out that the captain cannot go anywhere else but to Rio de Janeiro and draws his attention to the fact that this is in the interests of his expedition. Finally, he intimates that if the captain does not agree of his own free will, he would be compelled to do so. I must confess that I wish with all my heart that he will accede to our request of his own accord, for what an extreme course of action it would be to use force!

As the weather has improved tonight, I am able to leave my bed and dine in the main quarters. It is one of the greatest vexations of our passage that we have to be in the company of insignificant strangers, the majority of whom are ill-mannered, while the rest have such strange habits that they sometimes disgust me. Frequently at the table

Rio de Janeiro harbour
E. Aubert
Baie de Rio de Janeiro: Vue de Praya Grande c.1822
engraving; 23.8 x 32 cm
Louis-Claude de Freycinet, *Voyage autour du Monde ... Exécuté sur les Corvettes de S.M. l'Uranie et la Physicienne ... : Atlas Historique* (Paris: Chez Pillet Aîné, 1825), plate no. 5
Rex Nan Kivell Collection
National Library of Australia
Pictorial Collection (S7226)

they place a morsel on their plate which they have already started to eat, and if they don't like it, they put it back in the dish. Moreover, they are in the habit of helping themselves to the food by using their own forks. Fortunately, I am served first and I am careful not to take a second helping from any dish.

1 May 1820 – It seems that our captain is in a fine mess. His passengers have threatened to seize his ship if he persists on making for Rio, and Louis cannot agree to any other destination. Accordingly, he has asked Louis to permit him to stop for one or two days in Montevideo to allow his passengers to disembark. But seeing that Louis has granted this request, he also wants him to guarantee that his ship will not be seized by the Spanish Consul and the authorities in Rio. As you would realise, because he has no say in this matter, my husband has indicated that he cannot give such a guarantee. There is indeed a real danger that the captain's ship might be seized and that he might be imprisoned, as he is carrying weapons for the rebels and does not have an American commission, even though he flies their flag occasionally.

2 May 1820 – The weather is splendid, the sea beautiful. Louis and I are in good health. The captain, still in a dreadful dilemma, has just made another plea to Louis. But since the political situation in Buenos Aires is not at all favourable to the expedition's preparations for the return journey to France, it is stipulated in the contract that if he stops there, he will not be entitled to his fee. However, he is greedy for money and he would not like to forfeit the 18 000 piastres we have promised to pay him for our passage to Rio. All this puts him in a most difficult position. He has no idea how to resolve this problem.

3 May 1820 – The weather is still superb and we have already noticed a marked change in the temperature, although in this hemisphere it is winter. Very early this morning a French ship was sighted. We established contact with it; the captain came on board the *Mercury*. It is a whaler from Le Havre, the *Harponneur*, which is fishing along the coast. But the large number of whalers competing in this area prevents the fishing from being lucrative. The whaler has caught only three whales in five months since its departure from Le Havre. The captain informed Louis that there are no less than 100 ships in the vicinity engaged in the same type of fishing and that sailing here is very perilous. It often happens that 16 or 17 vessels are within sight of one another. As the favourable season for whaling is about to start, he hopes to be more successful along the African coast and plans

Theatre, Rio de Janeiro
Jean Nicolas Lerouge (b.1776)
Vue de la Salle de Spectacle sur la Place Do Rocio, à Rio de Janeiro
c.1822
engraving; 23.8 x 32 cm
Louis-Claude de Freycinet, *Voyage autour du Monde ... Exécuté sur les Corvettes de S.M. l'Uranie et la Physicienne ... : Atlas Historique* (Paris: Chez Pillet Aîné, 1825), plate no. 7
Rex Nan Kivell Collection
National Library of Australia
Pictorial Collection (S7228)

to return to France in 14 months' time. He did not want to stay for lunch and returned without delay to his ship.

The captain of the *Mercury* has made a new proposal: he is now asking Louis to buy his ship from him at the price agreed for our passage to Rio de Janeiro, plus 2000 piastres. Louis called a council meeting which considered the proposal. The officers argued that the captain would receive 18 000 piastres for our passage to Rio in any case and that we would have nothing to show for it. On the other hand, if they convinced him to give up the extra 2000 piastres which he was asking for the ship, for the same outlay as we would pay for our passage, we would have a ship all rigged out and armed, which perhaps would not require many repairs. The captain agreed to the conditions laid down by these gentlemen. The bill of sale was drafted and translated into English. Now, it has been agreed that the ship is no longer his, but that he remains in command until Montevideo where we shall stop for three days only, just long enough for him to offload his goods and passengers. Thereafter, Louis will take possession of her, fitted out as she is at sea, with her cannons, masts, etc ... She will be renamed the *Physicienne*. All this is preferable to coming to blows, for in his response to Louis, the captain stated that if my husband decided to take his ship by storm, he would meet with strong resistance. Think of the impression this would create if news were to break that the crew of the *Uranie*, after being rescued by a foreign ship, had attacked her captain and seized his ship, etc. ... People would see only the heinous

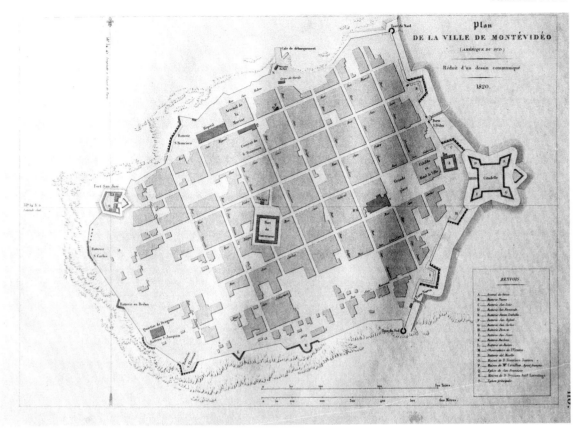

crime, and no-one would dare say that this foreigner had taken
advantage of our situation by blackmailing us and had refused to fulfil
his pledge to take us to Rio; in brief, that he wanted to put us ashore
in a country in the grip of a revolution, where we would have found
neither resources nor protection ... I repeat, people would see only one
side of the story, and this would be detrimental to the honour of France.

4 May 1820 – It is so fine today and the heat is beginning to be so
oppressive in our small prison that I have decided to go on deck for a
breath of fresh air. I spend very little time on deck, for I still have a lot
to do to fix one or two dresses, as almost all of mine were lost during the
shipwreck. They were in a trunk which could not be salvaged in time and
was completely submerged in seawater. The colour of the trunk's lining,
of the wood and of the locks has come out on to the clothes and I don't
think it will ever fade. Furthermore, it so happened, sadly, that all my
muslin and embroidered percaline dresses, which had been well pressed
at Port Jackson, were in the only trunk which was soaked. Fortunately,
I had pieces of percaline and muslin which I am now stitching together.

Map of Montevideo

Plan de la Ville de Montévidéo
1820
Louis-Claude de Freycinet, *Voyage
autour du Monde ... Exécuté sur les
Corvettes de S.M. l'Uranie et la
Physicienne ... : Atlas Historique* (Paris:
Chez Pillet Aîné, 1825), plate no. 110
Rex Nan Kivell Collection
National Library of Australia
Pictorial Collection (S7321)

5 and 6 May 1820 – These last two days have been very dull for me. Calm weather and light breezes have detained us almost in the same spot. However, the breeze is a little fresher today.

What seems quite extraordinary, especially to one who is not at all familiar with the approaches to the Rio de la Plata, is that we are sailing in only ten fathoms of water without sighting land. I was reassured and told that, depending on the approach, one sometimes sails in four fathoms, and yet land can only be sighted from the top of the masts. The sea along the coast is exceedingly low and one must consult reliable charts of previous soundings to establish one's position by the depth. I am fed up with our passengers; they are so peculiar that it is a strain for me to be at the same table with such barbarians. One of them calls himself an envoy of the French and Spanish governments to the rebels and puts on airs, but he looks like no-one of any significance. To cap it all, with the heat intensifying, our cabin has become unbearable; we have no window; there is little fresh air nor does it circulate if the door is left open.

7 May 1820 – At last we are sailing upstream but the breeze is so light that the ship is hardly moving forward. At sunset, the sky was aglow with lightning which flashed in different directions. Around 8 p.m., a dreadful storm broke; first, there was thunder, followed by strong gusts of wind. I was terrified, knowing that we were not far from land and in the middle of sandbanks. We hoisted small sails but the storm died down after a few hours.

8 May 1820 – It is foggy this morning and, although the captain estimates that he is 7 or 8 leagues from land, he cannot see it because of the fog. As he does not know his exact position in the middle of the sandbanks which surround Montevideo, our American captain furls all his sails and at 8 a.m. drops anchor in 5 fathoms. Around midday, we get under sail again because the captain recognises the entrance to the harbour at a spot where he believes he can see a brig leaving. The breeze is fresh and at 6 p.m. we anchor near the town. In the harbour, there are a superb English vessel and a shabby Portuguese frigate. As it is dark already, no boat will be sent out to the town tonight.

9 May 1820 – This morning M. Lamarche went to pay his respects to the Governor and to explain our situation to him. He was made most welcome. The Governor speaks French fluently.

The news from France is distressing; several European princes have died. Louis received on board a number of captains of French merchant ships. He went to pay a visit in person to the Governor and the Admiral. They received him well, as did a French merchant who acts as French Consul. He also met a French General, named Brayer. I derive great pleasure from eating European fruit, such as peaches, apples, etc ..., which are plentiful here.

10 May 1820 – Our passengers are not hastening to vacate their quarters. Two, however, have booked a passage on an English vessel this morning and have removed their belongings, thereby ridding us of their trunks. Louis went ashore to dine at the home of M. Cavaillon. He only returned about 6 p.m. He informed me that a Spanish merchant, an intimate friend of M. Cavaillon and of his brother-in-law, had most graciously offered us quarters in his home for the duration of our stay in Montevideo, which Louis was forced to accept on account of the repeated pleas of M. Cavaillon whose home is not large enough to accommodate us.

11 May 1820 – I have, therefore, decided to go ashore, as my health is not the best and I worry about falling ill on board. Around midday, I left in a boat and set foot for the second time in America, now notorious for its upheavals and revolutions. I have been greeted in the most charming and sincere manner possible by M. and Mme Juanico who beseech us to look upon their home as our own and insist that they are genuinely pleased to have us as their guests. Mme Juanico is a woman in her thirties who was once exceedingly pretty and still is. Her husband and she are unaffected and are the kindest people in the world. All ceremony is banned from their house. Although I found this very pleasant, the first few moments spent in their company were a little strange, as I have become accustomed to the stiffness of the English.

We dined at 2 p.m. and after dinner we went to spend the evening at the home of a relative of M. Juanico, whose birthday it was. I had a lot of fun meeting this family of 14 children, several of whom are married. Their parents, though quite old, were cheerful and in good health. We danced all night, the kind papa as much as everyone else. Spanish women dance a lot of minuets quite instinctively, without any formal training. As a rule, they are graceful and have pretty feet. Their dances resemble English ones in their formations, but the tempo is much slower.

12 May 1820 – As my doctors have advised me that hot milk can help me recover, M. Juanico is kind enough to send me some every morning. My thinness scares me. It is much more noticeable now when I undress than it was on board. I am pale, yellowish and have sunken eyes; in short, I look like a ghost. Louis goes on board each morning to discuss business with Captain Galvin, who is extremely greedy. We are able to read French newspapers.

On 13 May, Louis and the Abbé paid their respects to the Governor on the occasion of the birthday of the King of Portugal. They dined at his residence that night. There was a ball in town but we were not invited. Louis was very surprised that the Governor had not invited the staff of the corvette to dinner; the Governor apologised, alleging that his premises were too small. At 8 p.m., invitations to the ball arrived. Our clothes were still on board, and as the weather was dreadful in the harbour, I was obliged to miss the ball, which I would have enjoyed. Louis attended and noticed a lot of beautiful women dressed very elegantly in expensive clothes; almost all had beautiful ankles!

I hardly go out, being very weak; shopping tires me out, but I am not bored because the Juanico family are so charming. M. Juanico himself is very fond of music. Having found a piano and having more free time, I have resumed singing and playing. We have guests almost every night. Among the people who have come to make our acquaintance was the Chevalier de l'Hotte, an extremely amiable gentleman whom Louis had already met at the Governor's residence. He is a true knight of old; he has that characteristic air and deportment: tall, thin, handsome, with lively eyes and a small curled-up moustache which gives his face an unusual appearance; he is tactful, distinguished, very gallant towards women and pleasant to everyone. He is an Italian who has served for some time in Austria and is at present in the service of the King of Portugal. He is on the military staff of the fortress and is well respected by his soldiers. His conversation, enlivened by his natural wit, is very varied on account of his travels in almost all the civilised countries of Europe. He speaks French and English quite fluently and I believe that he has learnt German during a long stay in Vienna. He also knows Portuguese, as well as his own native language. All this makes him good company among foreigners here. His behaviour is so eccentric that, on first meeting him, one would think him peculiar, but one needs to get to know him to appreciate all his personal qualities fully.

20 May 1820 – I have been busy all morning writing letters to be sent to Gibraltar. They were finished around 1 p.m. After lunch, I sat at the piano until nightfall. Mme Chapus arrived tonight with several officers. We also had a visit from the Chevalier de l'Hotte. He had lent his album to Louis who, upon returning it, offered him a medal of the expedition, which seemed to please him greatly.

21 May 1820 – Whit Sunday. I went to the Abbé's mass very early in the morning and, as the weather was splendid, we went for a short walk on the outskirts of the town with the Juanico family. We made the acquaintance of Colonel Frangini, a pleasant Portuguese who is well educated and busies himself with art. He draws, paints ... and speaks French fluently. He served in France in 1814 with the troops of the Duke of Wellington. He has put his private box at our disposal, and we often take advantage of it. The theatre is small and, although the plays are in Portuguese, I am sufficiently familiar with this language to follow them. We also saw ballets which were very well performed. The contrast between our experiences in the Malouines and our stay here leads me to enjoy this kind of spectacle even more than I would have done in the old days.

We spent a day in the country with M. Juanico. The surrounding districts of Montevideo have been devastated during recent wars, but the soil seems very fertile. M. Juanico's house is located on the bank of a small river which runs into the harbour, a short distance from his garden. Hence, one can reach his home by sea. However, some of us travelled in M. Juanico's carriage and others went on horseback. The house has been damaged by the soldiers who have occupied it, but its location is very pleasant. It was in the process of being repaired. The gardens are well stocked and carefully looked after. We had dinner under the trees, in a grove close to the river. The scene was idyllic. My health is a lot better, a fact which I noticed during this outing in the country where I went for walks without feeling too tired. At Mme Juanico's house, we frequently met French people who took a great deal of interest in us. Among them were Captain Kervan and M. Morez, a very noble gentleman who repeatedly offered us his services.

6 June 1820 – As he had to go on board today, Louis took his leave of various people this morning. While I was getting ready to go and bid farewell to Mme Chapus, she arrived to be with me during the last moments of my stay on land. Our hosts made us stay for dinner once more and, soon after, we set off towards the landing. All day, I had a heavy heart, not just at the thought of leaving behind a family who had heaped kindness on me, but appalled above all by the prospect of putting out to sea in our wretched ship. I was extremely depressed, for this last month, spent on pleasure and entertainment, seemed so short and so different from the kind of life which I had led for the last few months. With a sorrowful heart, I dragged myself to the harbour where the attractive boat of the customs chief awaited us. All the ladies who had accompanied me to that point wanted to make the most of a superb day and went aboard with us. I was somewhat ashamed to receive them in our ugly vessel and especially in our hideous bedroom. I asked for their indulgence; I offered them white wine and pastries, which fortunately I had bought for us. Night fell and they returned to town. I was deeply moved when I kissed the amiable Mme Juanico goodbye.

7 June 1820 – Preparations are underway on board the *Physicienne* to set sail. Captain Hervaux is already alongside us with his schooner; he is tacking as he waits for us. Louis ordered a 29-gun salute for the fortress which returned a 16-gun one. He was about to lodge a complaint when the Chief of Staff, with whom he had been on good terms during his stay in Montevideo and who had come to bid him farewell, went ashore promptly to remedy this situation. Indeed, a few moments later, the salute was returned, this time in full. A salute was then given for the Admiral, and the Portuguese frigate duly returned it. The wits on our ship, commenting on the noise made by the poor cannons of the *Physicienne*, claimed that the tremors and sound made by the cannons of the Portuguese frigate were more noticeable on board than those of our wretched barge. At last, around 11 a.m., we set sail and the wind, having changed direction, remained favourable long enough to allow us to round the dangerous headlands. That night, the breeze was light and contrary; once more we dropped anchor. Having moored his schooner alongside the ship, the captain came to visit us, and as we had not yet dined, he sat down to dinner with us. The night was peaceful, and scarcely had day dawned than the *Physicienne* set off on her way again. The schooner came with us until we had rounded Flore Island and the English reef so fatal to ships. It went ahead of us as far as possible and guided us through those difficult channels. At midday, we bade farewell to the captain and the schooner headed towards Buenos Aires where M. Hervaux was to take on a cargo of leather.

10 June 1820 – Yesterday the wind was contrary, and today the weather has become very stormy. The sea is very rough and our bowsprit broke off level with the deck. The crew tried to salvage the rigging, but the weather was so tempestuous that they were forced to let it all fall into the sea. We were extremely lucky that, as it was dragged alongside the ship, it did not cause any damage. I went through agony when I heard this news, for I knew that all the other masts were attached to the bowsprit and that its loss might have severed them. Indeed, a few minutes later, with the sea still stormy, I was informed that the foremast had just snapped. I commended my soul to God, but this last rumour was fortunately without foundation. The mast had indeed been badly shaken and had suffered some damage, but it had not broken and was able to be repaired.

In a heavy swell, M. Lamarche suffered a rather serious fall and his temple was pierced by a nail. He lost consciousness and took a long time to come to. His wound was not critical, but he was covered in bruises.

The weather is too bad for the bowsprit to be replaced. This damage is especially unfortunate in that it slows down our progress and forces us to stay longer in these fatal seas. The wind has abated a little tonight but the sea is still choppy.

11 June 1820 – As the sea was not as rough today, the crew were able to replace the bowsprit. The carpenters have worked on it all day. M. Lamarche has not yet recovered, but this does not prevent him from going on deck to supervise the repairs; he cannot be persuaded to stay in his room. Yesterday, we suffered a very sad loss in view of the possible repercussions; the sea dragged away a boat which had been hoisted at the stern. This same boat unfortunately contained the hay destined for my poor merino sheep during the voyage to Rio, the only survivor of the pair from Port Jackson.

15 June 1820 – The sea continues to be very rough, although the wind is a little lighter. I feel dreadfully tired from all the rolling, which is much harder on the body than it was in the *Uranie*. M. Lamarche is much better; he no longer feels the effect of his fall. A ship is sighted and identified as the *Bacchus*, a French vessel which was taking on a cargo of mules in Montevideo during our stay there and which set sail a few hours after us. We were shocked by her lack of consideration for us; she saw the pitiful state of our ship, as we had not yet managed to repair the bowsprit because of the bad weather, and yet she sailed to windward of us without offering any help, which fortunately we did not need.

17 June 1820 – The sea is a little calmer and, with the wind becoming quite fresh and favourable, we sighted land early this morning. We hope to enter the harbour tonight, but the breeze has died down and we are obliged to spend the night carrying small sails.

18 June 1820 – I would have sworn that we were due to spend the night in the harbour and that we would see our friends today, but an almost dead calm has detained us during the entire day at the entrance to the harbour. And tonight will be just like last night. I am sorry for my poor Louis, who cannot go to bed when we are near land, and this has been the case for several nights. On the other hand, this short delay is useful to me, for it allows me to put the finishing touches to a black silk dress which I purchased in Montevideo for fear that the French Embassy in Rio might still be mourning the death of the Duc de Berry and that I might need to pay my respects in person to the Ambassador's wife. We notice several ships coming out of Rio and a small schooner which, like us, is waiting to sail into the harbour.

20 June 1820 – Yesterday we spent the entire day tacking, and it was not until around 8 p.m. that we were able to enter the harbour. When we rounded the channel, which is quite dangerous because of its strong currents, the wind abated suddenly and we were forced to drop anchor immediately to avoid being dragged once more towards the coast by the current which pulled strongly in that direction. When the breeze freshened up, Louis decided to cast anchor outside the harbour, so as to be sheltered from the weather if it were to deteriorate. He thought it wiser to sail into the harbour in daylight. This morning, the wind was more favourable and, just as we were about to get underway, a pilot arrived and offered to guide us to a safe anchorage. The breeze was fresh and in no time at all we entered the harbour. On this occasion, we have anchored at the far end of the harbour to carry out necessary repairs.

There are countless ships here, among them several English vessels and other warships. As we went past all those ships, we felt quite ashamed of the unwarlike appearance of our *Physicienne*, for, in addition to the damage incurred during the voyage, she was generally in poor condition. She looked so unlike a state-owned vessel that the city's merchants sent envoys to enquire if our ship was the *Cecilia* from Le Havre, the *Mutuelle* from Marseilles, etc … I must admit that I felt humiliated and, to cap it all, customs officers came on board for an official visit. They almost felt like crawling into a hole when Louis proudly explained to them that their presence was unwarranted because his was a military vessel.

Soon after our arrival, we received the usual visits from Portuguese officers. Louis sent his respects to the Admiral of the port and went with the purser to see the French Consul to discuss without delay the arrangements to be made for the ship.

While Louis was ashore, I had a visit from a Frenchman who is a merchant here and whom I had met during my first stay. I was delighted to see him again; I have the feeling that I have already set foot back in France by meeting such old friends again ... He gave me some news of our native land. I found very few newspapers here which contained more up-to-date news than that which we had received in Montevideo. I was very pleased to hear that Mme Sumter was still here with her family and that pregnancy had prevented her from leaving for America. The French Ambassador has not yet arrived; he is expected any day. We found only two French merchant ships in the harbour and not a single French warship.

21 June 1820 – Louis has not received any important dispatches. He found our Gascon in the same frame of mind. He invited Louis to dinner today and also sent me an invitation, but as Louis knew that I would not enjoy the occasion, he thanked him but declined, saying that I had no intention of going ashore until we found a house to stay in.

My husband left this morning to go to the harbour to pay his respects to the Portuguese Consul and to the English Admiral who yesterday sent one of his officers to compliment Louis on his arrival. Louis must then go with the Consul to see the Navy Commander to request assistance with the repairs to our ship. All morning, I have been hastily writing a few lines to you, dear Caroline, to my dear mother and to M. and Mme Freycinet to inform them of our safe arrival in this port. My letters need to be quickly taken on board a ship leaving for Le Havre tomorrow morning. Louis went to Mme Sumter's house and found the three oldest daughters to be quite grown up, but all three were suffering from a rather severe bout of whooping cough. Their mother, also stricken, is pregnant and is staying in the country with her two youngest children.

22 June 1820 – Although we do not yet look warlike, we saluted the town, as well as the Admiral of the Fleet. This morning, accompanied by M. Lamarche, Louis went to select and reserve in the Royal Arsenal the items needed for our repairs. The Minister had already sent orders and our officers found that everyone was willing to help. Despite pains in his legs, the Comte de Gestas came very early this morning and agreed to have breakfast with us.

23 June 1820 – Today men came to unmoor and take the *Physicienne* to the naval dockyard, and thence alongside a former warship in which all our equipment will be temporarily stored and the officers and crew of the corvette billeted. I went ashore to see Mlle Durand, the sister of a wealthy French merchant who has settled here, and from there I went to visit Mme Sumter. We found them at the dinner table and sat down to dinner with them. I thought Mme Sumter's daughters really charming; the eldest, who is 17, has grown in beauty and is as fresh as a rose. The younger sister, who looks like her mother, appeals to me much more than the others; she has a sweet and melancholic face which I find enchanting. Unfortunately, her health is very delicate. The third daughter, although very pale and pleasant, will shine more on account of her lively mind and her rather eccentric behaviour. As I had seen a lot of their mother during my first voyage, they welcomed me with a great deal of warmth and kindness. I confess that I was equally delighted to see them.

Tonight, M. Sumter took me in his carriage to the house of M. Maler and Mme Gi... (a Spanish lady for whom M. Juanico of Montevideo had given me a letter of recommendation), and then to the home of M. Durand, where I had business to attend to. We received some news which I dreaded and which spread gloom among the officers of the *Physicienne*: the list of promotions for the year 1820 has been received and only two midshipmen have been promoted, while many others were entitled to be and were expecting it. It is truly disheartening to sacrifice one's happiness and peace of mind and to endanger one's life for such an ungrateful government!

24 June 1820 – I never see St John's Feast pass without remembering how dear this date is to us! A thousand memories flood into my mind, and I recall all the joyful moments we spent at my mother's side. How happy were those days of hope and enchantment, devoid of anxieties! Since they cannot be recaptured, I console myself reliving them in my mind. But the protagonists are so far from each other at present that my heart is full of sorrow. I have but one hope, to gather around me in my small cottage my mother, my sister and my Caroline, when I am finally able to cover the distance which still separates us! After asking God to bless a Jeanne who is so dear to me [Rose's mother?] and to bestow sweet comfort on her, I headed for the house of M. Durand who had invited Louis and me to dinner. From his window I was able to watch the procession on its way to pay homage to the King, who goes by the name of Jean. Louis has been presented to him by M. Maler. His Majesty recognised him and spoke very kindly to him, bidding him to return in order to recount his voyage. He was also presented to the Queen and princesses. It is said that he coped very well with the thousand bows, but that was because of a rehearsal conducted by the Consul the night before, which we had found most entertaining.

25 June 1820 – I dined with Mme Sumter. Other guests were present, including several Frenchmen and other citizens I had met during my previous visit. The next day, I was invited to dine at the Consul's residence. He was very courteous towards me and had me fetched and driven back in his carriage. His sisters are very kind-hearted and made me feel very welcome. We dined with Abbé Boiret, a French émigré ecclesiastic, who had for a long time been attached to the court as French tutor to the princes. I have already mentioned him to you during my first stop here; he is pleasant and very witty.

27 June 1820 – M. Maler came to see me on board and accepted our invitation to lunch. He left with Louis to visit the Admiral to thank him and the harbour master for the repairs to the corvette and to urge them to speed up the rest of the work. It is only today that the court has gone into mourning for the death of the Duc de Berry; this has been delayed by official mourning for other earlier deaths. We are obliged to wear black; I am vexed, for I shall have to purchase a richly ornamented dress, having only one silk dress which is rather simple. As mourning crepe, gauze and tulle are very expensive, I have been forced to choose a light black satin gown, with a lace bodice and crepe sleeves.

At last, a house has been found for us, but it is a long distance away. This has been an urgent matter, for the ship is about to go into dry dock for careening. Louis has gone to inspect the house and if within two days he has not found anything better, he will take it. Tonight, Louis went to visit the King at St Christopher with M. Maler. He was shown in after quarter of an hour and the King talked to him for half an hour about the voyage, the death of the Duc de Berry, etc ... My husband then went to pay a visit to the Minister for the Navy, who was out at the time.

28 June 1820 – I am weary from packing, but I press on. When shall I be peacefully settled in a house for a while, and shall I ever stop being moved from pillar to post? I think that I won't have the strength to get to the end; sometimes I believe my patience is about to run out and what remains of it is so altered that a mere trifle makes me impatient and cross, something which never used to happen before.

30 June 1820 – Yesterday, we dined at the house of the Abbé who gave us an excellent meal. Several French acquaintances of ours were present, as well as the Comte de Gestas who found me more melancholic than during my first stay here, while on the other hand, he found my husband to be in better spirits. It is true that everything I have endured during the last two years has given me such a sombre outlook on life that I have become a philosopher and that the gay, wild and scatterbrained Rose has become serious. As for Louis, he likes my company and is proud to be returning me in good health to those who never thought they would see me again. Moreover, as he has fulfilled his duty well and has achieved more during his voyage than could have been hoped for, he has an extremely clear conscience.

Today, Louis reserved the house which is located outside the town, for he has not found any other. While he went to dine at the house of the Prussian Ambassador, Count Flaming, where he found as many ambassadors as possible gathered, I sent some people to clean our new home. I plan to go ashore tomorrow morning.

1 July 1820 – At last around 11 a.m., we left in the rowboat with our baggage and our trunks and landed safely. However, we do not have a single piece of furniture! As M. Maler had promised us tables, chairs, beds, etc ..., Louis went to explain our predicament to him, namely that there was no furniture for hire in the town. He was not at home, but that night he promised that we would be able to collect a camp-bed the next day. I am writing to Mlle Durand to ask if she would be kind enough to send me a bedstead and some chairs.

Although we were tired, we were obliged to go and take tea at the house of Mme Lizaur and, worst of all, to go on foot. We were amply compensated for our pains, as we heard a musician play the guitar exceptionally well with an instrument no bigger than his hand. This man managed to produce some extraordinary and amazing sounds from it. Finally, we also saw an actor from the *Théâtre Italien* who sang very agreeably. By my side almost the whole evening sat the Spanish Ambassador, the Comte de Marialva, who is very pleasant, speaks French fluently and has very distinguished manners. From among the diplomatic corps, I cannot fail to single out the Marquis de Grimaldi, a Minister of the King of Sardinia, a very witty man. We spent the evening in the apartment of the secretary to the legation. He has a very fine piano on which he played some waltzes for us. I discovered many new pieces of French music and asked the secretary to be kind enough to lend me some of them. We retired early, as Louis was a little tired.

15 July 1820 – My husband had a visit from the English Minister who brought him his barometer, but he was so sick that he could hardly speak.

Yesterday, two officers called on us to ask after him; we were touched by their thoughtfulness.

16 July 1820 – Louis, who is still unwell, wanted at all costs to take me to the home of M. Maler, who had asked us to dinner and who was to take us to the Royal Chapel in the evening. My husband stayed behind at Mme Maler's while I went off with Mlles Maler and their brother to the chapel. I had the pleasure of being seated opposite the royal family, whom I could observe quite comfortably. My foreign face drew their gaze, but they knew my identity, the Consul having warned His Majesty that I would attend the service. The King is handsome but not very majestic. The Prince Royal is tall with a rather attractive face, but his manners are deplorable and he seems rather common. He wore brown tails and nankeen trousers, a somewhat absurd costume at 8 p.m. for a grand festival and a public appearance. Although simple, the King's apparel was much more suitable. Moreover, he is an elderly man who can be forgiven for most things. I could not find in the appearance of the Princess Royal the noble and ceremonial air of the Austrian court; she neglects her manner of dress here and has a slovenly look. For this festival (which can only be compared to a concert of sacred music given at the opera), everyone, including the princesses themselves, is dressed in silk or tulle dresses. Our poor Austrian was wearing a grey riding-coat made of a rather common cloth, with a pleated short-sleeved blouse; her hair was dishevelled and pinned up high with a tortoiseshell comb. Her face, however, is not unattractive and I am convinced that if she were properly dressed, she would look quite beautiful. All the other princesses were dressed in velvet or satin and wore either flowers or feathers in their hair. Princess Isabelle-Marie is now the eldest of the unmarried princesses; she is 18 and prettier than her two sisters, both still very young. The youngest looks witty and very alert. Isabelle is very kind but does not appear to have a lot of personal qualities. The eldest daughter is the widow of an Infante of Spain; in my view, she is the prettiest of them all and has a noble and distinguished appearance.

Although the ceremony was rather long, I did not get bored thanks to the beautiful music. I was charmed by the castratos who surpassed themselves that night.

After the service, we went to take our positions in one of the corridors adjoining the palace to see the King and his family pass. I curtseyed to them right down to the ground and I received gracious bows from each one of them. The ceremony finished at midnight.

We went back to collect Louis, who had spent the time reading newspapers and who felt a lot better for having spent a peaceful evening.

I wonder, dear friend, if you have noticed how different our Consul's conduct has been during this stopover, compared to his behaviour in 1817. I don't know how to explain his kindness and the attentions which he showers on us each day. What have we done to deserve all this?

17 July 1820 – Today, I went to hear mass said by our dear Abbé, accompanied only by my servant because I feared the morning chill for Louis ...

We go and visit Abbé Boiret almost every day and walk with him in the garden.

15 August 1820 – I have received a very beautiful bouquet, some fine cakes, and a very kind letter. I also visit Mme Sumter from time to time.

The French fleet, commanded by M. Jurien, has arrived in Rio. It is made up of a ship, a frigate and a schooner. Louis went on board to pay his respects to the Admiral. On St Louis' Day, Admiral Jurien gave a dinner for all highly placed officers under his command and for the captains. Louis attended while I had dinner with a French Abbé at the house of Abbé Boiret.

September 1820 – As I fed my large pet monkey, he bit me cruelly. One of its teeth pierced my skin just one millimetre from an artery. I was in considerable pain and was unable to visit General Ogendorp [Hogendorp]. Louis went with Abbé de Quélen. The General sent me fresh butter, which is extremely rare here. The next day, I was invited to Tijouka to say goodbye to Mme de Roquefeuille and to attend a charming luncheon given in our honour by Comte de Flaming. I was unable to go, and regretted it. I would have liked to reacquaint myself both with the house which has a pleasant location and with its strange menagerie. I was also very sorry not to have seen Mme de Roquefeuille again. As I felt a little better, I went to say goodbye to all my friends in town.

I went on board and while still in the harbour I received news that Mme Sumter had given birth. At last we are leaving.

October 1820 – The crossing was without incident and we reached Cherbourg, the end of our voyage and of this narrative which is dedicated to you.

After the Voyage: Ennui, Illness and Isolation   Epilogue

A selection of Rose de Freycinet's letters to her sister-in-law Clémentine de Freycinet (1823–1830)

The letters that follow are to be found in manuscript form at the Archives de Laage—the Archives reference is given at the beginning of each letter. The translation closely follows Rose's original letters, even as far as the punctuation is concerned. Whenever a word or expression has proved impossible to decipher, [?] has been placed in the translation.

[Laage 240–7]

Madame de Freycinet,[1]
St Denis, Ile Bourbon

Paris, 5 August 1823

I send you a few words today, my dear Clémentine, to accompany both a letter from my father-in-law and the portrait of our darling little Louis,[2] which your father had dispatched to us to have a copy made for grandfather Freycinet. A friend of M. Allègre who sails on the frigate of M. de Villory has been kind enough to take charge of it. I think that in the absence of your dear child, his portrait will please you greatly; it will give you pleasure on two counts, since it is also a kind gesture on the part of one of your friends. This is, in my opinion, the direct result of your charms! We have received your letters of last October; we await others with a great deal of anxiety, especially those that concern Henriette, for we are on such strange terms with the directress of her school that we would be glad if this state of affairs were to come to an end. We think that Henri will have realised the urgency of replying at once and that he will have sent us the instructions which he wishes to see carried out. From time to time, we receive news of all your dear ones at Rochefort;[3] everyone was in good health ten days ago. Martial is also well; he dined with us on Easter Sunday and was in perfect health; he is still well disposed towards his studies and we have no doubt that he will cover himself with glory at the end of this year. As for us, our health is quite good; we long only for the happiness of being reunited with you, since to live so far from all the members of one's family is to vegetate. Louis joins me in sending his love to Henri and to you. Please allow me to express once more my genuine affection for you and my never-ending friendship.

Your devoted sister,

Rose de Freycinet

1   Clémentine de Saulces de Freycinet, née Bézar (1795–1878), who married Louis Henri de Saulces de Freycinet (1777–1840) in 1815.
2   Louis [Lodoix] de Saulces de Freycinet (1820–1877), Captain in 1864, Rear-Admiral in 1876, son of Clémentine de Saulces de Freycinet.
3   M. and Mme Bézar, Clémentine's parents.

[Laage 240–12]

Madame de Freycinet,
St Denis, Ile Bourbon

Paris, 20 November 1824

I must confess my laziness to you, dear sister, for it is quite some time since I wanted to answer, and ought to have answered, your kind letter of May. I must even seem to you ungrateful to have waited so long before thanking you for the kindnesses which you have lavished on my sister and the encouragement you gave her to return to France! In addition to a little laziness, several events have prevented me from putting pen to paper, and I shall describe them to you below. In spite of my position as the *So much the better* sister, I must admit that, for some time now, I have taken a gloomy view of things. How is it, indeed, that I am not delighted to learn that my sister's return,[1] which I have longed for, is at last going to occur! Alas, I see that her state of health is such that a three-month journey is perhaps going to be beyond her endurance! My apprehensions are based on the state she was in when she arrived in Bourbon after a journey of only a few hours! I am also inclined to think that she was ill on her return to Mauritius, for not even you have received news from her since 18 May! Surely several ships have arrived since her return. Moreover, she had promised to write to me as soon as she got back to Mauritius, and she has been there now for seven months, and not a word from her! It is not for lack of ships, many of which have arrived since then, for Louis has received a number of letters from people in Mauritius which were written after my sister's return to the island! Imagine my anxiety when I think that she has perhaps been taken ill among strangers! How distressing it must have been for her when she had just been treated so lovingly by you! In spite of a number of possible explanations, I cannot accept the fact that, being back in Mauritius for two months, my sister would not write to me if she were in good health! This thought haunts me and I will confess to you that it is one of the reasons for my apathy; I was reluctant to bore you with my worries and each day I hoped to receive news which would restore my peace of mind. But I cannot put off the moment any longer to send you news of us, especially as I have been quite ill for several months. If you were to hear about my indisposition from a third party, you would worry on account of your friendship for me. I have been tormented all summer by nervous migraines and by the symptoms of an illness which, however frightening it might be, perhaps awaits me at the end of my life. On the one hand, by my sterility I am an extraordinary creature; on the other hand, what is unusual in my wretched person is that the illness which I fear generally afflicts only women who have borne a lot of children!

I went to the country last autumn to try and restore my poor health, but we rented a house next to that of Caroline de Nanteuil.[2] As she and her child were ill continuously during my entire stay, I did not derive all the benefits that I might have done from my holiday. On our return to Paris, Caroline brought to me her eldest son who was ill with a cerebral fever which lasted much longer because of the serious circumstances which accompanied this terrible illness. You know how fond I am of this poor child and how keen I must have been to provide some relief to Caroline and her mother; I spent seven or eight nights at this darling's bedside. Fortunately, he recovered, when I had given up all hope for a few days. However, unaccustomed as I am to worries and to fatigue of this kind, I subsequently became ill. I am feeling much better now, but I think that I shall not recover completely until I receive treatment for my previous illness.

You can see, my dear friend, how weak my mind is and how incapable it is of executing a plan; I had started this letter with the intention of expressing my gratitude to you for your generous acts towards my sister and for the kindness you have shown her. Yet, I cannot find the right words to express fully my thanks for such affability. Believe me when I say that I am as sensitive to your obliging behaviour towards my sister as I would have been if it had been directed to me. How pleasant it must have been for that dear child to find herself in the company of two people who displayed such fraternal friendship and affection towards her. Her heart was so full of gratitude that she conveyed her feelings to me in a most moving manner, and she explained how she had such fond memories of the happy time which she had spent in your home.

I am most upset that the bonnet which I sent to my godson[3] is too small for him; he must have a very large head, for the shopkeeper had assured me that it was for a child of between 18 months and 2 years, and my godson was hardly that age when the bonnet reached you. I shall try to send him something else and pay more attention to the size next time, for I don't want what I send him to be put aside for a little niece! We have recently received news of our jewel of Rochefort through one of our friends who has seen him and who has assured us that he is charming and endowed with remarkable intelligence for a child of his age. Your entire family was in good health at the time; your sister had recovered from the illness which had detained your parents in the country a little longer than planned. We have also had news of our parents from the Dauphiné; they were both well. Casimir[4] and his family are also in good health and send you their love. Louis joins me in sending to you all our love and and our best wishes.

Rose de Freycinet

1 Stéphanie Pinon, who went to Mauritius as a governess in 1818.
2 Caroline de Nanteuil, née Barillon.
3 Charles de Saulces de Freycinet (Bourbon 1823– Rochefort 1881), Rear-Admiral, who married Camille de Garnier de La Boissière on 24 April 1851.
4 Frédéric-Casimir de Saulces de Freycinet (1787– 1862), botanist, brother of Louis and Henri.

[Laage 240–17]

Madame de Freycinet,
St Denis, Ile Bourbon

Paris, 5 April 1825

It is very painful for me and very tedious for you, my dear Clémentine, to see that my letters always begin with laments. Indeed, how can I get used to your prolonged silence! I would like to believe that, since 20 May, the date of your last letter, you have not forgotten to write to us; if so, what has become of your letters? It is most unfortunate that the packages which contained your letters for us should have gone astray whilst those addressed to the Minister should have reached their destination safely. Since 8 May, the only news that we have had of you is that you are alive, but it is not enough for us. I had been without news of my sister for a long time, but I have received three letters from her in one month; there is some evidence that two of her letters have been lost, namely the ones which she wrote to me on her return to Mauritius after having spent 20 days with you. In my sister's last letter, I see that she has resolved to stay in Mauritius until the arrival of a new governess. I must admit that, although I was prepared for her decision, it still caused us considerable distress, for from one year to the next, time passes and we don't see each other and we vegetate far from each other! Who knows if other circumstances would not keep her far from me after those eight or nine additional months which she has agreed to devote to the family! I have not been, I confess, the *So much the better* sister for a little while now; I had cherished the hope that we were nearing the end of the long wait, but my courage is at a low ebb; the isolated existence which I have led for the last four years is so painful for my heart to bear that I am afraid I might be close to contracting consumption. I had always hoped that you or my sister would be near us around this time, and it would seem that Providence had also wished it, for it gave me just enough courage to last until now. But my patience is at an end, I think. Moreover, my health is no longer good and some sort of ennui has robbed me of any illusion of happiness which I might still have harboured.

With each passing day, I am confirmed in my opinion that I shall never bear a child, and such a thought is unlikely to cheer me up. It is in this gloomy mood that news has reached me of Stéphanie's return. I have not confided in my sister about the sadness which I have felt because I did not wish to dampen her spirits, for at present she needs all her strength. So, my dear sister, please do not tell her of my distress; it would only worry her.

It is most unfortunate that Martial has been chosen to serve in a ship bound for the Levant station, whilst there are several state ships leaving for Bourbon Island; it would have been so pleasant for you both to meet after so many years of separation. In the last few days, we have received a letter from him from Smyrna written at the end of December; it seems that this dear child is happy in the navy and shows great enthusiasm; his health appears to be good despite his fatigue. We have received news from Rochefort; all the members of your family were well at last after many bouts of fever and other illnesses; your sister and your father have been quite seriously ill this autumn. It appears that our little darling has also been ill with fever. What a dreadful climate! Our dear parents from the Dauphiné are in fine fettle and their health is bearing up extraordinarily well; they are about to send me letters for you but, since these have not yet arrived, they cannot leave on the *Pomone*; they complain, as I do, about the lack of news from you. I must say, my dear friend, that if I knew that there was a share of laziness in your behaviour, I would admonish you sternly, for your actions would be most reprehensible if you were guilty of tormenting so many people who hold you so dear!

We still await the return of Captain Roquefeuille and we cannot understand why he is so late; I think that his behaviour has put our friend [Rey?] in a most difficult situation; he is not yet wealthy, and he counted on the return of this ship to indulge in new speculations, which have been rendered impossible by this delay. I would not want this to be detrimental to the interests of our dear relative. I still hope that M. de Roquefeuille will agree to take charge of my shawls; M. Duperrey[1] who is in command of the *Coquille* will perhaps undertake to do so in place of the Captain. I said my shawls because you told me that you received another from Henri today which you thought was for Stéphanie, but I had asked Charles[2] for two others and it was probably in response to one of my requests that he sent you one. It is sad to note that no one to date has agreed to bring them to me; I am sure that if one of the gentlemen I have named did not wish to take charge of them, Captain Allègre, who is in India and who is to stop at Bourbon Island on his return journey, would agree to take care of it, for he is a friend of Louis and has a great deal of affection for us.

We have not seen our friend Raucomet [?] for six months; he went to visit his mother in Liège and to take a short holiday in Brussels, but the poor lady broke her arm and her son was forced to stay by her side. This also proved distressing for us, since we had got used to seeing our dear friend every day. All our relatives whom we have recently seen, as well as Louis, send their regards and their love. The Barillons are still in financial difficulties; however, Giles [?] has just set up another trading company in Marseilles in which Chonchon [?] has invested 35 000 Francs which have been reimbursed to him, but the company does not seem to have been very successful since its establishment eight months ago; we hope that it will become more profitable within a very short time. Mme Barillon[3] and her mother stayed in Paris for the sake of George's education; he hopes to become a lawyer; her two children are now in good health.

Please give Henri all my love, my dear friend. I send you my very best wishes. Hugs and kisses to my darling little Charles. I beg you to speak of us often so that he may get to know us better and love us a little in anticipation of meeting us.

Love,

Rose de Freycinet

1   Louis-Isidore Duperrey (1786–1865) sailed round the world in the *Coquille* (1822–1825) and called at Bourbon Island 17–23 November 1824. He was named Officier de la Légion d'honneur in 1836 and became a member of the Académie des Sciences in 1842.
2   André Charles de Saulces de Freycinet (1783– Calcutta 1823), brother of Louis and Henri.
3   Caroline de Nanteuil.

Madame de Freycinet,
St Denis, Ile Bourbon

Paris, 18 June 1826 [?]

I have entrusted to Mr Gucit, my dear Clémentine, a small box containing some toys for our dear little Charles; I thought that during the crossing, this may serve to entertain him; Stéphanie who knows his taste has helped me choose, but I had to be content with a few items in order not to burden Mr Gucit; please excuse me, therefore, if I send such trifles from so far away, but if this can amuse your child for a quarter of an hour, I shall deem myself happy. Louis and I send you and Henri all our love.

Yours ever,

Rose de Freycinet

[Laage 240–24]

Madame de Freycinet,
St Denis, Ile Bourbon

Paris, 20 June 1827

I have waited for an opportunity to start this letter, but in vain until today, my dear Clémentine. As I am rather lazy in putting pen to paper, I send it to you in spite of the fact that it is out of date, because it contains details which it would take me a long time to copy again in view of all that I have to tell you today. We have at last received a letter from you, but it is the second one and not the one which Mr Maillin has taken charge of; this young officer has followed your husband's instructions to the letter and has refused to post your message; he has made a point of waiting until he could come to Paris to deliver the letter in person. He has just written to Louis to announce his impending departure for the capital. Before receiving the letter in question, we had just learnt from your dear father of your plans for your dear little Louis. You can well imagine how the message which has been relayed to us has both astonished and delighted us. However, I must confess that a shiver ran through my whole body when I thought that this little cherubin, whose health is so delicate and who has been ill so often, might be unwell in my care, either because of the journey, or because of the change in climate. I hope, nevertheless, that he will quickly get used to that of Paris. In any case, the weather is generally pleasant except on very hot days, but we intend spending the rest of the fine season in the country, which in my opinion will be good for him. However, we are close to the Tuileries and I shall take him out often for a breath of fresh air until we leave for the country. Our departure will almost coincide with his arrival amongst us, for your dear papa has announced that he will leave Rochefort around 4 July, and our plans were to go to the country around the 12th. Your dear papa has answered our most earnest prayers by volunteering to bring this dear child to Paris himself. Louis would gladly have travelled to Rochefort to fetch him, if his grandfather had been unable to accompany him, for however much one might trust one's friends, one can seldom be sure that they will look after one's children properly, especially as such a delicate child requires meticulous care on the first occasion that he undertakes such a long journey.

In spite of our apprehensions as we await the arrival of your dear child, believe me when I say, dear Clémentine, that I shall be extremely happy to have this little angel near me. I can assure you that I shall take the best possible care of him,

because it is so natural and so simple for us to do so. You already know this, but I want to set your mind at rest in one respect, namely your fear that I might spoil him. No, my dear sister, do not believe that I shall do so; know that I am fully aware that a spoilt child is affected all his life by the weakness shown towards him in his childhood, and I would never forgive myself if one day you came to regret having entrusted into our care such a precious little creature. I do not concur with the view that one cannot dearly love a child without spoiling him. However excessive love might be, it does not prevent one from forming the character of a child and admonishing him mildly whenever necessary. I call this to love them for themselves, while I can only condemn as selfishness a blind love which shields the child from any punishment. I don't claim to be better at it than anybody else, but I shall use all my know-how to do my very best, assisted by your advice and Henri's; we shall try to be worthy of the trust you have put in us, until such time as you may be able to take charge once more of the education of that dear child.

I am busy taking care of your errands, my dear friend, and I shall do my utmost to please you. I think that in a few days from now, I will have finished everything and that I shall be in a position to send you the box at the beginning of July. I shall write to you again then to tell you about the errands. Today, I close this letter in order to dispatch it with the one which Louis is writing to your husband. I send you all my love, dear sister.

Yours ever,

Rose de Freycinet

Please give a big hug to little Charles for me and talk to him about us and our great affection for him.

[Laage 240–28]

Madame de Freycinet,
Cayenne,
French Guyana

Paris, 29 May 1828

I ought to have written to you ages ago, dear friend, and I had even composed a letter in the early part of this month which I wanted to send through M. Millot who was supposed to warn me in sufficiently good time for me to dispatch my letters, but his business prevented him from coming to see me early enough and the ship sailed without my letter. I had a good mind to admonish him, but he left for Normandy. I consoled myself with the thought that he must have written to you and sent news of your dear child, since he had seen us all just a few days earlier. We enjoyed conversing with M. Millot, but I must say that I have not seen enough of him, for it seems to me that there were a thousand things I wanted to ask him which escaped me at the time. In truth, his arrival coincided with an event which he must have mentioned to you; it made our meetings less frequent because of the difficulties which preceded or followed it. I refer to the wedding of my sister. I wanted to write and let you know beforehand, but time passed so quickly that the event was over before I could find any free time to do so. I am sure that you will take an interest in the matter and that you will share in our joy on this occasion. This marriage was decided upon very quickly, and we were in a quandary on numerous occasions, especially as so many things had to be attended to in such a short period of time. The person who helped to arrange this marriage is one of our friends who had known my sister's husband for several years and who was in a position to vouch for his character. We needed his assurance, for we had been acquainted with

him for only six weeks when my sister said the momentous *yes.* We also tried ourselves to obtain as much information about him as we could and everything we were told was favourable. My brother-in-law's name is Maillard; he belongs to a good Poitou family; he has been very well brought up, is employed at the Ministry of the Royal Household as deputy chief clerk. He is well regarded by his superiors amongst whom is one of our most intimate friends, and he will be promoted in the very near future. He has an excellent temperament and has everything, I think, to make a woman happy. A quality which does not add to one's happiness, but which does not detract from it either, is the fact that he is physically attractive. The only criticism which, in my opinion, could be levelled at him is that the two spouses' age is not well matched, M. Maillard being just three years older than my sister. However, it suited them; in any case, there must always be a weakness in any arrangement and this *minor flaw* is preferable to many others. After a long search and many unsuccessful attempts, we found an apartment which is quite close to mine. It takes a mere six minutes to travel from one to the other. In Paris, long distances are so wearisome when people visit one another frequently. My apartment was not large enough to be shared by two couples and the bedroom which my sister occupied has become our bedroom. Having always thought that my sister would one day marry, we had chosen to put ourselves out and occupy a very cramped room, which now serves as a second study for Louis, rather than rent an additional large room which would have made our dwelling larger but would have been of no use to us after my sister's marriage.

I hope to be able to dispatch your orders through the *César* which leaves Nantes at the end of this month and by which I am sending my letters, but I was unable to find freshwater pearls mounted on 10 carats; here they are always mounted on 20 carats. I was, therefore, forced to have them made, as well as the coffee pot, but before all the measures were taken, time passed so quickly that I found myself at the end of the week without having achieved very much. I know that there is a ship leaving Nantes in April and I hope to be able to send you all your orders, except for your dresses, since I have been forced to have a bodice embroidered and I shall need all the time available between now and M. Millot's departure to have it made. I think that he is leaving in the early part of May; in accordance with your wishes, I have chosen cheap porcelain. Nevertheless, I hope that you will be satisfied, considering the price. Far from complaining and finding you indiscreet in your requests, dear friend, I wish, on the contrary, to thank you; it gives me an opportunity to be of service to you and to please you. There is nothing dearer to my heart. How many times a day I long to have you near me, dear sister, so that we might share the joy of gazing upon a child endowed with such an amiable nature and such endearing qualities! I cannot begin to tell you how charming he has become; at present his mind is developing surprisingly fast and he spends all day asking endless questions! He wishes to have everything he sees explained to him and, halfway through the question, he makes the most amiable and delightful observations. I can assure you that whenever I feel such happiness, I wish you were near me, for mothers deserve to witness such moments to compensate them for the suffering they endure when giving birth to those little creatures. However, I urge you not to rue the fact that you are not there to see our ward grow up, for he is such a good child that one day he will give you a great deal of satisfaction! I repeat what I have told you, namely, how apprehensive I sometimes feel at the thought of the enormous responsibility we have taken on! If this child were not to be brought up in accordance with your philosophy and in a manner which you would approve of, and if you were to judge him not to be to your liking when next you see him, how sad I would be, for he has such a good nature that it will have been entirely my fault. In truth, I do everything I think fit, but, my dear sister, please try to convey to me your tastes and your views so that I might understand you better and that the poor darling might not regret having been so far from you! My main preoccupation, I must tell you, is to elevate his soul, to edify him and to foster in him principles of honour and charity and a revulsion for anything that resembles lies and deceit ... You would be moved to see the candour with which he comes of his own accord to confess the faults of which he has been guilty and which are unknown to me. He displays, for example, a personal pride which is at times a little excessive but which I think ought to be largely preserved, though moderated when out of place, since it is a very strong motive in education. Emulation is nothing more than disguised pride and incites us to overcome many an obstacle in intellectual pursuits and in the entire course of a young man's education. I have mentioned to you his tendency to cry, but we are making steady progress in this respect and I hope that the stronger he becomes, the more self-control he will exert. His health is indeed very good and his constitution is improving; during the whole of winter, he has had only two colds which did not last long. At the moment, I make him take some vermifuge, as we think that he is plagued a little by worms. Recently, we have started taking him to a gymnasium in accordance with the instructions of a good doctor who found that his muscles were not sufficiently developed for his age. He does not look like an eight-year-old, and yet he will be eight next month. I myself accompany him and watch his exercises. You must not fret about this, for I sometimes wonder whether you worry about the fate of that poor child lost in the hustle and bustle of Paris. He never, I repeat never, crosses our doorstep without being accompanied either by Louis or myself or Mme de Nanteuil, who occasionally comes to collect him by car to go for a walk with her own child. Please have no fears on this count; I treat him as I would my own children. He is always with me or with his uncle. To come back to the gymnasium, I will tell you that children of his age are asked to do exercises which are meant to strengthen their muscles and make them more nimble and skilful; they climb up straight, diagonal and vertical ladders. But there is always someone to keep an eye on them. [Incomplete]

[Laage 240–29]

Madame la Baronne de Freycinet,
Cayenne,
French Guyana

Paris, 9 June 1828

The Superior of the Sisters of St Joseph, who is going to Cayenne, has been kind enough to take care, my dear friend, of part of the shopping which was not ready at the time of M. Millot's departure. I have handed over to her a small box and a parcel containing shoes for little Charles. I think that M. Millot will already be near you when this letter reaches you and that he will have given you news of us and especially of your dear child; I would very much like to be a fly on the wall when he shows you the portrait and gives you a few details about our dear ward. I am sure that your maternal heart will overflow with happiness and with the desire to see for yourself a precious part of yourself who is so amiable and so interesting! I wish also that M. Millot would

tell you that we long to see you and that I cannot wait to make your acquaintance. I cannot help reflecting on the strange nature of our correspondence, for Henri and you have put so much faith in a person whom you have never met and you have entrusted to her a child of whom, in truth, you have seen little, but whose fate must be so precious to you! Your trust in me must be, I repeat, considerable! I sometimes wonder if that is not the reason why you hesitated for so long before entrusting him to me! Is M. Millot going to reassure you in this respect? This matter preys on my mind. As I have frequently told you and as you will discover for yourself one day, it would be unfair to judge me by my mother and my sister whom you have met, for the one has passed on to the other her intellect and her education, and poor Rose, devoid of the first of these assets, has only acquired the second with great difficulty, but Nature has largely compensated her by giving her a kind and loving heart. This is not sufficient in the world we live in but, within a family, these qualities make amends for many weaknesses.

I think, dear friend, that M. Millot's sound mind will have formed an opinion of me and that he will be able to reassure you as far as your dear child is concerned; I am sure that you were impatient to see him and that you had countless questions for him! May you not be disappointed in your expectations and may you find peace of mind from the information which he has given you! Since the departure of this kind administrator, your dear child has been in good health; he has passed the spring without any sign of illness and I hope that months of good health lie ahead of us. May you find him strong and grown-up when you next come to visit us; that is my most earnest wish and almost my sole preoccupation. We await the arrival of your dear parents any day now; they are coming to Paris to see their grandchild; they want to wait for the arrival of M. Eugène who is returning via Le Havre, but as we are to spend three months in the castle of Vice-Admiral de Ferrière near Chartres, I have just written to them to urge them not to postpone their visit too long, for they might find us gone and hence not achieve their sole objective since we would be 30 leagues away.

The arrival of ships from India is so unpredictable at times that it would be unwise to rely on it. I am waiting for their reply in which they will confirm their departure date. We are so looking forward to showing to your dear Eugène and his mother all the unusual sights of Paris.

Your embroidered dress, which is in the box, has met with a most unfortunate accident; imagine that the dreadful Mme Thomas entrusted to two workers the corsage to embroider, and one of them seemingly understood that there was no need for any lining. It was only when the dress was brought to me that I noticed the flaw, so that I was unable to have it altered; you will only be able to wear it with a cape. Next, the laundry woman damaged it so much that I had to give it to the seamstress, who has spent two days on it. I am also sending you six pairs of shoes for Charles of which two are one size bigger than he needs; I think that you will be pleased with them and with the small items of clothing.

My sister has asked me to give you and Henri her love; we are all waiting for news from you in reply to the five letters which M. Millot has delivered to you, for by now you will have a clearer picture of your future plans.

We have received good news from the Dauphiné; our dear mother is quite well. Please receive the love of all your relatives here. Louis and I, as well as the little darling, send all our love. A thousand kisses to our dear little Charles.

Rose de Freycinet

[Laage 240–30]

Madame de Freycinet,
Cayenne,
French Guyana

Château de Ver, 29 July 1828

Your boxes and your orders have left, my dear friend, but I have delayed them because of what I told you through M. Millot. However, after dispatching everything, I remembered that the trimming which you had requested would not have been useful for St Charles' feast and that you needed some other trimming to adorn those dresses which you planned to wear. I therefore thought that the lace which would have been much dearer than you could have imagined, if it were to match the height of the existing flounces, would have cost too much, would have had little effect and would have been of no use to you in France. On the day of the feast of St Charles, you could substitute your poplin dress for it; it would, accordingly, be much wiser to use a light trimming which would make the right impact and would be fashionable on your dress of Indian poplin. I shall send you, by the Indian ship which is about to leave, some very nice cotton tulle which we manufacture in France almost as well as the English, together with a small quantity of lace tulle which you might wear flat around the edge; this will make two flounces which are in fashion nowadays. If this does not suit, please return them to me at once, since capes and ruches are so fashionable that I shall always be able to put them to good use; don't hesitate to do so. We have fashionable clothes here which are very convenient for small evening parties, especially in the colonies; these are cotton tulle dresses (which can be made to measure). They are designed in one piece with skirts which have two large flounces in several layers. The whole dress thus finished costs only 100 Francs; I have just sent a charming one to a friend of mine and she seems delighted with it. By wearing a satin dress or a white muslin one underneath, one is more or less well dressed. This year, dresses with sewn sequins are not in fashion; I have not been able to find any; on the other hand, smooth material is worn a lot. I am sending you some because it lasts a long time and is not very dear. Your hat with all the trimming costs only 13 Francs. You will be able to renew it often. I wanted to send you two of them. Would I have been right? I trust that you will find the flowers and trimming to your liking, for they looked so charmingly refreshing. These days, ladies wear single flowers on their heads; your trimming cost 30 Francs and your flowers 10 Francs. Henri's hat has not yet been paid for; the hatter had not brought us the bill before our departure. The satin is the bluest that I could find. I insisted on black for your shoes and I hope that you will be happy with them. I also enquired about necklaces; amethysts are rarely worn, but women of your age wear them because it is understood that they have been acquired through marriage. There is some very attractive costume jewellery made with agates which would cost around 400 to 500 Francs, but, just like amethysts, this stone does not have any real value, except that it is fashionable. To purchase a small necklace of polished stones, such as rubies, turquoise or emeralds, one must pay up to 1200 Francs for each. Gold is worn a lot and is suitable for mourning clothes, white dresses and indeed of any colour; this kind of necklace is very pretty when worn on semi-formal occasions, and hairpins or earrings cost only 500 Francs. In addition, there is garnet which is becoming more popular and which makes for a very attractive necklace costing up to 600 Francs. Coral can be repolished; although it is quite dear, it is beautiful and I have been told that it is worthwhile. However, it is going out of fashion nowadays. There are many *respectable* people who wear fine necklaces made of *imitation* pearls; these cost only 200 Francs and are very well set. As for bracelets, you are quite right not to look for gold ones, for in a very short time they will no longer be fashionable. Some quite attractive ones are being made, and you would swear that the ones costing 30 to 35 Francs per pair are made of real gold. Many an elegant woman in Paris owns nothing else, and rightly so. I have enclosed in the box the 'Northern Pimple Cream'; one of the best apothecaries of Paris has assured me that it is not affected by humidity, so I have not sent it in a tin.

How I regret, dear friend, having used the word 'deformity' to explain to you that the upper lip of your dear child did not have the desired shape. Thank God, he is not deformed, as his portrait will confirm. Moreover, M. Millot will be in a position to confirm this; when his mouth is closed, it is hardly noticeable and, far from making him ugly, it adds to his charms, but when he laughs, he is less attractive, for his upper lip is cleft in the middle. Take heart, he will not need beauty to be a charming child; I think that I have somewhat exaggerated the problem so that you may be pleasantly surprised. It was a certain measure of coquetry on my part which I unconsciously indulged in. The fact is that I judged your reactions by my own; I would rather have a pleasant surprise than an unpleasant one, if I were in your shoes.

Don't hesitate, my dear friend, to send me many details about Charles; I take such a genuine interest in him that I would never tire of hearing you speak of him; the similarity between his personality and that of Lodoix pleases me greatly, since they will get on famously together. How happy they will be to play with each other!

I have to restrain myself in order not to praise your dear child to the skies. Perhaps I show too much enthusiasm; you cannot imagine how docile and assiduous he is; he has never, I repeat never, shunned work; he tackles his homework with as much pleasure as others play games, and I must add that he also willingly plays games and is quite good at them. At the end of his homework, he shows the same enthusiasm as at the beginning; the slightest remark increases his assiduity, and I must tell you that as his health is good at the moment, I make him work a little harder.

We are at present staying at the residence of M. le Comte de Ferrière, one of our retired navy generals who has a lot of affection for us. We intend spending one or two months in his castle where Louis, your child and I are trying to build up our strength. This is especially beneficial to Lodoix who is pink and healthy, as his portrait shows. I am in charge of his education here and I try to carry out all the habitual duties of his teachers, being determined that he will not regress during his absence. In fact, his teachers would be surprised since, far from regressing, he is making further progress. His appetite for knowledge is most pleasing and I shall give you an example of it; at the end of each dictation and after the grammar lesson I make him write one line for each word which he has misspelt. Two days ago, after I had given him this task in addition to all the others, he said: 'Auntie, tell me to write out several times such and such a word, which he pointed out to me, because I have misspelt the word frequently and, by writing it several times, I shall at last get it into my head.' How many children are there who ask for nothing better than to shorten their homework, as is the norm! Your child is not brilliant, but he is very intelligent and very diligent. With these qualities, he will do well in his studies. He is in good health and grows

stronger each day. I have not noticed that work tires him out. You can rest assured that I would never expect him to make progress at the expense of his health. This is my main concern. Do not doubt that I have the highest opinion of you; I appreciate your gentleness, your great kindness and your sensitivity. As for your indulgence, I crave it so much and I shall continue to do so; only then will I dare to appear in your presence. Louis has sent his brother the book, which he has requested, in a box which left with yours; he will also write a letter which will travel in the Indian ship leaving port in two weeks' time. He joins me in wishing both of you well and in sending you our love. Yours ever,

Rose

Your dear child sends a thousand hugs and kisses and the three of us send our love to dear little Charles. The present Governor of Martinique has been recalled and everyone in high society is saying that Henri is going to replace him. However, Louis has not heard anything on the subject at the Ministry of the Navy.

Please give our regards to your kind Commissioner; we hope that meeting his old acquaintances once more won't make him forget his new ones.

[Laage 240–34]

Madame de Freycinet,
Cayenne,
French Guyana

Paris, [June 1828?]

Because my letter was not ready in time, it has missed the ship leaving Nantes, sweet and kind sister. This happened because I wanted to add to it a small box which I had even mentioned to M. Clemausin; it was to contain bracelets which I knew you wanted, but I was misled; they were ready too late for me to send them to Nantes. M. Clemausin told me that there would not be another ship leaving for a long time, nor was there any navy ship bound for Cayenne. Therefore, my letters remained behind. Today, I am busy writing some which will be delivered to you by M. Mercier, a retired navy officer who has just been named harbour master in your colony; he is an officer about whom we know very little but who is interesting on account of the large family which he supports with a zeal and selflessness worthy of the warmest praise. Hence news of his posting as the harbour master in Cayenne has been well received by those who are acquainted with his private life. M. de Neuville has signalled his Ministry by remarkably equitable decisions. It appears that Ministry officials are astounded to see a Minister follow his own judgement and do so with such equanimity. M. Mercier is willing to take charge of the little box left behind containing the bracelets. I have taken up painting and as the current fashion permits ladies to wear small scenes painted on bracelets, as did our grandmothers, I have taken the liberty of having mounted on the bracelets two little drawings which I have done for you. Not only are they my first attempts at painting, but they are also my first experiment with this art form. Because I was not very experienced with this type of painting, they faded a little when applied on the glass. In order to preserve their original colour, it would have been necessary to make the coats of colour much thicker, which I did not do. If I had had time, I would have started all over again, but as the oil has to dry for two months before it is applied on the glass, this process would have taken too long. I therefore hope that you will be lenient, and I trust that

you will be willing to wear this little memento of my friendship. One of the little drawings shows the interior of a chapel in Rome and the other the ruins of an abbey in Europe.

In the parcel, you will find two letters addressed to you in Paris which reached us several months ago. I beg you, dear friend, to pass on my apologies to Henri for my absent-mindedness, for twice I have failed to enclose them in my parcels; they were in the drawer of my desk where I had completely forgotten about them. Besides, I must warn you, my dear sister, that both you and dear Henri must be patient with me, for I am the most scatterbrained of all women; it is a defect which is natural in me and which indicates that I am getting older, for they say that the defects of the mind and of the body become more pronounced when one is nearing old age, and at 34 and a half years, a woman is no longer young ... how sad! One must make the best of it, so they say, but it is not easy. If the Ministry were to hinder your return in some way, the two of us would finally see each other when our faces are wrinkled and old and our hair white, while the two brothers themselves would no longer be in their prime! You will find my poor sister quite changed, for her health has deteriorated greatly and she is constantly afflicted either with an inflammation or with other illnesses; she would need at least some peace of mind to cure herself at leisure, but far from it, she is in a very difficult situation.

Unfortunately, M. Maillard, who first thought that he wanted to take a wife both to make her happy and to enjoy domestic happiness himself, has had a complete change of heart; he has gone back to a most dissolute life as a bachelor and to the most unacceptable debauchery. He has behaved towards my sister in a most inconsiderate and disloyal manner. I do not know how all this will end, but we shall try to make sure at least that he will not spend the fruit of my poor sister's labour on his vile pleasures! You can well imagine how sad and distressing all this is for her! Luckily, she has no children, for it would perhaps have been an impediment to many future arrangements!

It is impossible for me to tell you how upset we are when we think of your boredom and your impatience during the time that has elapsed since the moment when you were ready to leave the colony! How you must have cursed the delay which had prevented you from taking your holidays, until the day when you received our letters! Your anxiety has been prolonged because winter, being even harsher than usual, delayed the departure of the vessel which was to convey the good tidings to you. Had it left around 12 January, as it had planned to do before the arrival of the ice and snow, you would not have remained so long in the dark. If you only knew how much I share your irritation and how often we have talked of this in front of the fireplace! However, your kind letters of November, which ought to have filled us with joy if we had not been forewarned about the other events, have reassured us; we were becoming a little anxious, since we had not received any letters from you for a long time. I was beginning to think that dear Charles had caused you more problems. I do not remember if in my last letter I told you of the measures taken by the navy to send you news of your appointment.

De Guéridon must have written to you about it in detail. M. Brou has not yet left Toulon, because his ship is not ready, I think, and the detour which he is making to Senegal will prevent him from arriving with your replacement before the month of May. All this postpones your return by quite a bit, but we hope that, as you are allowed (or so Louis was told at the Ministry) to take your holidays after a few days' stay in Martinique, we shall be able to see each other this summer in France; we await impatiently your decision in this respect. Your silver service is ready and we wait for your instructions as to whether we should send it to you in Martinique or not. If you are to stay there only a few days, it might not be worth our while sending it out to you, but on the other hand, maybe you would like to have it for the first dinner party which you plan to give in honour of your arrival. Please let us know your decision; we shall follow your instructions to the letter. All the silver is in a large box constucted in the shape of a trunk very well covered with leather and with well-made compartments in which each item can travel to the ends of the earth without suffering any damage. The knives and spoons are in two boxes, one for the dessert cutlery and the other for the large diverse cutlery of different kinds; the shapes are attractive and pleasing and the service displays an elegant simplicity. It will make a considerable impact on a table of 40 place settings, and it won't be the least bit out of place when you have set up home. I hope that my brother and you will approve; the silversmith has agreed to keep it in his shop for a while, and we are pleased, for it is safer there and better looked after. He has been asked by the Delegate for the Colonies to hand it over to us so that we might be able to send it on. Louis has instructed the silversmith to inscribe the arms which the Colonial Office wanted.

Recently, a young man, to whom Louis has given a letter of recommendation for Henri, left for Martinique; he is an interesting young man in his own right but he is also the nephew of one of our childhood friends, Mme Fessart. We would be very grateful if you could make him feel welcome; he is going to the West Indies to recover funds for a Paris bank; his name is M. Alphonse Blaison.

[Incomplete]

[Laage 240–36]

Baroness de Freycinet,
Rochefort

Paris, 26 May 1830

You will find in the small box which I am
sending you, dear sister, the two hairpins which
M. Devillère has made for you. I have decided not
to wait for the departure of the other box, since
I think that you are in urgent need of this.

I cannot tell you, dear friend, how sad I have
felt since your departure! I had grown accustomed
to seeing you each day and to hearing your
children around me, and it was so sweet to me
that being deprived of it has made me extremely
sad. I suffer from incurable ennui and I
experience a feeling of emptiness which I cannot
overcome; at all hours of the day I expect to
see you, I long for your presence and I become
gloomy when I remember that it is now four days
since you have left to travel so many leagues and
be far from us! I am also most anxious to know
how you have borne the past three tedious nights.
You were already tired and unwell; it seemed to
me that when I saw all of you in the coach, you
were in a terrible crush; the coupé appeared
narrower than when we last sat in it with you.
You must have been greatly troubled by the heat
the day after you left if, as I think, you had the
same weather as we did; it was hotter on Sunday
than it had been until then, and at night there
was a violent storm which lasted several hours.
I cannot hope to receive news from you quickly,
since on your arrival you will need several days to
rest, and the sweet feeling of being once more in
the midst of your family will take your mind off
the folk in Paris! However, dear friend, once the
initial moments of excitement are past, be kind
enough to look back and think of the happiness
you will cause by devoting a few minutes to us.

Consider our isolation and our sadness;
imagine what my poor heart must be feeling,
accustomed as I am to your dear child! I feel as
if you have deprived me of part of my life! I had
already that feeling of emptiness when you took
him back, but I found some solace after a few
hours in your presence. Now, on the other hand,
however long I wait, come and go, I neither meet
nor see those I seek! My only consolation is to
attend to your business and to the preparations
for our journey. Fortunately I have a lot to do
here in the next month or so, and time, which
flies when one is happy, will not slow down to
while away my impatience.

My mind and heart were so overtaxed at the
time of your departure that I forgot to send our
greetings for your dear parents; please mention
us to them and pass on our warmest regards,
especially to the amiable Eugène. I can well
imagine how happy she is to see you.

I hope that our little ones will sometimes think
of us. Please give them a hug for us, as well as to
their father to whom we send our love and best
regards. Louis joins me in sending you his love
and the assurance of our devotion and friendship.

Yours ever,

Rose

⊷ ⊰✦⊱ ⊶

Rose de Saulces de Freycinet, née Pinon, died
in Paris on 7 May 1832 while nursing her sick
husband who was struck down by cholera during
the epidemic of 1832. She was first buried in
Paris, but her remains were transferred to Saulces
cemetery on 19 September 1849. Louis-Claude
de Saulces de Freycinet died at the age of 63 on
19 August 1842. Rose was 37 when she died.
The voyage had finally taken its tragic toll.

Index